IMAGINING WINDMILLS

D1380802

Imagining Windmills presents a compilation of scholarly chapters by selected authors of global standing in the arts therapies.

This book reflects the theme of the 15th International Conference of the European Consortium for Arts Therapies (ECArTE), held in Alcalá de Henares, Spain, birthplace of Miguel de Cervantes. This innovative work seeks to further understanding of arts therapy education, practice and research and incorporates current thinking from art therapists, dance-movement therapists, dramatherapists and music therapists. Writers from Belgium, Germany, Greece, India, Israel, Italy, The Netherlands, Spain, Sweden, UK and USA combine to give an international voice to the book, which celebrates cultural distinctiveness, while also presenting shared intercultural developments in the professions. This interdisciplinary publication explores questions of the unknown and the imagined, misconception, delusion, truth and trust in the arts therapies. It enquires into ways in which education and the practice of the arts therapies engage with the imagination as a place of multiple realities, which may lead us closer to finding our truth.

This book will be of interest and relevance not only to those in the arts therapeutic community, but also to a broad audience including those in related professions – for instance psychology, sociology, the arts, medicine, health and wellbeing and education.

Marián Cao is an Art Therapist and Professor of Art Education and Art Therapy at the University Complutense of Madrid, Spain. She teaches and lectures in Spain and internationally. Founder director of the AT master's programme at University Complutense of Madrid, and former director of the Ph.D. programme on Art, Art Therapy and Social Inclusion, she has coordinated several Latinoamerican University programmes.

Richard Hougham is Principal Lecturer at Royal Central School of Speech and Drama, University of London where he is course leader of the MA Drama and Movement Therapy programme. He is Chair of the Executive Board of European Consortium of Arts Therapies Education (ECArTE) and has a particular interest in intercultural dialogues and epistemology in the international teaching of the arts therapies.

Sarah Scoble is Honorary President of ECArTE. She served on the Executive Board of ECArTE for over twenty years and was Chair from 2009 to 2017. Founder trainer in southwest UK in Dramatherapy and former director of Masters in Dramatherapy programmes, University of Exeter, she is Series Editor with Diane Waller for the annual *International Research in the Arts Therapies* publication with Routledge, in association with ECArTE and the International Centre for Research in Arts Therapies (ICRA), Imperial College, London.

IMAGINING WINDMILLS

Trust, Truth, and the Unknown
in the Arts Therapies

Edited by
Marián Cao, Richard Hougham, Sarah Scoble

Routledge
Taylor & Francis Group

LONDON AND NEW YORK

EUROPEAN CONSORTIUM FOR ARTS THERAPIES EDUCATION

First published 2022
by Routledge
2 Park Square, Milton Park, Abingdon, Oxon OX14 4RN

and by Routledge
605 Third Avenue, New York, NY 10158

Routledge is an imprint of the Taylor & Francis Group, an informa business

British Library Cataloguing-in-Publication Data
A catalogue record for this book is available from the British Library

Library of Congress Cataloging-in-Publication Data
A catalog record has been requested for this book

ISBN: 978-0-367-62673-0 (hbk)
ISBN: 978-0-367-62669-3 (pbk)
ISBN: 978-1-003-11020-0 (ebk)

DOI: 10.4324/9781003110200

Typeset in Bembo Std
by KnowledgeWorks Global Ltd.

CONTENTS

FIGURES

BIOGRAPHIES

Editors

Marián López Fdz. Cao, PhD, is Professor and Chair of Art Education and Art Therapy at the University Complutense of Madrid, Spain. She was the founding director of the University's Art Therapy master's programme and formerly the director of the PhD programme on Art, Art Therapy and Social Inclusion. She teaches and lectures both in Spain and internationally and has coordinated several Latinoamerican University programmes. Marián Cao has published several books on women and art, art therapy and trauma and the social functions of art. She is the director of the Research Group 941035 "Social Applications of Art: art therapy and education" and main researcher of ALETHEIA, "Arts, art therapy, trauma and emotional memory." Marián has directed several national and European research projects, including DiverCity, ("diving into diversity in museums and in the city"), ARIADNE (Art and Intercultural integration) and MUSYGEN on gender and museums.

Richard Hougham, MA, is a Principal Lecturer and Course Leader of the MA in Drama and Movement Therapy at the Royal Central School of Speech and Drama, University of London, England. He has a special interest in storytelling and the language of myth as part of the Sesame approach to dramatherapy and as a teaching pedagogy. He is currently Chair of the European Consortium of Arts Therapies Education (ECArTE). Richard continues to develop his interest in the connections between analytical psychology and the arts. Publications include Hougham, R. and Jones, B. (Eds.) (2017) *Dramatherapy: Reflections and Praxis.* London: Palgrave Macmillan, and Hougham, R. & Jones, B. (Eds.) (2021) *The Nature of Interruption.* London: Routledge.

Sarah Scoble, MA, is Honorary President of ECArTE and Series Editor with Professor Diane Waller of the *International Research in the Arts Therapies* publication, with Routledge. She is also one of four collaborators for the International Centre for Research in Arts Therapies (ICRA), Imperial College, London. She served on the Executive Board of ECArTE for several years and was Chair from 2009 to 2017. Formerly, Head of the Centre for Performing Arts and Media at South Devon College, UK, where she was also a founder trainer of the UK's first southwest postgraduate Diploma in Dramatherapy. Later, Course Leader of the Exeter-based Masters in Dramatherapy programmes and Director of the Southwest School for Dramatherapy Limited. She has edited many ECArTE publications and continues to develop her long interest in community theatre.

Authors

Irit Belity, MA, was formerly a lecturer and supervisor at the School of Creative Arts at the University of Haifa and the Kibbutzim College in Tel Aviv, Israel, and has been an art therapist for 20 years. She works in the education system as a manager and supervisor of therapists, and in private practice. Publications include: Belity, I. (2017) 'A relationship between the art therapist - parents within the educational system'. In: Snir, S. and Regev, D. (Eds.) *When art therapies meet the Israeli educational system, practical aspects.* Israel: University of Haifa Press, and Belity, I., Regev, D. & Snir, S. (2017) *Supervisors' perceptions of art therapy in the Israeli education system.* International Journal of Art Therapy.

Tania Ugena Candel, PhD, holds a doctorate in Education at the Complutense University of Madrid in addition to her Master's degree in Art Therapy and Art Education for Social Inclusion and Bachelor's degrees in Anthropology and in Social Education. Tania trained in Flamenco and Classical Dance. She is currently director of Sunflower Art Therapy in Motion; Professor of the Degree in Performing Arts – Antonio de Nebrija University and Nebrija Institute of Professional Skills; and collaborator with Education Area in the National Prado Museum. Art therapist at the Community Health Centers-CMSc Joven-of Madrid City Council (2017–2018). She has experience with children, adolescents, families and women at risk of social exclusion, as well as people with mental disorders, Alzheimer's disease and disabilities in general, affective-sexual education and drug addictions.

Oihika Chakrabarti, MA, is Co-Founder and Chairperson of The Art Therapy Association of India (TATAI). Oihika (MFA, RATh, DAT-c), a Masters in Fine Arts (MFA) from Visva Bharati University, Santiniketan, was awarded the Commonwealth Scholarship in 1997 to pursue postgraduate training in Art Psychotherapy at Goldsmiths College, University of London, UK. She pioneered Art Therapy in India, spearheading the first art psychotherapy clinical service at the Tata Institute of Social Science's Child Guidance Clinic at Wadia Children's Hospital, Mumbai, in 1999. In 2004, Oihika founded Manahkshetra Foundation (art for social change) and has over two decades of clinical, developmental, rehabilitative, post-disaster/humanitarian and training experience working in India. She has contributed to several international publications on art therapy and is core faculty of art therapy on the PG Dip Expressive Art Therapy programme at St. Xaviers College, Mumbai. Oihika is in the final stages of completing her Professional Doctorate in Art Therapy (DAT) from Mount Mary University, USA, and her doctoral research on decolonising the curriculum aims to contribute to the creation of the first culturally relevant Masters in Creative Arts Therapy in India.

Nina Cherla, MA, is Course Leader of Musikverkstan at Furuboda Folkhögskola, Yngsjö, Sweden. Nina has a Masters in Music Therapy (MA, MT) form University of South Wales, UK. She is a clinical music therapist based in Malmo, Sweden. Her professional experience includes a decade of work in public healthcare working for individuals with special needs in Sweden, India and the UK. She has collaborated with many well-known organisations such as Music as Therapy International, Shankar Foundation and The Music Therapy Trust. Nina Cherla is the founder of Musikterapi Syd, south of Sweden's biggest co-operative for music therapists. Nina currently works as a clinical music therapist specialising in children with social and communication difficulties. She frequently conducts workshops and training programmes and is an advocate for music therapy both in Sweden and in India.

Sibylle Cseri, MA, is a lecturer and supervisor at various university art therapy programmes in Spain and teaches on the Art Therapy Master's programme in Berlin, Germany. Based in Barcelona, Spain, Sibylle has been a practising clinical art psychotherapist for the last eighteen years, working principally with children and adolescents, having specialised in the field of post-adoption services and foster care. She is a frequent international guest lecturer, as well as an active voice for the development of the art therapy profession within Spain and Europe. She is co-founder and registered member of the Spanish Art Therapy Association (ATE), of the Spanish Federation of Art Therapists (FEAPA) and has also recently co-founded the European Federation of Art Therapists (EFAT), where she is member of its research group.

Einat Shuper Engelhard, PhD, is a research associate at the School of Creative Art Therapies at the University of Haifa, Israel, and Head of the Dance Movement Therapy training programme. She is a dance movement therapist (DMT) and psychotherapist. She served as Head of the Dance Movement Therapy training programme at Seminar Ha'Kibuzzim (2013–2017). Her clinical experience includes therapeutic work with Holocaust survivors and therapeutic work with children and adolescents with emotional difficulties and developmental problems. Her research focuses on DMT with couples, DMT with adolescents, DMT interventions, movement as emotional expression, body image and DMT training.

Maitri Gopalakrishna, PhD, is a dramatherapist, counselling psychologist and practice-researcher. She has a PhD from the Tata Institute of Social Sciences (Mumbai) and an MA in Counselling Psychology with a focus on dramatherapy from the California Institute of Integral Studies (San Francisco). She is also a registered drama therapist (RDT) of the North American Drama Therapy Association. Maitri works in community building, preventative care, mental health support, psychotherapy and training in a variety of institutional and community contexts. She has experience of working with issues of gender, sexual trauma and childhood sexual abuse. Maitri's recent areas of practice-research include drama as an intervention for sexual trauma, therapeutic theatre and drawing on theories and practices from the Natyashastra in therapeutic work.

Joy Gravestock, MA, is a music therapist in private practice in the UK. She has been the adoption clinical lead for a Nottinghamshire NHS Trust and also a member of the adoption panels for Nottinghamshire and Leicestershire local authorities, offering both her professional and personal experiences to panel. A specialist in music therapy with children in adoption, Joy works with local authority and charitable adoption agencies providing music therapy for families funded by the Adoption Support Fund. Current work (detailed in her chapter) focuses on adopted children with complex physical and learning disabilities, where often a disability discovered at birth led to the relinquishment of a baby. Her PhD research explores how relational attachments in adoptive families may be enhanced by moments of attunement occurring within a music therapy relationship. Publications include Gravestock, J. (2019) Psychoanalytic relational music therapy for children with high-functioning autism in specialist school placements. In: Dunn, H., Coombes, E., Maclean, E., Mottram, H. & Nugent, J. (eds) *'Music therapy and autism; a* spectrum *of approaches'* London: Jessica Kingsley Publishers, and Gravestock, J. (2021) *Music therapy in adoption and trauma.* London: Jessica Kingsley Publishers.

Uwe Herrmann, PhD, is visiting professor in art therapy and deputy course leader on the MA Programme in Art Therapy at Weissensee University of Art, Berlin, Germany. Professor Herrmann trained in art therapy at the University of Hertfordshire and Goldsmiths College, London University. He developed the art therapy service at the State Training Institute for the Blind (LBZB) in Hanover, Germany, where he has practised for the past 30 years. Since 2000 he has lectured on the MA Programme in Art Therapy at Weissensee University of Art Berlin, where he was appointed visiting professor in art therapy and deputy course leader in 2014. He has published widely, most notably on the subjects of disability, vision and blindness in art therapy, and has lectured across Germany, the EU, the UK and in South Korea.

Andrea López Iglesias, MA, is a Pre-Doctoral Research Fellow at Complutense University of Madrid (UCM). Andrea is an art therapist, artist and researcher with a Master´s Degree in Art Therapy and Art Education for Social Inclusion and a Bachelor's Degree in Fine Arts. She is currently collaborating with the Research project I+d+i Aletheia: Art, Art Therapy, Trauma and Emotional Memory and she has been a member of a research team EARTDI (Applications of Art for Social Inclusion) at the Musacces Consortium. Art therapist at the Community Health Centers -CMSc Chamberí- of the Madrid City Council (2017–2018). As an art therapist, she has developed her profession nationally and internationally with children who have learning disabilities, those who have suffered from health problems in the dialysis unit, adults with mental health disorders, women's collectives and elderly people.

Jean-François Jacques, PhD, is an independent dramatherapist, clinical supervisor, educator and researcher with more than 15 years of experience in the National Health Service and in private practice in the UK. His current areas of research focus on therapeutic theatre, trauma, shared meaning, aesthetics, embodiment, intersubjectivity, otherness and spectatorship. He is editorial board member and reviews editor of the *Dramatherapy* journal. He is also the creative director of the Theatre of Lived Experience whose mission is to foster dialogue through performance. He is published in the field of dramatherapy and has presented at conferences in the UK and internationally. Recent publications include a paper in *The Arts in Psychotherapy* (2020) on "Investigation into the Production of Meaning in Autobiographical Performance in Dramatherapy," a chapter on "Otherness and Meaning in Performance" in the edited volume *Cultural Landscapes in the Arts Therapies* (University of Plymouth Press, 2017), and a chapter on "Intersubjectivity in Autobiographical Performance in Dramatherapy" in the edited volume on *The Self in Performance* (Palgrave Macmillan, 2016).

Bryn Jones, MA, teaches drama on the MA in Drama and Movement Therapy at the Royal Central School of Speech and Drama, London, England, and is a dramatherapist and clinical supervisor. His current commitments include clinical practice with individuals in London, group work with adults on an addiction therapy programme and therapy with families for a bereavement service. Bryn continues to develop his combined theatre arts/dramatherapy practice through long-standing associations with an arts-based social welfare initiative in Tokyo and an environmental arts project in Kyushu, Japan. His most recent publications are: Jones, B. (2021) 'The Shakkei of Dramatherapy'. In: Hougham, R. & Jones, B. (Eds.) *Dramatherapy: The Nature of Interruption.* London: Routledge and Jones, B. (2021) 'An Unresolved Poem of Walking, Noticing and Composing'. In: Butte, C. & Colbert, T. (Eds.) *The Listening Body: Embodied Approaches to Supervision.* London, Routledge.

Tripura Kashyap, MA Psych, pioneered dance movement therapy in India in 1990. She received a MA in Psychology from Annamalai University, Tamilnadu, India and studied Movement Therapy at the Hancock Centre for Dance/Movement Therapy in Wisconsin, USA. On her return she worked as a movement therapist at half-way homes, special schools, treatment/rehabilitation centres, senior citizens' facilities and with individual clients for the next 10 years. Tripura received fellowships from the Ashoka International Foundation and Indian Ministry of Culture for her innovations in dance therapy and contemporary dance. She authored *My Body, My Wisdom* a book on creative dance therapy and *Contemporary dance: practices, paradigms and practitioners* published by Penguin and Aayu publications. Tripura is the Co-Founder of Creative Movement Therapy Association of India (CMTAI).

Ana Serrano Navarro, PhD, is associate professor on the Master's in Art Therapy and Art Education for Social Inclusion at the Complutense University of Madrid, Spain, and collaborates as a teaching partner in different trainings in art therapy. She is an art therapist, artist, art educator and researcher. She developed her doctoral research at José Germain Children and Youth Hospital, which continues to focus on trauma and mental health. In 2017–2018, she conducted a research project for Madrid City Council into the possibilities of art therapy in a health promotion context, and she collaborates with the research project I+d+i Aletheia: Art, Art Therapy, Trauma and Emotional Memory. Currently, she provides art therapy services in private practice, individual and group sessions.

Salvo Pitruzzella is Professor of Arts Education at the Fine Arts Academy of Palermo, Italy and, since 1998, Dramatherapy course leader at the "Centro ArtiTerapie," Lecco, Italy. Salvatore is a pioneer of dramatherapy in Italy. Starting from a background as an actor, playwright and puppeteer, he has been working as dramatherapist for over twenty-five years. He has published widely on dramatherapy, educational theatre, and creativity theories. Salvo is an international Member of the BADth (British Association of Dramatherapists), and member of the Editorial Advisory Board of Dramatherapy Journal. Honorary Member of the SPID (Società Professionale Italiana di Drammaterapia). Salvo is a member of Executive Board of the EFD (European Federation of Dramatherapy). He is the Italian Representative with ECArTE (European Consortium for Arts Therapies Education) and external examiner of the MA Drama and Movement Therapy at the Royal School of Speech and Drama, London, UK.

Robert Romanyshyn, PhD, is Emeritus Professor in the doctoral programme in clinical psychology at Pacifica Graduate Institute, USA. A Fellow of the Dallas Institute of Humanities and Culture, he co-founded in 1972 an interdisciplinary programme in existential-phenomenological psychology and literature at the University of Dallas. In 1991, he moved to Pacifica Graduate Institute to create a doctoral programme in clinical psychology. On his retirement in 2015, he was elected Emeritus Professor in that programme. He is the first non-analyst elected as an Affiliate Member of The Inter-Regional Society of Jungian Analysts based upon his scholarly contributions to Jungian psychology. In addition to on-line webinars, interviews, lectures, workshops and keynote addresses at international conferences, universities and professional societies in the US, Europe, Australia, South Africa, Canada and New Zealand, he has published eight books, numerous articles in psychology, philosophy, education, literary and poetry journals, written a one act play about Frankenstein, and in 2009, he created a multi-media DVD entitled *Antarctica: Inner journeys in the Outer World.*

Celine Schweizer, PhD, is a lecturer, supervisor and researcher at The Department of Art Therapy, Academy Health at NHL Stenden University of Applied Sciences, Leeuwarden, The Netherlands, and coordinates, supervises and teaches at the Professional Founding Programme for art therapists at Master Arts Therapies of HAN University of Applied Sciences, Nijmegen. She is an experienced art therapist, member of KenVaK, Research Centre for Arts Therapies, The Netherlands, and member of Research Group Small n-designs of NHL Stenden University of Applied Sciences. Celine chairs the research committee of EFAT (www.arttherapyfederation.eu) and teaches art therapy papers, masterclasses and workshops all over Europe. She obtained her PhD about art therapy for children diagnosed with Autism Spectrum Disorders at Faculty of Social and Behavioural Sciences, Groningen University, Groningen, The Netherlands.

Maya Vulcan, PhD, is Head of the Dance Movement therapy training programme at Seminar Ha'Kibuzzim, Tel Aviv, Israel. She is a dance movement therapist (DMT). Her clinical experience includes therapeutic work with infants and caregivers, focusing on psychosomatic disorders and medically unexplained symptoms, and therapeutic work with children with emotional difficulties and developmental problems such as ASD. Her research focuses on DMT education and training, DMT with couples, DMT with infants and caregivers, the experience of therapists working with autism, DMT interventions in autism, and issues of professional identity in the field of DMT.

This publication follows a series of ten previous books, all inspired by and emerging from ECArTE's biennial international conferences. This is ECArTE's first such publication with Routledge.

In memory of Professor Wita Szulc

EUROPEAN CONSORTIUM FOR ARTS THERAPIES EDUCATION (ECArTE)

The European Consortium for Arts Therapies Education was founded in 1991. It is a non-profit-making organisation, which was established with the support of ERASMUS.

ECArTE is a consortium of Universities. Its primary purpose is to represent and encourage the development of the Arts Therapies and Arts Therapies education in Europe; in particular, the courses offering nationally validated and professionally recognised training for Arts Therapists. (The Arts Therapies include art therapy, dance therapy, dramatherapy, play therapy and music therapy).

The Universities of Hertfordshire, Münster, Nijmegen and Paris founded ECArTE in 1991. Currently it comprises 34 member institutions from 13 European countries.

The Consortium's work includes:

- Creating stronger European links in the Arts Therapies through the international exchange of staff and students
- Promoting research into methods of Arts Therapies practice within Europe
- Working towards opportunities for international study and exchange in Arts Therapies training programmes
- Promoting recognition of qualifications in the Arts Therapies at a European level
- Supporting the development of appropriate, academically recognised, nationally validated Higher Education courses for the Arts Therapies
- Publishing academic texts on current practices, philosophies and research in international Arts Therapies
- Offering opportunities for professional communication and development at its international conferences
- Working towards mutual collaboration in all aspects of Arts Therapies development and practice across Europe

- Supporting the design, development and validation of new programmes in all member states
- Communicating with policy and strategic departments to educate and inform them about the discipline of the Arts Therapies

European Network

ECArTE is working towards establishing mutual recognition and compatibility in educational and vocational training for Arts Therapists within the European Community. The criteria for membership to ECArTE is subject to a changing educational and social landscape. There are complex articulations of qualifications in different European Countries and ECArTE is keen to remain observant of these differences and inclusive in its practice.

ACKNOWLEDGEMENTS

We would like to thank the following for their contribution towards this publication and the Alcala conference.

First of all, Carmen Alcaide Spirito, University of Alcala, for her generosity of both spirit and place and for hosting much of the conference in the wonderful "Aula de Bellas Artes." We also extend our thanks to the Vice Rector Dra. Dna. Maria Jesus Such Devesa, who supported the conference from the outset. Thanks to the Fundacion General de la Universidad de Alcala for its hospitality and welcome.

A special thanks to the Vertebradas Artes Escenicas for their opening performance at the Cervantes Theatre: Molinos ¡A mí! (Windmills come to me!). This group creation was based on an idea of Marta Lage de la Rosa and Laura Suárez. Thanks to all the actors, musicians and technical support involved in this production. This theatrical performance brought us closer to Cervantes, and to Quixote and Sancho Panza at the very beginning of the conference. We extend our thanks to the Cervantes theatre for collaborating with us for this performance, the opening ceremony and the keynote.

We would also like to thank David Gamella Gonzalez, University Center Cardenal Cisneros, for his work on the conference logo as well as the filming and photography throughout the conference. Thanks too to Marta Lage de la Rosa for her filming and photography.

Thanks to all the contributing authors who have worked on the chapters in this publication and to Matthew Gammage for his impeccable skills in proof reading.

Thanks to Laura Hussey and Swati Hindwan at Routledge for their support in developing and producing this publication.

Finally, we would like to thank all the delegates of the ECArTE conference for contributing to such a lively and collegiate happening in Alcala de Henares, Spain, in the late summer of 2019.

PREFACE

"Imagining Windmills: trust, truth and the unknown in the Arts Therapies" sets out to reflect the theme of the 15th International Conference of the European Consortium for Arts Therapies (ECArTE), held in 2019. The location of the Conference was the university city of Alcalá de Henares, Spain, birthplace of Miguel de Cervantes, who is largely regarded as the greatest writer in the Spanish language. Alcalá de Henares symbolises the presence of a large part of the multicultural European heritage, from its first Cetiberian inhabitants, later with one of the most important Roman settlements in the Iberian Peninsula -Complutum-, the Visigothic settlements or the Arab culture, which gave it its name, Alkal'a Nahar. With the subsequent Christian conquest, it became one of the most important places in the Kingdom of Castile, turning it into a cultural centre of great prestige and where, as in Toledo, Jews, Muslims and Christians lived together in harmony for almost 400 years.

"Imagining Windmills" alludes to the famous passage in Cervantes' masterpiece "Don Quixote," in which the protagonist, on one of his missions as a knight errant, begins to attack windmills, thinking they are giants. This act, one of his many misguided adventures, reflects both hubris and an imaginal capacity, a contrast evident throughout the book and one of psychological significance. Guided by this literary masterpiece, the Conference theme invited people to wrestle with ideas of misperception and delusion, truth and trust and the paradoxical delight and vitality brought about by Quixote's madness and purpose. The prospect of actively imagining windmills plays with consensual reality and provokes questions of the unknown and the imagined. How does the education and practice of the arts therapies engage with the imagination as a place of multiple realities in ways that can lead us closer to finding our truth? Picasso's suggestion "art is a lie that helps us realise the truth" points to this capacity in art.

The space of art and creation is not a space of certainties or answers. Nor is it a closed and limited space that can be defined in a few words. On the contrary, the space of creation has to do with openness, vulnerability, the unknown, the vacuum. The therapeutic space, in turn, opens up as an invitation to a journey where these ingredients – the unknown and the uncertain – are present as assiduous companions.

Cervantes accompanies us in this process, introducing us to multiple levels of significance, making us enter into the game of truth which includes questions of authorship itself. Indeed, who is the author of Don Quixote? Cervantes, Cide Hamete Benengeli? Or perhaps Pierre Menard? As in Don Quixote, the space of the story, of storytelling oneself, oscillates between fiction and reconstruction in a never-ending narrative, which can be told in many different ways. As in Don Quixote, the subjects of creation move between the search for truth, trust and the unknown, trying to find a place of goodness, where and how to do the right thing, not knowing even what the right thing is. In a world in which the media increasingly manipulates and digitalises the image, how can the arts therapies offer the opportunity for the imagination and story to emerge spontaneously through the art forms of dance, drama, art and music in meaningful ways? How do arts therapies education and practice help reclaim storytelling and engage with the imaginal, building towards practices of trust and discourses of truth?

So, in the fields of art and medicine, art and psychology, the arts therapies, how do we conceive of truth? Are there multiple truths, in a postmodern bricolage of social construction, or an essential truth and experience of Self which transcends these concerns? And how do we consider trust? How is it transmitted, cultivated, broken? And how do trust and truth relate to the as yet unformed, the unconscious, the unknown?

It is of note that Cervantes wrote Don Quixote whilst in prison. His masterpiece was not conceived through looking out upon beautiful vistas, but kindled from the interior of his own being. He then turns outward to face afresh his world with all the subtelty and intricacy of a storyteller capturing the essentials of the human soul, with its capacity for adventure, inflation, idealism and purpose. And all shot through with acerbic wit, satire and mockery. The aim of arts therapies is, in a way, to find lightness, balance, just as Don Quixote must undertake a journey to find the calm his soul needs. On the way, as in the artistic and therapeutic process, the windmills rise up like giants, confusing us, trapping us and at the same time abandoning us. The arid Castilian plateau is a landscape where the horizon we long for is always far away. This is the setting of this work, its guiding thread, its backdrop.

Coronavirus, on the other hand, has presented itself as an unavoidable guest, which could not go unnoticed in this process. Somehow, the words that run through this book have been written, rewritten or corrected in partial or total confinement – as with Cervantes when writing Don Quixote. There is an attentive eye on the number of people occupying the world's Intensive Care Units, with the awareness of a body that had felt unnoticed until 2020. The body appears again, emerging from a pretended digital simulacrum where we thought we lived, and with it the presence of vanitas, which was so important in the Baroque period, an era that also experienced a pandemic. Uncertainty and unpredictability, so present in the creative process and previously so far removed from today's society, a society that had become accustomed to reigning and controlling the future, have raised awareness of the importance of human vulnerability, fragility and mortality. COVID-19 has also shown the gravity of the acts of attachment and loss in human life, so present in this pandemic, which are the pillars of artistic creation and arts therapy.

The aim of the book is to reflect, together with the authors, on the ideas that we have described in these lines, accompanied by the spirit of Don Quixote, but also by the feeling of fragility that a pandemic leaves behind. The book presents a compilation of thirteen scholarly chapters by selected authors of global standing in their field, all of whom were presenters at the Conference and that are not only from Europe but also from India, Israel and USA.

Marian López Fdz. Cao opens the sequence of chapters with a haunting narrative, written with a world in crisis during a Coronavirus lockdown. Inspired by María Zambrano's assertion that "art is the awareness of a lost life and it is the means to recover it," Cao considers deeply the nature of space; spaces of imagination and creation, of possibility, the interstices between absence and presence. A personal narrative, three works of fiction and the work of a visual artist connect us to the shifting and potentially transformative qualities of space and kindle her argument in this thought-provoking paper.

With reference to Cervantes' masterpiece, Robert Romanyshyn offers a guide for the education of the imagination. With the text at the heart of his chapter, Romanyshyn rallies around a central idea of the story as a "collective cultural-historical dream that is still dreaming us." In so doing, he destabilises any poststructuralist reading of Don Quixote and instead offers new positions, different angles and amplifications of images. All challenge and wrestle with conceptions of the very basis of education in psychotherapy. Educating the "Quixotic imagination" is a central part of this process, moving away from the "tyranny of the real" and towards a capacity to live with multiplicity and paradox.

The subject of truth and its relation to art therapy is explored in the work of Uwe Herrmann against the backdrop of historical, political, philosophical and artistic ideas related to it, and matched against a debate in psychoanalysis. The author reflects on such important concepts as Αλήθεια, the Greek word for a concept of truth as something that must be actively procured from its hidings, presenting an idea of truth related in form and meaning to the word trust. Through a single case research, the chapter questions the client's and therapist's changing binary conceptions of "true" or "false" from three temporal perspectives: in therapy, post-therapy and revisiting the material many years later.

In a keenly observed contribution to the publication, Richard Hougham and Bryn Jones present a playful and searching analysis of ideas emerging from their dramatherapy workshop at the Alcalá Conference. The writing is insightful as they test and examine themes of aesthetic sensibility, connection and constellation in the play space and the impact and reverberations of the introduction of unorthodox materials. Persuaded by the work of Peter Slade and Gaston Bachelard, this chapter jostles with fascinating questions and stirs with gentle curiosity.

Salvo Pitruzzella offers a new paradigm for dramatherapy. With consummate skill and dexterity in his language and design, he interrogates and disarms accepted notions of the Self. In its place, we are introduced to the "Dramatic Self paradigm," a concept and emergent dramatherapy philosophy that draws on intersubjectivity and sees the very structure of drama as a pattern of understanding human nature. As the shape of the new paradigm emerges, we trace a diversity of influences including complexity theories and neuroscientific ideas including the structured coupling of the brain. However, the drama remains ever-present as Pitruzzella's boldest claim rings through; "Theatre is the realm of consciousness."

Jean-François Jacques quotes Marianne Hirsch in his chapter, stressing the importance of developing connective structures to survive in vulnerable times. His chapter is an invitation to reflect on ways in which the arts therapies can provide such connective structures, at the time when our disconnections could easily overshadow our inner needs for connection. It explores aesthetics as a relational process that enables access to unknown truths and the unveiling of unsuspected imaginaries through dramatherapy.

Irit Belity leads us into the second section of the book, which focuses on cultural and intercultural connections. Her chapter explores the important topic of encounter between clients and therapists from different traditions, beliefs and cultures. Belity suggests the creation of a "third space" in the encounter; one of possibility and growth. In particular, she examines issues arising from the practice of intercultural therapy between a Jewish secular art therapist and Muslim religious Arab clients.

Chapter 8 – Oihika Chakrabati et al. – combines the experiences and expertise of four pioneer arts therapists, from the fields of art, dance-movement, drama and music, in India. The chapter presents an authentic record, combining commitment and collective wisdom in the task of establishing culturally-relevant models of practice, pedagogy and training. The writing points up the critical issue of decolonisation in the keen endeavour to gain professional recognition for the arts therapies in India.

Inspired by the idea of Don Quixote with his nobility and compassion at the service of those he encounters in his adventures, Ana Serrano et al. propose a chapter that shows how art therapy can be approached from a community-based perspective, working in collective spaces to promote health through accompanied creative processes and support networks among participants, institutions and health agents. Moods, anxiety, stress and depression, self-esteem, loneliness, general satisfaction, group cohesion and interpersonal relationships were observed and evaluated through mixed research methods.

Einat Shuper Engelhard and Maya Vulcan's innovative research into Dance Movement Therapy for Couples demonstrates ways in which a combination of movement and verbal processing can disclose multiple truths in relationships. In this chapter, dance is shown to serve as a bridge to the unconscious. The authors analyse the use of diverse experiences through movement to uncover and give insight into subjective embodied material, which can influence experiences in a couple's relationship.

Joy Gravestock offers a beautifully crafted and moving account of her music therapy work with a young girl with disabilities. The chapter charts the therapy as it spanned several years, taking the reader into the subtleties and nuances of the therapeutic relationship and shared music making. This is a moving and tender account that also educates as to the psychodynamics of music therapy, offering a framework for understanding the inner experiences of the client and how music can be a profound bridge for shared experience.

Celine Schweizer outlines and discusses her work and research as an art therapist with children diagnosed on the autistic spectrum. Whilst looking at the nature of the practice and its inherent challenges, she also opens up valuable questions about the languages of treatment in art therapy, how they sit within an interdisciplinary context and the growing demand for evidence. Through referring to her Doctoral research, she suggests new languages and collaborations, along with an outline of a model of working.

Finally, Sibylle Cseri closes the book with a chapter that, moving from inner states of alertness and mistrust, tries to connect to a place in art therapy where the exploration of unknown territories becomes possible. The chapter focuses on children who have a fragile sense of trust, derived from a history of early childhood loss. The text examines a therapeutic journey where the exploration of unknown territories becomes possible. As in the case of Don Quixote, who faces unexpected challenges, children and the art therapist must confront fears, anxieties about the unexpected, through the creative process.

This publication, as with previous ECArTE books generated from conferences, brings together these international contributions. All concerned with the innovative and everchanging ideas within the arts therapies, each author has wrestled with and elaborated on the theme of the conference. The story of Don Quixote and Sancho Panza is a story of adventure, genius and ultimately the power of wonder and imagination. In a zeitgeist in which this imagination is all too often explained away rationally, or undermined by monolithic structures of truth, the multiplicity of the psyche and of human experience can be elicited and expressed through the arts therapies. The evidence is in the chapters of the book – as the authors destabilise the truth by looking out for what is truthful and mobilise the genius of creativity in their teaching and practice.

THE EDITORS
Marián Cao, Richard Hougham, Sarah Scoble
2021

1

ON THE UNKNOWN THAT ART ADDRESSES

Space, vacuum and awareness in the arts

Marián López Fdz. Cao

Abstract

Through this chapter, we will have a glance at how artists, be they writers, painters, dancers or musicians, have looked for spaces of imagination and creation. Spaces where emptiness calls us to otherness, to the artist him/herself, to the interstice between absence and felt presence. The field of art introduces us to an empty space and an anachronistic time – a space without coordinates, a time without past or future. It proposes an "operated spacing," where the object becomes, like the trace, the sign of a loss, as Didi-Huberman (2014) would say. As Cervantes says in *Don Quixote*, only the poet can recount or sing about things not as they were, but as they should have been.

Art has the potential to create a state of exceptionality. It can generate a space of possibility, an encounter with the visible and tangible, which opens up and evolves before our eyes. Four cases accompanied by a personal narrative will explain this thesis: the pandemic autoethnographic narrative; the space taken away in Julio Cortazar's *The House Taken Over* (1951); the labyrinth as a refuge from external violence as embodied by Isabel Allende's *The House of the Spirits* (1982); the paradoxical space of Juan Rulfo's *Pedro Páramo* (1997). In turn, we will reflect on the longed-for, impossible space shown in Doris Salcedo's artwork *Shibboleth* (2007). Aesthetic perception opens up a new spatiality; the painting as a work of art is not in the space it inhabits; dance and theatre are developed in a space without objectives and without directions: it is a suspension of our history. Arts therapies unravel the ambiguous, contradictory and multiple sense of the space that humans have inhabited, still inhabit or create around them, making a space for transformation and transcendence. As in Cervantes' work, the space of the arts fluctuates between what is perceived and what is felt, the trace of what has been and the yearning for its apprehension.

DOI: 10.4324/9781003110200-1

Keywords: unknown, space, creation, aesthetic, emptiness, heterotopia

Abstract in Spanish

A través de este capítulo, veremos cómo los artistas, sean escritores, pintores, bailarines o músicos, han buscado espacios de imaginación y creación. Espacios donde el vacío llama a la alteridad, al propio artista, al intersticio entre la ausencia y la presencia sentida. El campo del arte nos introduce en un espacio vacío y en un tiempo anacrónico -un espacio sin coordenadas, un tiempo sin pasado ni futuro-. Propone un "espacio operado," donde el objeto se convierte, como el rastro, en el signo de una pérdida, como diría Didi-Huberman (2014). Como Cervantes cita en *Don Quixote*, sólo el poeta puede contar o cantar sobre las cosas no como eran, sino como deberían haber sido.

El arte crea un estado de excepcionalidad, la experiencia de lo visible y lo tangible se hace y se rehace ante nuestros ojos. Cuatro casos acompañados de una narración personal explicarán esta tesis: la narración autoetnográfica pandémica, el espacio arrebatado en *La casa tomada* de Julio Cortazar; el laberinto como refugio de la violencia exterior de *La casa de los espíritus* de Isabel Allende; el espacio paradójico de *Pedro Páramo* de Juan Rulfo. A su vez, reflexionaremos sobre el anhelado e imposible espacio entrevisto en la obra de Doris Salcedo, Shibboleth (2007). La percepción estética abre una nueva espacialidad; la pintura como obra de arte no está en el espacio que habita; la danza y el teatro se desarrollan en un espacio sin objetivos y sin direcciones: es una suspensión de nuestra historia. Las terapias artísticas desentrañan el sentido ambiguo, contradictorio y múltiple del espacio que los humanos han habitado, aún habitan o crean a su alrededor, haciendo un lugar de transformación y trascendencia. Al igual que en la obra de Cervantes, el espacio de las artes fluctúa entre lo que se percibe y lo que se siente, la huella de lo que ha sido y el anhelo de su aprehensión.

On space and sustained inter-corporality

This text was conceived months before the time of the coronavirus pandemic. It raised the idea of a symbolic space that opened, could be glimpsed or closed over on human beings, where they slipped their life into its cracks and fissures more than into the full and open space. Human beings who breathed and recognised themselves in the voids and in the interstices, caught up in the instant, opened themselves to not knowing.

> Life itself seems crazy. Who knows where madness lies? To be too practical is madness, to seek treasure where there is only trash, to surrender dreams may be madness.
>
> Too much sanity may be madness, but maddest of all is to see life as it is and not as it should be.
>
> *(El Quixote, Miguel de Cervantes, 1994)*

The following lines have been written during a lockdown agreed upon by a society that thought itself complete, seamless, closed, without bodies or vulnerable organs. A society of defined spaces, with an opening and a closing, and with an instruction manual that could only be understood in one way. An Excel life, neo-positivist, capable of being fully recounted in effective versions and in terms of efficiency. Life, however, is neither efficient nor effective. We live to die, while trying to circumvent death. Confinement has confronted us with it head on. The human being, doomed to its end, according to Sartre, is nothing more than "a useless passion."

In this framework, the issues that I proposed to address, given this situation, and that now come as a premonition, make even more sense: "Art is the awareness of a lost life and it is the means to recover it," pointed out the philosopher, María Zambrano (1971, p99). Poetic spaces reveal the absences, what has been lost, the invisible, that which is no longer more than a hint of what was but is not now. Such is this time of waiting, such is this space that is not, that still is not. A strange silent space reigns, a strange known space that turns out to be new. There are no persons, bodies establish distance, a void without words and an uncertain space. "But now, how few people I see," wrote Samuel Pepys during the pandemic of 1665, "and those walking like people that had taken leave of the world" (Bucholz & Ward, 2012, p317). Merleau-Ponty challenges us, relates us to the other, another who today becomes unknown, like oneself:

> How to name something, how to describe it, as I see it from my place, that experience of another which, however, is not anything to me because I believe in another – and which, on the other hand, concerns me, since it is there as another's vision of me? (…) my private world is no longer just mine; it is now the instrument with which another acts, the dimension of a generalized life that has been grafted onto mine.
>
> *(Merleau-Ponty, 2010, p17)*

I walk to the grocery store – the only thing allowed during the lockdown, feeding the body to keep it alive – in a state of national alarm. My street, in silence, returns its usual image, this time cleaner and clearer, and calmer than usual. There is nothing tangible that allows me to think of an alarm. My body, the perception that emanates from my body, in fact provides me with the opposite experience: it is spring, the trees are beginning to flower and they are covered with small mauve flowers, which will fall in a few weeks, letting their leaves appear. The sky is that blue that made me fall in love and was one of the reasons that made me choose Madrid as my home. It smells good, there is a pleasant freshness that floods my body after breathing it. I struggle with my mind, the one that informs me that I am deeply and existentially wrong. More than ever, as Merleau-Ponty points out, my private world has to be mine alone and I have to interact today, in a way that is contrary to what my body would do and is used to, in need of touch and contact with the other.

I walk, and I am also careful not to touch myself. I must believe that touch, the contact that constitutes me with the other, implies the contamination of the body (March 2020).

As Carolina Meloni points out:

> everything, as material as it is somatic, as impure as it is erotic, that brings us closer and communicates with each other, has been invested by the paralyzing fear of possible contamination. If there is one thing that defines coronavirus disease 2019 (COVID-19), it is its potential to transform us into abject persons. And the only motto that is transmitted to us, as a moral imperative that we must abide by without question, is the supposed responsibility to assume our own abjection.
>
> *(Meloni, 2020, p1)*

> *My own touch is therefore an abject agent, ready to make my body a sick territory. The emptiness is not such, it is loaded with a meaning that I do not know but to which I must pay attention. I do not see it, but I must think about it. It is the invisible. Seldom has the air become more symbolically dense, the void so threatening. Nothing has changed. Everything has changed. Now, when I see another person, we look at each other from afar, we measure the distance; we smell good, we look good, but we turn away.*

Materiality descends upon us all at once. As Meloni points out, we are ontologically vulnerable, physically, emotionally and affectively precarious. We are entwined with the other and yet now the encounter is denied, we break the physical bond that binds us to other. Our inter-corporeal knowledge, which Merleau-Ponty pointed out, is denied even to ourselves.

> *I write in plastic gloves. My fingertips are typing on a keyboard now unknown, after so many texts typed, in a threatening space, a train. And only at this moment am I aware of the importance of the touch, my fingertips not recognizing the surface, my hands touching and being touched.*

An unreal, uninhabited, naked, frightening space appears. A leaden, heavy air, similar to the air that one breathes in Comala, the town, or perhaps better to say non-town, where the novel *Pedro Páramo* takes place. Rarely has the paradox of perception taken on more meaning and returned us precisely to the foundations of phenomenology and existentialism. I am, insofar as they are; I move in a presumed realm of the visible and the tangible, which extends further than that which I currently see and touch. Hell is other people, as Sartre said. In the face of the supposed invisibility and panopticality of the modern subject, this confinement, this awareness of the space we inhabit that we miss, paradoxically brings us back to existence, to das-sein, to the existence that is configured as a vulnerable and violated and potentially violating body. No longer are only the other the vulnerable ones, those who vainly did not look, drowned again and again in the Mediterranean Sea. Now the bodies are us. Now the non-existent space becomes real, materially real, in the purest Lacanian sense. It is the space of not knowing. The air that exists, enters our lungs, modulates our vocal cords, makes us speak and sigh.

Creation, as a space of exceptionality

The work of art emerges as a citizen of two, almost three worlds, at one time belonging to the world of sensitivity, but also claimed by the world of meanings (Lutereau, 2010, p32). The relationship with the world is through knowledge and feeling, understanding feeling as the access to sensation, both internal and external. In some way, taking up Husserl, the artistic work confronts us with the two horizons of things: their external horizon and their "internal horizon," that "darkness crammed with visibility whose surface is the only limit" (Merleau-Ponty, 2010, p128). The work of art, its practice, marks the silence, the absence and the absent. Emptiness is neither hollow space nor lack of it. The void would, on the contrary, be a place linked to existence, to being. In art, in artistic production, empty space is endowed with meaning: "The void is nothing. Nor is it a lack of something. In artistic embodiment, emptiness plays in the manner of a seeking-projecting instituting of places (suchend-entwerfenden Stiften) places" (Groth, 2018).

The work of art, both in the artistic process and in art therapy, shows us that space is not something already there, as physics teaches us. The work of art guarantees that singularly human places will exist. Places that are the symbol of absence, like the long corridors designed by Eismann in the Jewish Museum in Berlin, so that we can inhabit absence, or like Alfredo Jaar's closed boxes, which contain photographs of the 1994 Rwandan genocide. Another of his works, from 2002, means that, when walking through it, the visitor finds a screen of white light or two equally luminous panels that close like a sarcophagus of light and plunge the place into darkness. Jaar does not offer images that leave us with a feeling of absence, in them he offers an absence that can provoke a presence. Again, emptiness.

Creation opens a symbolic space, to the Heideggerian *Raumgeben*, and in that opening it discovers at the same time that what is irreducible of the difference starts from the experience of the world, in the world. In the subjects we will find *gestalt* and meaning, structure and imagination. But, beyond them, we will find our experience of them, our inter-corporality through the visible and the tangible, confronted, accompanied by the experience of others. As Hegel pointed out, and Merleau-Ponty remarks, "to enter into oneself is also to leave oneself" (Merleau-Ponty, 2010, p54).

So, it is worth this special, suspended time, this space of intimacy that is constantly crossed by the public, of going out and coming in, to come in and therefore, to be able to go out. It is worth this heterotopic space, this "other" space in our own house, where the resonance and the repercussion mentioned by Bachelard act simultaneously. The resonance as an inner listening, that discovers us and our intimate and fragile spaces, that connects us with unseen corners of our own home, with spaces and times hidden behind a book on the shelf. The repercussion, from which time and space summon us to the threat, the fear, the limit, the prohibition, the friction between confinement and freedom. This is also the time and space of art, a suspended time and space, which reveals its fissures and paradoxes. Don Quixote traced an unprecedented and extraordinary journey through everyday passages, in the same way that the space of art discovers the unheard of in the ordinary. It is most likely the artists that can best live these moments.

From this personal pandemic narrative, we have chosen four works, three novels and one from the visual arts as spatial-temporal and sound axes: *The House Taken Over* by Julio Cortazar; *The House of the Spirits* by Isabel Allende; *Pedro Páramo* by Juan Rulfo and *Shibboleth* by Doris Salcedo. All four are open to sound, space and time simultaneously. And through them all, the work of Don Quixote reverberates like an echo where the being seeks him/herself, beyond him/herself. The works presented are connected in a special space and time that opens up in a dialectical space and time, beyond the Cartesian coordinates, just like this suspended time from a new plague. Art stops us, extracts us from *chronos*, just as the character of *The Plague* by Camus (1948), Doctor Bernard Rieux, stops before a dead rat lying in the middle of the landing.

The utopia, the heterotopia

Utopias are places that do not exist: imagined, as the horizon of our thoughts, they guide our society as a horizon, but they do not materialise. Heterotopia describes places functioning in non-hegemonic conditions and that are simultaneously physical and mental. By this definition, heterotopia is a physical approximation of imaginary utopia or a parallel space that makes utopia possible somewhere else.

> We do not live in a homogeneous and empty space (...) The space of our primary perception, the space of our dreams and that of our passions hold within themselves qualities that seem intrinsic: there is a light, ethereal, transparent space, or again a dark, rough, encumbered space; a space from above, of summits, or on the contrary a space from below of mud; or again a space that can be flowing like sparkling water, or space that is fixed, congealed, like stone or crystal. Yet these analyses, while fundamental for reflection in our time, primarily concern internal space.
>
> *(Foucault, 2002, p231)*

The spaces we present in this chapter are heterotopias: places that expel their inhabitants, places that unfold and become labyrinths, places that drown, or forbidden places whose only entrance or exit needs a password.

The House Taken Over is revealed as a false utopia, a conformable and stable space that, nevertheless, revolves and expels its inhabitants; *Pedro Páramo* presents the unstable, dense and disconcerting space of the town that has not been able to die completely and where everything and everyone dies again and again, without finding calm, an uncomfortable and guilt-ridden heterotopia. *The House of the*

Spirits is, by contrast, a heterotopia of salvation and affection, where the clandestine and unstable spaces multiply to shelter the rebels, those who do not settle down. Finally, *Shibboleth*, the dramatic piece created by Doris Salcedo, refers to expulsion, to the non-places denied to life, where beings, refugees from the violence of others, wander without a destination, denied again and again through the word that grants knowledge and the possibility of survival.

And Quixote, as a classic heterotopia, hovers over this text. In all the works there is a journey. It can be a journey without return, as in *The House Taken Over*, *Pedro Páramo* or *Shibboleth*. Or a journey that returns to the origin, which appears in *Don Quixote* and *The House of the Spirits*. A journey that, like that of Ulysses, returns home without, in some cases, ever having left it. Perhaps the confinement of 2020 can be considered a profound journey without having left our own home.

In all of them, the sound, the air, the whispers. The footprint of a life – or a death – that passes by, floats through the places, as premonitory elements of an action that happens.

The air, the voices, the whispers

> Our voice is the music that
> the wind blows through our bodies.
> *(Daniel Pennac, 2012, p31)*

Throughout the works addressed, the sound, the right word, the lack of it, is present, flooding the spaces of life or highlighting the lack of it. Merleau-Ponty points out that we can often grasp the feeling of what we are experiencing in its absence (1975). When we experience its limit, the lack of it, we are aware of what it means. Didi-Huberman talks about the experience of air in breathing (Didi-Huberman, 2017), about Marcel Proust's asthma and quotes Benjamin (2007, p317):

> Asthma entered into his art (…) His syntax imitates, with its rhythm, that fear of suffocation (…) On a larger scale, death comes to be that which Proust had continuously present, especially while writing, the brutal threat of Breathlessness.

> *One symptom of Covid19 is shortness of breath. I talked to a friend about her daughter and the illness: "Every night, around 2.00 AM, she wakes up with no air and this causes her an anxiety that only our presence, together with small crumbs of bread, which she swallows bit by bit, manages to calm her fear of suffocation." In the most serious cases, the nurses have to intubate the patients laying face down, so that the air can reach their lungs. In order to do this, they have to sedate them, eliminate their speech, leave them in semi-consciousness. In many cases, the disease presents itself in the form of "silent hypoxia," where patients are showing up to the hospital in worse health than they realize but their lungs are clearly not effective. They are unknowingly suffocating.*

Air which enters our lungs every few seconds and allows us to live. When we are accustomed to writing, we forget about the voice, that sound that emanates from our bodies and the air and comes to us. In his work *Of Grammatology* (Derrida, 1967), Derrida makes an interesting distinction between the written and the vocalised word, between writing and voice, between writing as a sign detached from the natural. Somehow, we forget where we come from, where the word refers to the voice, to the sound, to the body, to the flesh, to the earth: "We end up forgetting that we learn to speak before we learn to write, and the natural relationship is reversed" (Derrida, 1967, p74).

Air is the vehicle, the handle of the word, because there is no word without a breath: "The breath is not suspense or lack of word but its very condition" (Didi-Huberman, 2017, p16). To speak, as Levinas points out, suggests "a breath that opens up to the other" (Bataille, 1973), and is distinguished from the written word, from the discourse, which does not follow the enunciation, because its experience passes through it. "It is the will, that adds to the discourse, of not adhering to the enunciation, of forcing oneself to feel the cold of the wind, to be naked" (p23).

The air releases a movement, and it is the wind that will take shape in the artistic work, in the dance, in the waving of a flag, in a gesture. When we inhale "the ambient air, matter par excellence of the exterior, penetrates our body to the depths of our lungs, very low, almost to our entrails. When we breathe out, it is the very matter of our interiority that seems, inversely, to diffuse into the surrounding space" (Didi Huberman, 2017, p30). In a way, the word is the imprint of the air, which is made "in the moving mould of the mouth, the palate, the tongue" (p32).

In the spaces, the air modulated by the voices resonates and affects other spaces, other times that overlap. Murmurs behind the curtains, falling objects. The objects, as transitional elements of the family memory, which embrace superimposed generations, crossing them. The bodies themselves are air crossing the flesh. The murmurs of Comala, in *Pedro Páramo*, make the protagonist's journey unbearable, because they arise continuously among the lamentations of its dead inhabitants. As in *The House Taken Over*, they oppress and trigger the next expulsion. In *Shibboleth*, it means – revealing the body that names – to be or not to be definitively expelled. In *The House of the Spirits*, the cry marks the change of the house, of the space and its inhabitants, as well as the self-imposed silence of Clara, general or selective, pointing out when it is worth speaking or who does not deserve to be spoken to or heard. However, only *The House of the Spirits* receives the warnings of the spirits who shelter its inhabitants.

The House Taken Over: the womb or the life beyond

The space of *The House Taken Over* is an interior space, dense, loaded, stable, heavy. It is the space of the family house, where the old wood of the different generations creaks. *The House Taken Over* tells us, in a few pages, how the peaceful, monotonous and self-absorbed life of two adults, brother and sister, whose life passes by, is altered by sounds that come from inside the family home and that, night after night, gradually occupy the different rooms of the great house:

> "I went down to the kitchen, heated the kettle, and when I got back with the tray of mate, I told Irene: 'I had to shut the door to the passage, they've taken over the back part.'
> She let her knitting fall and looked at me with her tired, serious eyes.
> 'You're sure?' I nodded.
> 'In that case,' she said, picking up her knitting again, 'We'll have to live on this side.'"
>
> *(Cortazar, 1951, p4)*

What exactly are the murmurs heard in *The House Taken Over* that force the characters, first to live in a reduced space and, later, to leave their home? For many experts, these murmurs are situations that have been experienced in the past, something like the ghosts of the past, which the characters have not been able to face. These metaphysical "ghosts" appear in the house and haunt the characters who do not have the courage to face them:

> We stood listening to the noises, growing more and more sure that they were on our side of the oak door, if not the kitchen, then the bath or in the hall itself at the turn, almost next to us. We didn't wait to look at one another. I took Irene's arm and forced her to run with me to the wrought-iron door, not waiting to look back. You could hear the noises, still muffled but louder, just behind us. I slammed the grating and we stopped in the vestibule. Now there was nothing to be heard.
> "They've taken over our section," Irene said.
>
> *(Cortazar, 1951, p5)*

Like the legend of Lot, they do not even dare to look back, for fear of being trapped again by the past of others. Gaston Bachelard makes an interesting analysis of the poetics of space in the house:

> With the image of the house, we support a real principle of psychological integration. Descriptive psychology, psychology of the depths, psychoanalysis and phenomenology could constitute, with the house, this body of doctrines that we designate under the name of topo-analysis. Examined in the most diverse theoretical horizons, it seems that the image of the home becomes the topography of our intimate being.
>
> *(Bachelard, 1961, p27)*

The House Taken Over, that inherited space, full of objects from previous generations, holds the two, brother and sister, dragging them into an inherited life, where Irene sews and unsews, like Penelope, the same cloth, a fabric that endlessly repeats one stitch after another, towards death. As the house is taken over, the beings, abandoned to the open space, paradoxically start to live.

Pedro Páramo, the lifedeath

- Is he dead? What about?
- I do not know. Maybe sadness. He sighed a lot.
- That's bad. Every sigh is like a sip of life that one discards.

(Rulfo, 1997, p102)

The central character of the novel is the town itself. In it, only souls who wander in sorrow live. At first, Juan Preciado tells of his journey to the village in search of a father he never knew, and he begins to perceive the ghost of Comala. The structure of the story changes as the novel progresses. It is no longer only the protagonist who tells the story, but the voices of the inhabitants of Comala are intermingled. Juan Preciado talks with the living and the dead, the events told by the inhabitants overlap indistinctly, present and past are no longer categories of a temporal order.

Comala's atmosphere is one of emptiness and ruin. Death is seen as a transition, a journey into another realm, something you live with. Juan Preciado, the son of Pedro Páramo, does not know that it is a journey with no return. About halfway through the story, Juan says, "I was killed by the murmurs."

The space of Comala is non-existent and at the same time, heavy and asphyxiating. Time and space are suspended, and the dead intervene at the wrong time and place. They appear and disappear haphazardly, in a fragmentary way, because there is no chronological time that orders their appearance. Time overlaps. The past and the present coexist, like life and death, in the same space. The orphanage, the lack, the radical absence of the other emerges. Comala means the loss of Eden and at the same time, as Muñoz highlights (Muñoz, 1985), it is the search for one's origins:

"Why are you crying, Mother?" he asked, for as soon as he put his feet on the ground, he recognized his mother's face.
"Your father is dead," she said.
(…) Outside in the courtyard, footsteps, as if people were walking around. Quiet noises. And here, that woman, standing in the doorway, her body preventing the arrival of daylight; letting in, through her arms, bits of sky, and under her feet, traces of light; a light sprinkled as if the ground underneath her was flooded with tears. And then the sobbing. Again, the soft but sharp cry, and the sorrow twisting her body.
"Your father has been killed."
"And who killed you, Mother?"

(Rulfo, 1997, p89)

Pedro Páramo's space is the catastrophe. In it, Juan Preciado tries to give meaning to a fragmentary time, devoid of memory, that superimposes the past on the present, and to a dense and rotten space, like the bodies that inhabit it. In it he lives and dies simultaneously, in a sterile search for his father. A journey without return to an origin that he does not find. As Muñoz (1985, p387) points out, "the dominant figure of the Father, the expulsion of the original couple, the wandering of the children without affiliation, the wandering of the souls in pain, the atrocious suffering of the condemned, parricide as an act of justice…, are forms in which the mythical thought expresses itself and affirms the existence of a parallel reality." *Pedro Páramo* is a work where the paradox emerges: paradise is hell, love is sadness or violence, fatherhood is abandonment, movement is motionless. There is no possibility of escaping a tragic destiny, of loneliness amidst lamentations, governed by arbitrariness and absurdity. In the narrative, the opposite unfolds: a mother looking for a child she did not have and a child looking for a father who does not exist. The characters yearn for what they thought they had without having it and do not get what they are looking for. At the same time, nostalgia for what one never had. The nostalgia for utopia in the heterotopic space that is a deep crack in existence.

There is no mercy in Pedro Páramo's space; beings, like space and time, wander in their devastation, eaten away.

The House of the Spirits

The spaces of *The House of the Spirits* mix reality and paradox and contrast with each other in their texture and rigidity. Contrary to La hacienda, an unalterable, rigid, ordered, patriarchal space where Esteban Trueba develops his dominant role, The House on the Corner, governed by Clara Valle, is a space of change.

> He could not have known that that solemn, cubic, compact and pompous mansion (…) would end up filled with protuberances and add-ons, with multiple crooked stairs that led to vague places, with towers, with windows that did not open, of doors suspended in the void of twisted corridors and portholes that linked the bedrooms to allow communication with each other at nap time, according to Clara's inspiration, who every time she needed to install a new guest, she would have another room built somewhere else (…) until she left the mansion converted into an enchanted labyrinth impossible to clean.
>
> *(Allende, 1982, p72)*

The space welcomes the inhabitants, allows them to hide, to rest, to make each space a shelter: "Accompanied by the spirits of air, water and earth, she was so happy that she did not feel the need to speak for nine years" (Allende, 1982, p63).

Gaston Bachelard points out four perspectives that can be used to interact with the interior of matter. The third one, refers to a perspective that reveals a wonderful interior, like a geode, where a crystalline, coloured world is revealed to us. An interior that holds arborescence, luminescence, that reveals a celestial interior (Bachelard, 1961). That's the space behind The House on the Corner.

Clara Valle builds spaces in The House on the Corner as she needs them, offering resting places to others and hiding places for herself. Later, her granddaughter, Alba, will use these spaces as a hiding place for fugitives from the dictatorial regime, a "labyrinth of secret corners" (Allende, 1982, p301). The house on the corner becomes, behind its bourgeois façade, a dynamic, changing labyrinth that serves as a refuge, generation after generation, for the intimacy of those who flee, who live differently, subordinates, who survive in the hostile, unalterable spaces planned in the light.

As Bachelard points out, the spaces of the house are impregnated with symbolism. In the house on the corner, the basement becomes the feminine space, the roots, where the past is accumulated, which will later be the space of love and refuge from violence. Spiritual, creative spaces of affectivity, turned over to the imagination and the feminine that undermine from within the base of patriarchal society, like the basement, exclusive to women in the house. It is the place where Alba plays and develops her creativity with the forgotten objects of the family. It is there that she hides, after Clara's burial, to meet the spirit of her grandmother. When she falls in love with Miguel, she recovers that space of her childhood to secretly enjoy her love. On the outside, the space in front. Behind the walls, Clara's space, the basement, the women's, clandestine. A labyrinth:

> Rooms, staircases, turrets and roofs began to sprout from the noble architecture. Whenever a new guest had to be accommodated, the same workers arrived and added another room. Thus, the big house on the corner came to look like a maze.
>
> *(Allende, 1982, p170)*

> The big house on the corner was a closed world where she grew up protected even from her own nightmares.
>
> *(Allende, 1982, p202)*

The House on the Corner is characterised by the forms of spirit, sensibility, affectivity, creativity, magic, secret love, marginalisation, social justice and revolution; in short, every transgressive element that departs from the patriarchal discourse of the powerful class.

The air and the voices

Voice, air and silence flood the space of *The House of the Spirits*. The silence, the mute, the moaning:

> (…) a terrible wailing of a lost ship was heard throughout the house. It was the first and last time that Barabbas made himself heard. He howled at the dead girl all day long, until he shattered the nerves of the inhabitants of the house and the neighbors, who came by, attracted by that wailing of the shipwreck.
>
> *(Allende, 1982, p21)*

At the same time, silence imposes itself, not as an absence, but as a decision and a choice, something solid as another space of inner refuge that occupies everything. Like her mourning, first for her sister and the vision of her lifeless body and then for the mourning of an act that leaves an open and unsolvable wound: "Silence occupied her entirely, and she did not speak again until nine years later." "I had come to understand that silence was my wife's last inviolable refuge" (Allende, 1982, p86).

The unsaid is present. The unsaid word, without form, becomes a metaphor of the unrealised, of what, even if it could, does not happen.

Shibboleth

> Seeing, thinking and speaking is thinking, but thinking takes place in the interstice, in the disjunction between seeing and speaking.
>
> *(Deleuze, 2004)*

In 2007, the visual artist, Doris Salcedo, built an empty space in the form of an irregular 167-metre crack on the floor of the Turbine Room Museum at the Tate Gallery, London. A terrible crack like a wound on the surface of culture. The insurmountable space between being and not being, between having and not having; being inside and outside. She calls it *Shibboleth*, that key word that appears in the Bible to distinguish with its pronunciation, in its speech and the body that enunciates it, those who are of the chosen people. From its pronunciation, membership is marked, those who must die – pointing out which are the "right" bodies that pronounce it properly and the "other" bodies that reveal its abjection and dispensability. Salcedo's *Shibboleth* ciphers a visual password into the mute mystery of the rift, made up of fractures, faults and saturated voids, paradoxical and negative space turned in on itself (Speranza, 2012). The use of the password also appears in *The House of the Spirits*:

> Alba came up to them and pointed to the mural across the street. It was stained
>   with red paint and had only one word written on it in huge letters: Djakarta.
> "What does that name mean, comrades?"
> "We don't know," they answered.
> No one knew why the opposition painted that Asian word on the walls, they had
>   never heard of the piles of dead in the streets of that faraway city.
>
> *(Allende, 1982, p277)*

Words, the border between the inside and the outside of the body, between abandonment, isolation and life with others. In the past, the lazarettos gathered the others, in that heterotopia, that dystopia that enclosed the unworthy. Sometimes, this heterotopia is the non-place, the space of death. It is the city of Comala, where all the inhabitants have died, and wander among the laments for the life they have not finished living, or for the pain that accompanies them. Operation Djakarta was a plan for the systematic assassination of leaders of Allende's Popular

Unity Government in Chile, where *The House of the Spirits* takes place. The organisation was named after the CIA (Central Inteligence Agency)'s bloodiest success, the military coup in Indonesia in 1965, during which one million people were brutally murdered. The CIA helped the military in Chile meticulously put together lists of 3,000 top-level and 20,000 mid-level leaders of people's organisations that were to be exterminated. Virtually everyone who did not flee the country was hunted down and killed. Lists with names whose significance hid vulnerable bodies sentenced behind one keyword: Djakarta.

In 2020, *Shibboleth* is a coin or symbol that saves those who possess it: the age that separates those who should and should not receive medical care, who have already lived long enough, from that Foucaultian panopticon that prescribes and proscribes. *Shibboleth* is a social class that may or may not have access to health services; *Shibboleth* is an origin that is configured as guilty and contaminated, that demonised "other" that separates the healthy and the sick, illness and death, which Susan Sontag so well pointed out in *Illness as Metaphor*. Art reveals that impudence, the scandal of human tragedy, the shame of those who participate in the siege or the barbarism of those who, dehumanised, let others die and do not look back. *Oedipus Rex*, by Sophocles, begins when a plague breaks out in Thebes and the citizens count on the king to resolve the situation. But Oedipus ends up realising that he is the source of the plague, where the origin and the end meet.

Conclusion

The field of art, by introducing us into an empty space, an anachronistic time – a space without coordinates, a time without past or future – and an inverse movement, proposes an "operated spacing," where the object becomes, like the vestige, the sign of a loss, as Didi-Huberman would say (2014). Creation, as a state of exceptionality, takes the experience of the visible and the tangible, and makes and remakes it before our eyes: in doing so, aesthetic perception opens a new spatiality, and it is a suspension of our history (Merleau-Ponty, 2010).

> *The streets of this city that I inhabit today are a reminder of what they once were: dialogues suspended in an empty space, whispers of a few laughs, the sound of cars stranded on the sidewalks. This parenthesis, where we hold our breath, that air in our body still warm, announces something that is no longer and has not yet happened. Something that will never be again. The murmur, like Greek Erinyes, like Sartre's flies, falls on the living as a recrimination of what has been done and not done, what has happened and what is still to come.*

These are the spaces evoked by the works mentioned in this text. This takes place in an inverse and paradoxical movement, which becomes a journey without return, as in *The House Taken Over*, *Pedro Páramo* and *Shibboleth*; or in a circular journey, as in *The House of the Spirits*.

The space opened by the arts therapies is similar to the one we have mentioned in this essay. In arts therapies time pauses, becomes anachronistic, opens a symbolic place halfway between heterotopia and utopia, where to return to a painful past from a safe space that becomes potential. The word recovers the materiality of the body, the body takes sense, acknowledges the unknown. Zambrano's words are fulfilled in the space of art as therapy: in the workshop, lost life and absence emerge as reflection and at the same time as a way to recover and create space for what is possible, but it's not yet.

Quixote returns transformed, and dies as soon as he recovers his sanity, after having travelled through an imagined and melancholic space, where he has learned from others and from himself. Alba, the granddaughter tortured by power, with long and beautiful green hair – like her great aunt, who made her grandmother mute for nine years – in *The House of the Spirits* has made the epic journey through her generations, of love and hate, of affection and violence, acquiring the wisdom of pain and forgiveness and opens the house as a space of wisdom.

The wind cannot be stopped, but one must know how to make windmills.
(Miguel de Cervantes)

References

Allende, I. (1982) *La casa de los espíritus*. Chile: Editorial Sudamericana.

Bachelard, G. (1961) *La poétique de l'espace*. París: Les Presses universitaires de France.

Bataille, G. (1973) *La experiencia interior*. Madrid: Taurus.

Benjamin, W. (2007) 'Hacia la imagen de Proust' en *Obras, libro II*, Vol. 1. Madrid: Abada.

Bucholz, R. and Ward, J. P. (2012) *London, A social and cultural history 1550-1750*. Cambridge: Cambridge University Press.

Camus, A. (1948) *The plague*. London: Hamish Hamilton.

Cervantes, M. de (1994) *Don Quijote de la Mancha*. En *Obras completas*, tomo II. México: Aguilar.

Cortazar, J. (1951) *La casa tomada*. En *Bestiario*, Buenos Aires: Hispanoamérica.

Deleuze, G. (2004) *Foucault*. Paris: Les Éditions de Minuit.

Derrida, J. (1967) *De la gramatología*. París: Minuit.

Didi-Huberman, G. (2014) *El hombre que andaba en el color*. Madrid: Adaba.

Didi-Huberman, G. (2017) *Gestos de aire y de la piedra*. Ciudad de México: Canta Mares.

Foucault, M. (2002) *Of other Spaces: utopias and heterotopias*. In: Mirzoeff, N. *The visual culture reader*. London, Routledge.

Groth, M. (2018) *Art and Emptiness: Heidegger and Chillida on space and place* THÉMATA. Revista de Filosofía N° 57, Ed.)

Merleau-Ponty, M. (1975) *Fenomenología de la Percepción*. Barcelona: Península.

Merleau-Ponty, M. (2010) *Lo visible y lo invisible*. Buenos Aires: Nueva Visión.

Lutereau, L. (2010) *Fenomenología de la presentación estética*. Buenos Aires: Universidad de Buenos Aires.

Meloni, C. (2020) *La comunidad intocable*. https://lavoragine.net/comunidad-intocable-meloni/ downloaded 2nd April 2020.

Muñoz, M. (1985) Dualidad y desencuentro en "Pedro Páramo". Cuadernos Hispanoamericanos, núm. 421–423 (julio-septiembre 1985), pp. 385–398, Madrid: Instituto de Cooperación Iberoamericana.

Pennac, D. (2012) *Diario de un cuerpo*. Madrid: Mondadori.

Rulfo, J. (1997) *Pedro Páramo*. Madrid: Fondo de Cultura Económica.

Speranza, G. (2012) *Atlas portátil de América Latina. Arte y ficciones errantes*. Barcelona: Anagrama.

Zambrano, M. (1971) *Algunos lugares de la pintura*. En: Zambrano, M. *Obras Reunidas*. Madrid: Aguilar.

2

EDUCATING THE QUIXOTIC IMAGINATION

Robert D. Romanyshyn

Abstract

Cervantes's text is an excellent example of what Jung calls a visionary work of art. Written in the spirit of the times, Don Quixote appears to us as a foolish knight errant, perhaps even mad and delusional in his attacks on windmills that he perceives to be giants. And yet, in this visionary book, Quixote's quest is rooted in the spirit of the depths where he dreams what seems to be an impossible dream. It is a dream we are still dreaming, a dream that is dreaming us, a quest that now in our time has become, perhaps, even more crucial. In his dialogues with his humble squire, Sancho Panza, we are eavesdroppers, as it were, who, line by line, page by page, chapter by chapter are slowly but irresistibly drawn into questioning fixed beliefs about who is mad and who is sane, be they wind-mills or be they Giants, what is true and what is false, what is real and what is unreal, what is familiar and what is strange and estranging in its strangeness. This is the stuff that psychotherapists are made on, and Cervantes's visionary master-piece is an indispensable guide for the education of the imagination. For, it is only through imagination that one can imagine windmills as giants, a possibility so unreasonable that our fixed dichotomies can be dissolved to reveal possibilities still to be dreamed.

Keywords: Imagination, imaginal, poetic realism, poetic sensibility, margins, psychotherapy

Introduction: Don Quixote is not Quixotic

I am reading Cervantes's text as a collective cultural-historical dream that is still dreaming us. Attending to the characters of Cervantes' dream, we are taken to the margins of his prophetic and visionary text, which, in its time having already

DOI: 10.4324/9781003110200-2

envisioned the world that has become our own, can unsettle us with its questions about who is mad and who is sane – be they windmills or be they giants, or is that dichotomy itself a piece of our own cultural complex? What is true and what is false, what is real and what is unreal, what is familiar and what is strange and estranging in its strangeness. For it is on the margins, and I would say only on the margins of our shared and individual lives, where the walls of our dichotomies might become more porous gates of transformation. Might become, I said, because nothing is certain when individually and collectively an education into a Quixotic imagination invites us to trust what speaks to us from the margins and seems so impossible. To trust even in the face of the fact that the character of Don Quixote has become an adjective to describe and dismiss what is dreamy, impractical, romantic, starry-eyed, capricious, unreliable and unpredictable.

Don Quixote is dreaming what seems to be an impossible dream, and, as I noted above, I am reading Cervantes's text as a collective dream that is still dreaming us. From this perspective, "his" seeming impossible dream, while coming through him, is more than personal. We might even say that Quixote is dreaming for all of us who fall into the enchantment of that dream when we cross the threshold into the place where the one who is reading Cervantes's book encounters Don Quixote.

In my psychotherapy practice over nearly fifty years I have on more than a few occasions witnessed such collective dreams and have come to appreciate this type of dream as a calling that is pregnant with the spirit of the depths that lingers below the spirit of the times in which they occur. They have a visionary and, we might even say, a prophetic quality.

Quixote's impossible dream shows us that such prophetic dreams present a vision of a life. They underline a quest that is like a myth that informs the destiny of one's life, that seeds a vocation, a dream, which, like a polestar, guides the direction of one's life and which at times modifies, supplements and even corrects one's path.

These corrections seem to arise especially in those moments when one might have unknowingly lost one's way. Or they might arise in moments when doubt or discouragement weigh heavily on the person. In this regard, Sancho Panza's repeated questioning of Quixote's actions is a brilliant psychological step, which illustrates the power of what is called a paradoxical intention. His questioning of Quixote simultaneously suggests the folly of his master's quest even as it re-enforces Quixote's vision.

In Cervantes' day, the character of Don Quixote's impossible dream is one that embodies and enacts the values of a noble, chivalrous, courtly knight whose world has passed away. On the surface of things, it is easy to dismiss him as Quixotic, a mad fool, as someone who is insane. And yet, the character of Quixote beguiles us so much that we begin to wonder if there is meaning in the apparent madness, wisdom in the seeming folly of the fool. Mounted on Rocinante, lance in hand he even disarms us, wounding us as the tip of his lance blesses us with the gift of imagination that bridges the divide between sanity and madness.

Visionary dreams are not as uncommon as they might seem and I have found them to be of singular significance in listening to the seemingly impossible dreams of patients, and, to confess, such dreams have played a major role in my life.

I would add here that the mood quality of such impossible dreams is often one of longing for something that seems lost, or forgotten, or left by the side of the road which, if not given a place in one's reflections, lingers as a kind of low-level depression, or maybe melancholy to use a less clinical term. In addition, such dreams often carry images of the orphan figure, the one who is, not literally an orphan, but one who does not feel at home. Our impossible dreams, these polestars whose dark light still lights the way, might very well be dreams of homecoming.

Imagine that! Don Quixote still lives within our collective imaginations as a guide home.

Part one: the art of psychotherapy

This phrase holds a key insight honed over fifty years of practice, teaching, supervision and writing about the necessity of the humanities and the arts in the education of psychotherapists. It is an insight that dawned on me in my work with actors. As I wondered about that magical pivot, so taken for granted and seemingly natural, where the person of the actor on stage would become increasingly invisible as the character being portrayed became increasingly visible, this pivot, I realised, was also the magic and mystery of psychotherapy. Thus, I would emphasise to my students that the threshold of the therapy room is a boundary where the quotidian world of *the person who comes to therapy* is transformed into a stage where *the figures who came for therapy could tell their still untold tales.* The primary lesson in the education of a psychotherapist was to learn how to differentiate the visible person from the subtle, invisible characters in the room.

My reflections on educating the Quixotic imagination addresses this point. It also addresses two key implications of this lesson.

Firstly, a psychotherapy that does acknowledge this difference takes place in a dramatic field with its cast of characters.

Secondly, to work within this dramatic field requires a thorough education in the humanities. Richard Hougham in his article on the Duende cites the Jungian analyst Rafael Lopez-Pedraza:

> Psychotherapy not founded on culture, or a psychotherapist who does not have a cultured view of life and is unaware that sickness has its roots in cultural complexes, is inconceivable.
>
> *(Hougham, 2015, p9)*

But it took me quite some time to realise and work through the implications of this first lesson, to learn that the craft of psychotherapy required a kind of education that could appreciate the healing power of making a place for the silenced stories of the figures to be told and felt in a dramatic, embodied way; and, as well, time to appreciate that the untold tales were part of larger stories, strands of the psychic DNA of the collective unconscious of humanity, imagined and depicted in myths, dramas, paintings, literature and film. As a patient and as a psychotherapist, I have witnessed how these larger stories contain and provide perspective for one's life and, as such, are therapeutic. The actor, Mark Rylance, makes the same point about drama:

> We need larger stories—mythological stories which touch upon the soul's need for experience in life, something deeper, something more mysterious. If you keep in contact with the older, more mythological stories, they are not productive, they are not functional, they are not going to get you a job, but they keep the road curvy and spirally, rather than making the road as straight as possible from A to B. That's a quick journey but it's a terribly boring journey and you'll be very sad when you die.
>
> *(Rylance in Hougham, 2015, p2)*

Does this not suggest that what still lives in psychotherapy is a hunger to tell one's story and find where it belongs in the community of stories that bind each of us to a tradition?

Does not this need persist even in the age of straightening out the patient in the quickest possible time?

Therapy is a kind of theatre and theatre is a kind of therapy. Both exist within the frame of a dramatic reality, which Salvo Pitruzzella notes "is a basic theoretical construct in drama therapy" (Pitruzzella, 2017, p107). In theatre and therapy, a shared space is created, which is "a different level in respect to what is commonly perceived as everyday reality." It is a reality that I describe as the poetic realism of the world.

In my own practice, the distinction between the person and the figure has defined the process of psychotherapy as the transformation of space into a place where the figures stage their stories. More often than not, the therapy room has been a place for a gathering of ancestors leaning in to listen to the untold tales being told by the figure(s), as if drawn to this moment by an emotional affinity between fellow wanderers.

In addition, there have also been on occasion fictional and historical characters through whom the untold tales of the figure have been presented.

One very dramatic example was a patient whose untold tale unfolded over a series of sessions through the story of Merlin. A drama major in an arts and humanities program where I taught, she suffered under the weight of her partner's criticisms. A professor of German philosophy, he routinely ridiculed and dismissed her work as mere fantasy. Leaving aside, for this presentation, the important clinical issues regarding transference, counter-transference and the dynamics of the power shadow of Eros in the story of Merlin, I offer this example to show how in the theatre of the therapy room, the person of the patient spontaneously lived into and embodied the figure of Morgana through whom her untold desires were given a place.[1]

Today we are witnesses to the tale of Don Quixote, the knight of the sorrowful countenance, the dreamer of impossible dreams, and his companion, Sancho Panza. While part one of Cervantes's visionary masterpiece was finished in 1605 and part two in 1615, the story of Quixote and his squire is not done. They linger with us.

What might we learn if we attend to their presence?

Part two: imagining windmills: absence and presence – a phenomenology of the empty bench

Have you ever stopped, even for a moment, beside an empty bench? Such a pause can be an invitation to something more than ordinary. As you linger there, maybe not even knowing why, you might discover that unexpectedly you have been stopped in your tracks by a question as if posed by the empty bench: "Can you linger for a moment to hear a story?"

In the daily mundane world, such a moment is like a miracle because there is no one who is present who has posed the question that has stopped you in your tracks. And yet, if you pause, perhaps feeling a bit foolish, you might discover that a curtain in the everyday world has been drawn aside and that there on the empty bench is a presence that is present in its absence. One day it might even be Don Quixote and his squire who are present in their absence even while absent in their presence. In such moments, the everyday world of things and thoughts becomes a stage and life itself becomes a drama with many stories within which you play your parts.

An empty bench is like Don Quixote's windmills and pausing to attend to who/what is present in its absence reveals an-other domain of reality – let us call it the imaginal – which is neither a matter of things nor thoughts, neither a matter of fact nor one of mind. An ordinary empty bench can be an extraordinary education into the Quixotic imagination. It can be an occasion where and when you are led out of yourself and drawn into an-other world.

Part three: bench reveries

When Don Quixote accompanied by Sancho Panza sets forth on his first adventure, he and his companion are clearing a path into a new style of education. To e-ducate and to be e-ducated is to be drawn or led out of oneself. Education is a journey that proceeds from what is known and familiar to what is strange and unknown. Or at least it should be. If it is, it can be a transformative experience, even an estrangement from who one is and has been.

The one who educates in this way does not simply impart information. On the contrary, he or she raises the disturbing possibility that what is might be otherwise than how it appears. This type of teacher is kin to Socrates whose way of teaching is characterised by the mood of irony and the mode of the question. This mood and mode of education, which turns things upside down and inside out can have a satirical, humorous, dramatic quality when one's beliefs are cracked open by what is unbelievable. It is also very often painful as attested to by Quixote's tale when his body suffers the blows from others for his seemingly unbelievable visions. The one who does educate in this way is, therefore, a fool, a dangerous figure because he or she challenges familiar, unquestioned, comfortable ways of being. Socrates was forced to drink hemlock for his educational improprieties.

Don Quixote and Sancho Panza complement each other, and both are foolish, dangerous figures. Indeed, their education is a seduction. It has an enticing even erotic appeal that can make you lose your head as it were, taking you away from yourself and leading you deeper into unfamiliar depths. Bench reveries with Quixote can lead you into those seemingly mad parts of yourself, to those unknown but beguiling places where you are paradoxically most sane even as it might appear to others you are not normal.

Bench work with Don Quixote is like waking up and being addressed by him and his squire whose tales of seemingly impossible encounters show you as other to yourself. As you read his story you fall into it as line by line, paragraph by paragraph, page by page and chapter by chapter you discover that the constant spoken and silent dialogue between Quixote and his squire is becoming a dialogue between the sane, normal, reliable and responsible parts of who you believe yourself to be, and those unknown, seemingly mad parts that you might never even imagined becoming.

Dare we trust such moments?

Dare we not trust such moments?

Don Quixote and Sancho Panza companion us into a dramatic and therapeutic education, not only stimulating our minds, but also whetting the appetite of our imaginations, feeding it with the nourishing food of their story. That is the genius of the knight errant and his squire, its terrible beauty, which lingers to this day. It is a complex tale that holds the tension between madness and sanity by refusing to split them into an either/or dichotomy.

In the deathbed scene, Quixote's housekeeper says to him: "Stay at home, attend to your affairs, go often to confession, be charitable to the poor…" While her voice is the voice of reason that would seem to dismiss her master's escapades as mere folly, Samuel Putnam (1949, p34) argues that her words do not necessarily suggest an unquestioned acceptance of things as they are. Rather they are a counterpoint that underscores the wisdom and value and even necessity for Quixote's impossible dream. Indeed, Putnam argues that Quixote had to become the knight errant; it was, we can say, his vocation, his destiny. Reminded of the housekeeper's words, Putnam quotes the following passage from the diary of Kathe Kollwitz, German painter and print maker in the late 19th century through the middle of the 20th century:

> I am not only allowed to finish my work, I am bidden to finish it. This, it seems to me, is the meaning of all the talk about civilization. It can exist only when each individual fills his own personal sphere of duty.
>
> *(Putnam, 1949, p34)*

While such words might seem like "a homely, prosaic lesson," one "may have to go through hell to learn it." Moreover, a thinking person, Putnam adds, "may have to draw aside a curtain that had best be left undrawn, since the tragicomic spectacle revealed is one that can only lead to madness in the eyes of those who remain on the other side" (Putnam, 1949, p34). Drawing aside that curtain lifts the veils that cloud our vision making the Quixotic therapeutic education a revelation. Indeed, a Quixotic education is in the root sense of the term an *apocalyptic* vision, a parting of the veils.

If a Quixotic education is truly apocalyptic, a parting of the veils, it is, in large measure, because it cultivates the *as if* quality of imagination as a legitimate and even necessary way of knowing and being in the world.

Part four: the image quality of the Quixotic imagination

Would Don Quixote be who he is without Sancho Panza?

Would the story be what it is and what it has become without this interplay between them: a visionary text that speaks to us from the depths of the collective, archetypal imagination?

Does not Sancho Panza reflect back to Don Quixote that necessary element of disbelief that deepens and enriches the character of Quixote, allowing us, in fact, to pause along the way with them to wonder about the primary question in this story: what is sanity and what is madness?

They twin each other, which is the same dynamic in Mary Shelley's visionary text, *Frankenstein, Or, The Modern Prometheus*. Indeed, in my recent book, *Victor Frankenstein, The Monster and the Shadows of Technology: The Frankenstein Prophecies,* that twinning is brought into sharp relief, because the twin in Victor Frankenstein's story is the figure of the Monster, who is a rather more disturbing presence compared with Sancho Panza.

And yet, as difficult as it is to attend to the Monster's side of the story, the story of Victor Frankenstein could not be the cautionary tale it has become. The Monster's story, which my book explores in terms of eight questions he poses to us as readers, reveals the hubris of his creator's dream to be a new god of creation and the consequences of his denial of responsibility for what he has created. For Victor Frankenstein, the scarred and disfigured devil, as he calls his creation, is an abomination to be exiled to the margins of humankind, ignored, a dark shadow of a flawed god, whose dream has become our nightmare. Attending to the Monster's tale on the margins allows us as readers to face a question that is haunting us today: who is the Monster?

But, of course, I am not saying Sancho Panza is a monster. He is, however, the other to his master as the "Monster" is to his creator. The point here is the issue of *the otherness of the other* that reflects back unrecognised and even unwanted aspects of oneself. Quixote and his squire mirror each other, and in that mutual reflexivity each presents an uncanny image of the other. A few remarks on the experience of the mirror reflection are in order here if we are to uncover some of the qualities of the Quixotic imagination.

Firstly, the mirror reflection is an image that throws back to the person look-ing in the mirror not a duplicate or carbon copy of him/herself, but an-other.

Secondly, the experience poses the question of who that strange yet haunt-ingly familiar other might be.

Thirdly, whoever he or she might be, the mirror image is a piece of magic that displays oneself as he/she is seen by others and/or reflects how one wishes, imagines himself or herself to be.

Fourthly, while the optical explanation places the image in the mirror, the experience of the reflection appears to be on the far side of the glass, as far per-haps from the surface of the glass as is the person on this side of the mirror. The mirror image is not a surface phenomenon. It is no superficial matter. On the contrary, the image matters as the depth of the person on this side of the mirror. Insofar as Jung says psyche is image, might we say that the mirror image is a deepening of mind into soul?

The mirror image that seems to regard you from afar dissolves the fixed sense of who one is. It is a piece of alchemy that the cover image of the 1958 edition of Jung's *The Undiscovered Self* suggests is an ongoing process of dissolution.

The image is not merely a negation of who one is. Rather, the image is a claim that asserts one is always who/what one is not, a journey that is always on the way.

With this brief excursion into the phenomenology of the mirror, I am sug-gesting the mirror can be an encounter with Quixote's windmills. As with his windmills

—Be they windmills or be they Giants?—

the mirror is not an object there in the world defined by its physical measures. It is a threshold, a doorway. The mirror, like Quixote's windmills, is a magical portal into a different domain of reality, the subtle reality of the image that is neither a matter of fact nor an idea of mind.

We are all mirrors for each other!
Portals of Possibility!

Quixote is for Sancho Panza, as Sancho Panza is for Quixote, an image of possi-bility. As such, each undoes the fixed identity of the other. Each is for the other a deepening of who and what each of them is. For each of them, the other is the one that gives flesh to the story and carries its dramatic action. We cannot and should not say, then, that Sancho Panza is the one who only carries the reality of the windmills as a given fact in the world. He is not an image of the conven-tional ways of the world. That would be a serious misreading of the story because it would set his view as the arbiter of what is truly real. Measured against that stubborn fact, Don Quixote would have to be regarded as mad, and then we would miss how, through his squire, Quixote is an image of necessity, courage and vocation to journey beyond the given norms, three values according to Jung that are essential features of the individuation process. And then, I would add, sadly for ourselves today, we would regard this magnificent tale as a prophecy of the diagnosed psychiatric patient and the DSM as the text, which, purporting to know the true and real story of Quixote, would spoil the story.

So, let us stay in the realm of the image and celebrate that while Sancho Panza does carry the lapidary reality of the windmills, his view is leavened by the magic of his master's visions. The stony gravitas of the windmills takes on some of the wispy fragments of Quixote's dream. Sancho Panza is changed through his relationship with Quixote.

In like manner let us celebrate that Quixote too is changed. While he does suffer his exploits in a very direct, embodied way, he is able to continue because Sancho Panza makes a place for the stories Quixote fabricates to make sense of his misfortunes. When Sancho Panza tells Quixote that the windmills are not giants, he is not a critic who would dismiss Quixote's experience. He is, rather, the companion who, as the word suggests, breaks bread with his master. He is the other who feeds and nourishes the imagination of his master.

Together, Quixote and Sancho Panza embody and enact the Quixotic imagination as a journey of soul making.

Together, they infuse the Quixotic dramatic, apocalyptic imagination with the qualities of a poetic sensibility, which Keats described as negative capability and Coleridge as the willing suspension of disbelief.

Is not such a poetic sensibility essential to an arts therapy education?

Part five: the mood quality of a Quixotic imagination

As Quixote and Sancho Panza set out on their adventures, they are enveloped in a specific mood, an atmosphere of possibility:

> As if windmills were giants!

It is the mood that grammarians call the subjunctive, which expresses a condition that is contrary to fact. It is a mood that is also used to express a wish, or a suggestion, or even a regret, as if, for example, I were to say: "If only I were a poet and not a psychologist."

But be that as it may be, the subjunctive mood highlights the power of the human imagination to see and say things as they might or could be and not just as they are. The subjunctive mood is, as it were, the gentle breeze of an angel's wing, which, uplifting the human condition, situates it in that domain between the material animal and the spiritual angel that Rilke (2009) describes so movingly in his *Duino Elegies*.

The mood of possibility is not only a key quality of the Quixotic imagination, it is also the salient feature of Quixote's character, the knight whose sorrowful countenance has the elegiac cast of one who, dwelling within the possibility of possibility, bears the lament for what is not while celebrating what might be.[2]

Quixote's mood is infectious and so delightfully infectious that the story, as I noted earlier, not only transforms Quixote and his squire. It also e-ducates them (and us today), leading them out and beyond themselves (and us today) into the possibility that the ordinary might itself be extraordinary. That is the wonder of this tale, the miracle of the mundane that is there, if one be in the right mood.

If one be in the right mood and something more: the embodied enactment of that mood!

Quixote acts in a way that accords with his mood. He is dramatic in his speech and his gestures, extravagant if you will, elegant, charming in their excess, and seductive in their appeals. To be in his presence tugs at his squire, Quixote's gestures transgressing the boundaries of the physical body and impregnating the flesh.

Part six: the dream of Don Quixote

In the beginning of my presentation I indicated that I would approach the tale of Don Quixote as if it were a cultural-historical dream that is still dreaming us. I return now to my starting point to show that the dream puts us in the right mood for an arts therapy education.

A phenomenology of the dream deals with the dream in the subjunctive mood. It stays with the mood of the dream as a possibility of possibility. In this context, education in dream work begins with a shift from making sense of a dream to sensing it, as if one were attending a performance staged in the night theatre of soul. In this context, I regard the dream as a dress rehearsal of possibilities to be played out in the waking world.

It is also a shift from talking about a dream to becoming the dream, enacting its characters as if they were dress rehearsals for who or what one might be in the light of day.

In this regard, each of us imitates Quixote's tale!

In this regard, each of us every morning has the opportunity to "tilt at windmills."

Part seven: final thoughts

In the context of the theme of this conference – *Imagining Windmills: Trust, truth and the unknown in the arts therapies* – I am persuaded that the cultivation of the mood of possibility is essential to balance the tyranny of the real, to educate therapists in the value of trusting what is unknown, and to recognise and applaud the truth of imagination. I hope that the examples I have given in relation to the text have shown that Don Quixote and Sancho Panza are exemplary teachers for an arts therapy education, and that my remarks are at least a preparation for a continuing dialogue between my work as a psychotherapist, which has been formed by my education in the traditions of phenomenological and Jungian psychologies, and the tradition of arts and drama therapies.

I conclude now with three questions:

Is it not vital to our world today that Don Quixote and his squire remain, like, I might add, Victor Frankenstein and the Monster, alive today as companions?

Indeed, what might we become if we do not insist on an education that not only fosters and feeds the literary and dramatic imagination, but also gives it a central place?

And as a corollary to the second question, what happens to the human world when and if imagination is no longer available to sustain the poetic realism of the world, a reality where outside the boundaries of convention, windmills can be imagined as giants, and where the world in its cultural and natural wonders display themselves and seduce the creative power of the human imagination, the spark of divinity gifted to us in our expulsion from paradise?

Notes

1 In this drama that unfolded within the theater of the therapy room, the clinical work, of course, required that the vehicle of this larger story had to be made conscious by the patient in her life. Insight into the inner traumas had to be made into another way of living in the world. This move is the ethical obligation of therapy, which poses these two questions for consideration:

What is the place of the ethical dimension in arts and dramatherapy?

How might education in arts and dramatherapy align with a Jungian clinical perspective? In this regard, I find myself very much in agreement with the remarks of Jean-Francois Jacques (in Hougham, 2017, pp275–86) regarding how dramatherapy is well suited to think about a relational ethics that is defined as one between a witness and the witnessed and is embodied. I would add that the work of Paul Ricoeur (1974) regarding the challenge of unconscious dynamics for any philosophy takes the same path regarding the witness-witnessed relation.

2 Perhaps it is not Don Quixote who is mad but we who insist on seeing the world only as it is; we who have forgotten how to dream.

References

Hougham, R. (2015) 'Not form, but the marrow of forms' Reflections on Lorca's duende in the arts therapies'. In Hougham, R., Pitruzzella, S. & Scoble, S. (eds) Through the Looking Glass: dimensions of reflection in the arts therapies. Plymouth, UK: University of Plymouth Press.

Jacques, J-F. (2017) 'In search of an Other: otherness and meaning in performance: a dramatherapy perspective'. In Hougham, R., Pitruzzella, S. & Scoble, S. (eds) *Cultural landscapes in the arts therapies* Plymouth, UK: University of Plymouth Press.

Pitruzzella, S. (2017) 'The intersubjective dimension of dramatherapy'. In: Hougham, R., Pitruzzella, S. & Scoble, S. (eds) *Cultural landscapes in the arts therapies*. Plymouth, UK: University of Plymouth Press.

Putnam, S. (1949) *The portable Cervantes*. New York: Penguin Books.

Ricoeur, P (1974) 'Consciousness and the unconscious'. In: Ihde, D. (ed) *The conflict of interpretations*. Evanston, Ill: Northwestern University Press.

Rilke, R.M. (2009) *Duino elegies and the sonnets to Orpheus*, Edited and Translated by Stephen, M. New York: Vantage Books

Romanyshyn, R. (2019) *Victor Frankenstein, the monster and the shadows of technology: the Frankenstein prophecies*. London: Routledge

3

CHANGING TRUTHS

Deconstructing and reconstructing the elusive in art therapy

Uwe Herrmann

Abstract

This chapter explores the subject of truth and its relation to art therapy against the backdrop of historical, political, philosophical and artistic ideas on truth, and in light of a debate in psychoanalysis, if anything can be known beyond the moment of the therapeutic relationship.

Looking at retrospective and collaborative single case research, the chapter explores the client's and therapist's changing binary conceptions of "true" or "false" from three temporal perspectives: in therapy, post-therapy, and revisiting the material many years later. Though "moments of truth" occurred at all three stages, their understanding changed considerably over time. It is proposed that art making, with its open and ambiguous nature, allows for a slow and mutable assimilation to the client's and therapist's changing ideas of what was "true" and thus facilitates a continuous critical investigation of something essentially elusive.

Keywords: art therapy, truth, ambiguity, case study, retrospective review, collaborative research

Abstract in German

Dieses Kapitel beschäftigt sich mit dem Thema der Wahrheit und ihrer Verbindung zur Kunsttherapie; dies geschieht vor dem Hintergrund historischer, politischer, philosophischer und künstlerischer Vorstellungen zu diesem Begriff und im Licht einer Debatte in der Psychoanalyse, ob es jenseits des Moments der therapeutischen Beziehung möglich ist, etwas als ,wahr' zu erkennen.

Ausgehend von einer kollaborativen Einzelfallstudie untersucht das Kapitel die veränderlichen, binären Konzepte von ,wahr' und ,falsch' bei Klientin und Kunsttherapeut aus drei zeitlichen Perspektiven: während der Therapie,

DOI: 10.4324/9781003110200-3

unmittelbar nach der Therapie und bei einer erneuten Untersuchung des Materials viele Jahre später. Auch wenn 'Momente von Wahrheit' in allen drei Stadien auftauchten, veränderte sich ihr Verständnis mit der Zeit erheblich.

Das Kapitel zeigt, wie das Schaffen von Kunst, durch deren offene und vieldeutige Natur, Klientin und Therapeut eine langsame und flexible Annäherung an veränderliche Vorstellungen von ‚Wahrheit' ermöglicht, und somit die kontinuierliche, kritische Erforschung von etwas, dessen Wesen schwer fassbar ist.

Introduction

"The truth is rarely pure and never simple," wrote Oscar Wilde (1895, p6), and the recognition that truth is a complex and at times thorny issue goes back to antiquity. In ancient Greek, the word for truth is Αλήθεια, and looking at the word's components "A-" and "λήθεια"shows that it can also be translated as a state of "un-closedness," "un-concealedness" or "un-obliviousness" (Liddell & Scott, 1887, p60). Inherent in this word is a concept of truth as something that must be actively procured from its hiding place. It is for this reason that in many European languages we use figures of speech hinting at truth's ambiguous and elusive nature. To find, uncloak and unravel truth, to arrive at "pure truth" or "naked truth," we must go beyond truth's "hidden," "untold" or "half" states. We may do this in the hope that by paring off layers of concealment we finally get to a "core truth," so we can glance at the "true" nature of a natural, physical, social, psychological or aesthetic phenomenon. Maybe we want to understand the core of a life story, of family dynamics, an illness, global warming, political history, class struggles or a piece of art. Art often seems to finds itself on the defensive when it comes to the question of truth, in as much as "true" is equalled with "genuine," "resembling," "believable" or "unyielding." This leads to very disparate questions, i.e. whether the artwork is an original masterpiece, the work of an acolyte, or a mechanical reproduction; whether the artist achieved a likeness that is true to his subject; whether the work succeeds in making the viewer experience it as relevant and believable; and lastly, whether the artist has managed to stay true to her or his own vision or has bowed to other forces, be it opportunism to a commissioner's predilections, social pressures or political intimidation.

Be it in art or science, relationships, politics or history, we strive for truth to solve a problem that is important enough for us to go through to the trouble of gathering facts, so we can consolidate our fragmented knowledge, possibly adjust our stance, and base our further actions on reason. But the onerous work of "un-concealing" truth may not always result in the blissful state of "knowing" that we fantasised. The terms "ugly truth," "painful truth" or "sad truth" indicate that there are reasons for concealing truth and that by revealing these reasons we come face to face with unpleasant or unbearable insights.

Notwithstanding, the question of truth remains vital to our very social and psychological being. Without truth we have little reason to trust; the German word "treu" – meaning faithful or trustworthy – derives from the same root as "true." The closeness of the two words indicates that knowing what is true and can be relied on – "true feelings," "true love," "true friendship," "true thoughts" – creates faith. If we put our faith into someone or something, we are prepared to make decisions on that judgement. Such faithful trust, based on believing in someone's good, true intentions, governs our individual and collective actions. On the other hand, misplaced trust and the intentional concealment of truth – be it in relationships or politics – tend to result in individual or collective misery.

Lessons on truth from history

The fabrication of "truths," notably in the form of propaganda, has taken its toll on the fate of entire societies. Looking at the early 20th century, fascism reveals a blueprint for this phenomenon. Josef Goebbels, the spin doctor of Hitler's Third Reich, claimed: "Propaganda should not be intellectually pleasing, but effectively popular. It is not the task of propaganda to discover intellectual truths" (1928/1934, p46). This mind-set and its strategies led straight into disaster. Wirtz and Godson (2002, p100) describe in *Strategic Denial and Deception: The Twenty-First Century Challenge*, how, setting up for WWII, Hitler told his generals on 22 August 1939: "I will provide a propagandistic casus belli. Its credibility doesn't matter. The victor will not be asked whether he told the truth." Not even two weeks later the regime fabricated a Polish attack on a German radio station and declared the subsequent invasion of Poland an act of self-defence. Consequently, and still ongoing, post-war Germany has been largely shaped, individually and collectively, by facing an abundance of painful and shameful truths about WWII and the Holocaust. Once uncovered, these truths can never be resolved or put to rest. They can only be remembered to determine the shape of the present and the future.

A mere 17 years after the end of WWII, we find another landmark contortion of truth: the socialist East German Head of State, Walter Ulbricht, said at a press conference on June 15, 1961 in East Berlin (Ulbricht, 1961):

> Nobody has the intention of building a wall. I know nothing about such a plan existing, because all construction workers in the capital are busy with building houses and therefore their workforce is fully exploited ... put to use.

The statesman's slip of the tongue, omitted in the conference transcript but recorded in the original film footage, revealed how Ulbricht's unconscious found a way to express his betrayal of truth and trust. A mere two months later, and prepared behind the scenes, the construction of the Berlin Wall began, brutally separating an entire city that, for almost three decades, stood for the entire world's division into two hostile blocs. Again, when the wall fell in 1989 and the East German regime collapsed, freedom came at a cost: many Eastern citizens had to face the ugly truth that close friends, neighbours or family had reported them as political dissidents to the secret police, which had resulted in their imprisonment, enforced labour or in losing their employment and barring their children from university.

While such examples may feel historically or geographically remote to many of us today, taking a look at our contemporary experiences reveals that the question of truth is as crucial to our political and social cultures as ever. Currently, facts have suddenly got new company, called "alternative facts." In 2017, Kellyanne Conway, former US Counsellor to the American president, used this phrase during a *Meet the Press* interview on January 22, defending a White House statement boasting about the attendance at Donald Trump's inauguration.

The incident seems trivial in retrospect and in comparison to developments to date; however, the new term "alternative facts" has spurred many, often visual, responses, i.e. in the form of political caricature. A fine example is a 2018 drawing by Pittsburgh cartoonist, Rob Rogers, showing D. Trump laying down a Memorial Day wreath, with a R.I.P sign affixed, in front of the grave of "Truth. Honour. Rule of Law." The newspaper rejected the drawing and Rogers' unwillingness to tone down his criticisms led to his losing the position he had held as editorial cartoonist for 24 years.

Political caricatures and memes, such as the sign "Alternative facts can be found in our fiction section," placed on a bookshop table, are among the numerous and creative reactions that portions of our liberal societies produce when our governments compromise truth. The question of truth is therefore not, as Goebbels claimed, a petty intellectual one. Rather, it concerns the people to whom we can entrust our lives and our future. It is about our societal, economic, cultural and psychological survival, and, as German 20th-century history shows, it determines under which denominator our past and our present will be viewed in future.

Checking facts and suspending our instant judgement in favour of a meticulous search is time-consuming. It involves our personal judgement as much as taking into account the judgement of others. Not knowing until we have formed an opinion on what is likely or reasonably true draws on our psychological faculties because we have to tolerate ambiguity. This requires us to have a resilient ego that can bear and navigate uncertainty long enough to form a judgement based on knowledge that we have accumulated slowly, scrutinised painstakingly and weighed cautiously. That propaganda can still undermine such careful deliberation becomes evident in the light of recent psychological research. Fazio, Brashier, Payne and Marsh (2015) found that, contrary to past assumptions in the literature, constant repetition of false information leads to an "illusory truth effect," which surfaced in their study subjects' neglecting their knowledge in favour of the lie and in spite of "knowing better." It is the fast, repetitious staccato of propaganda that seems to pose the biggest challenge to our ego's vigilance, because it disconnects our thinking from our established, contextual and internal knowledge.

However, individuals and societies are not without guidance in their search for truth. Traditionally artists and philosophers have, with their respective means, been among those who monitor their societies closely, offer us their reflections and administer advice for the problems of our times.

Philosophy's take on truth and art

Generations of philosophers have argued that defining and establishing truth is key to the human condition, unsurprisingly coming up with very different lines of thought, and they were eventually joined by natural scientists, psycho-analysts and psychologists. Art, however, has not always managed to earn the early philosophers' trust when it came to its reliability for pursuing and reveal-ing truth. Plato believed that the purest essence of things could not be found in the material world but rather in the form of ideas, existing only in non-physical form. Any physical manifestations of such ideas would be mere copies or shadows, and therefore inevitably flawed. A work of art would consequently constitute a copy from a copy, and Plato therefore thought the artist "...a man-ufacturer of images and … very far removed from the truth" (Republic, X, around 380 B.C.E, p320). This, Plato argued, made an artist range far below a craftsman, while the sensory and physical nature of art was essentially harmful to the human soul.

And yet, for centuries people have continued flocking to art galleries in ever-increasing numbers. I suggest that rather than seeking art out of a self-destructive drive, being drawn towards something noxious, people view art in the hope that it will give them answers to personal questions, possibly the most important being: who am I?

When going to a gallery, I find myself spending as much time watching the way people view art as I do watching the artwork itself. During one of these trips I observed an elderly lady who was noticeably drawn by a renaissance portrait of a young woman in white dress (Fig. 3.1).

Maybe her question to the picture simply was: is white a good colour? But her long, incessant and mesmerised gaze at the picture suggested otherwise. Maybe she wondered whom this portrait reminded her of, and, while ponder-ing, found an immortalised version of her younger self, rosy cheeked, with aspi-rations yet untarnished. And maybe she left the gallery enriched and consoled by refreshed memories, with a new perspective on what a strange thing time is and how a five-hundred-year-old painting can evoke something youthful and personal to her.

Such an understanding of art is closer to Aristotle, who revised Plato's verdict in favour of the arts. To Aristotle, art is born from the human urge to know, and consequently he thought of the arts as equal to scientific endeavours, able to express the core ideas inherent to all existing things by means of *condensa-tion* and *distillation*. In other words, art is still accountable to the truthful, how-ever, in Aristotle's conviction, a work of art is allowed to change and transform

FIGURE 3.1 Gallery visitor, Germany 2019. Uwe Herrmann.

reality in the service of revealing truth (Aristotle, Poetics, ca. 330 B.C.E./2013; Metaphysics, ca. 350 B.C.E./2004).

Since the times of Plato and Aristotle, philosophy's discourse on truth has amounted to a vast array of convictions, on which yet another philosopher, Friedrich Nietzsche, concluded in 1878: "Convictions are more dangerous enemies of truth than lies" (1996, p179).

Another philosopher who dared to tackle the problem of truth in spite of Nietzsche's verdict was Heidegger; in his essay *The Origin of the Work of Art* (2008), Heidegger revived the Greek idea of Αλήθεια, or un-concealment, and saw art as a paramount means of eliciting truth from its hidden state. To Heidegger, art does not only convey truth in a society, but engenders it through the engagement of the viewer and the entire community with the work. Art thus does not merely replicate or represent something that exists but creates insights that change a civilisation's idea of existence, thus continuously changing and adding to our perception of the world and of ourselves in it. It is noteworthy that Heidegger, a man of the word, made special reference to the materials used in making art and to the useful role of their inherent qualities for creating meaning and truth. However, it is equally noteworthy that Heidegger not only utterly failed to see truth when it came to the ideology of the Third Reich; since the posthumous publication of his *Ponderings/Black Notebooks 1939-41* in 2014 (Heidegger/Trawney, 2014), whatever doubt may have existed about his anti-Semitic stance at the time has been dispersed. This raises the hard question as to whether it is possible to separate thought from thinker, or, in other words, to find truth in someone's thinking who betrayed truth in thought and action when it mattered most.

Truth and art

Unsurprisingly, artists commented on philosophy's – especially Plato's – concern with the relation of art and truth, and, in keeping with their professional fortes, responded through art. One of the wittiest and best-known examples is René Magritte's 1929 painting *La trahison des images – The Treachery of Images*. It shows a large representation of a pipe, subtitled with the handwritten line "Ceci n'est pas une pipe" – this is not a pipe. Almost constituting an ironic picture book lesson on the difference between an artwork and the object it depicts, this and other paintings established Magritte as the prototypical modern, reflective artist. The picture's title seemingly acquiesces to Plato's grave accusation that an image constitutes treachery. But looking at the way the painting is executed reveals that it cleverly teases the viewer in a semiotic triangle between picture, depicted subject and spectator. "Calm down! The mere forging of reality," Magritte seems to say, "has never been my objective and just in case you might be confused about my intentions or your own perception, I'll write it under the image for you in my best, large-enough to read lettering."

Magritte's calculated denouncement of the image as "treason" constituted a critique of a utilitarian, simplistic view of art in relation to truth. And yet, questions continue to be asked, i.e. is this a true Rembrandt? Or was it painted by one of his students? Does this portrait show a true likeness? Does it resemble the physical, psychological and social reality of its depicted subject, or does it constitute an idealised piece of work, driven by the subject's wish to be seen, or the artist's wish to present him or her, in a certain way? Two fine examples of the latter problem are two portraits of Baron H.H. Thyssen-Bornemisza, on display in the Madrid museum bearing the steel tycoon's name and housing his and his wife's vast collections. One portrait of Thyssen, by Ricardo Macarròn, is placed in the museum's entrance hall. Larger than life and showing the magnate in a formal suit and posture, it seems painted to emphasise Thyssen's social status and power. It dwarfs the viewer by its scale and the way it is placed: we cannot help but look up to the Baron. In sharp contrast, another portrait of Thyssen, painted by Lucian Freud, can be found on the upper floors of the same collection. Much smaller in size, it presents Thyssen in a neat but moderate street suit, seated awkwardly against the muted walls of the artist's studio. Freud seems to have been far from any obligation or urge to flatter his sitter. As we share the painter's gaze, this time looking down on Thyssen, we become co-voyeurs in Freud's scrutiny of his subject's aging face and receding hairline. In the vacuum of Freud's studio, Thyssen's status and wealth seem to have evaporated, and this may be indicated also in Freud's titling his work, *Man in a Chair*, identifying his subject, as if only in an afterthought, as (*Portrait of Baron H.H. Thyssen-Bornemisza*).

Could anyone say which of the two paintings captured Thyssen's "true" persona better, if this was their intention at all, or which painter stayed more "true" to himself and his personal vision? Or might these paintings eventually reveal more about the artist than they reveal about their subject? At this point we are thrown back to the semiotic scrambling between the artist's, the subject's and our own subjectivities.

An even more difficult concern seems whether a work of art, beyond its mere phenomenological being, is able to give us an insight that we consider believable. Here, the acuity of an artist's vision is key, particularly when the work of art is concerned with something essentially un-representable. This certainly applies to many of Anselm Kiefer's paintings and installations from the 1980s, widely understood as the artist's grappling with German history and the Holocaust (Biro, 2003). These works, and the way in which Kiefer introduces rough and heavy materials in them, exemplify how art can add something to the viewer's understanding of the artwork's subject that feels surprising, revealing and shockingly "true." Maybe it is when facing a subject that is so hard to describe, understand and grasp as a whole that we can see how Aristotle's notion of the artwork's ability to show truth, or rather *create* it in the viewer by means of condensation and distillation, and Heidegger's idea of art as a revelation changing the individual's and the society's understanding of being, past and present, hold true. In front of Kiefer's works, we are left stunned, with a feeling of overwhelming sadness, evoked by the way the artist transformed simple materials into embodied grief, a grief so vast that words seem shallow to express it. Here, it is not that the image would promise "truth," leading to the redemption or resolution of something that is unsolvable and unredeemable; but it produces an experience in the viewer that goes beyond words and thus opens an avenue for feelings and thoughts that feel fresh, immediate and raw.

From Magritte's witty painting, as from Kiefer's substance-laden canvasses, it is a short leap to psychoanalysis, the most influential intellectual development at Magritte's time, which was a great inspiration to the surrealist movement of which Magritte was part. The ideas that things are seldom what they seem, so mockingly expressed by Magritte and so sadly and heavily present in Kiefer's work, and that truth was something needing to be freed from concealment, are at the core of psychoanalytic practice and theory.

Truth in psychoanalysis

The earliest and most fundamental question in psychoanalytic thinking is: what is hidden in the patient's and in the therapist's unconscious and how can it be revealed, recovered and made available to the patient's conscious mind in the service of recovery? In recent years, a postmodernist position – on the premise that nothing can be known and everything depends on everything – has made the goals, means and results of psychoanalysis appear somewhat relativist and fuzzy. This has resulted in several papers that argue whether truth can be known in analysis and, if so, under which premises (Allison and Fonagy, 2016; Blass, 2016; Busch, 2016, Hanly, 1990; Greenberg, 2016; Levine, 2016; Mills, 2017; Ogden, 2016; Steiner, 2016).

Greenberg (2016, p271) points to a conundrum that Freud left us with when trying to unearth the past in the present moment of analysis. Freud, in his article *Constructions in Analysis* (1937), restates the familiar point that therapeutic activity relies on enabling the recollection of repressed mental contents. However, Freud continues:

> "The path that starts from the analyst's construction ought to end in the patient's recollection; but it does not always lead so far. Quite often we do not succeed in bringing the patient to recollect what has been repressed. Instead of that, if the analysis is carried out correctly, *we produce in him an assured conviction of the truth of the construction which achieves the same therapeutic result as a recaptured memory.*" [Freud in Greenberg, 1937, pp265-266, italics added]. Greenberg concludes: "And yet we have no certainty about what 'truth' means, or, (…) about what it means to 'know' that something is true" (pp271-72). In essence, this is about whether we should retrieve or reconstruct what we believe was lost and must be remembered – or concentrate on the revelations of the here and now, the given, live relationship in therapy as the only thing that can be known by the witnessing and reflecting minds of client and therapist.

Allison and Fonagy (2016) tackle the issue further and suggest that

> "…the experience of knowing and having the truth about oneself known in the context of therapy is not an end in itself; rather, it is important because the trust engendered by this experience (…) opens one up to learning about one's social world and finding better ways to live in it."
>
> *(p275)*

They suggest that truth is a *process*, not a mental representation, which depends on the patient's ability to mentalise, i.e. to understand the mental state of others and of oneself. If mentalising breaks down in moments of great distress, it is impossible to recognise the truth in any therapeutic intervention. If mentalising is active, however, Allison and Fonagy describe it as:

> …marked by an intersubjective experience in which two individuals feel the psychological presence of the other, and the relationship between them feels real (not pretend or absent) and in that sense genuine and true.

This is a *"moment of meeting,"* stretching "into minutes and perhaps entire sessions," generating the "felt experience of truth" (pp286–7).

As Fonagy (1999) suggested in an earlier paper,

> …the only way we can know what goes on in our patient's mind, what might have happened to them, is how they are with us in the transference. They come to us with (…) a network of unconscious expectations or mental models of self – other relationships. Individual experiences that have contributed to this model may or may not be "stored" elsewhere as discrete autobiographical memories, but in either case the model is now "autonomous," no longer dependent on the experiences that have contributed to it.
>
> *(p217)*

Fonagy therefore stressed that such models "are not replicas of actual experience," that is, there is no way to establish that the transference gives us any reliable information about a "true" event or course of actions. Rather, he argues, any of these models transpiring in the transference is "undoubtedly defensively distorted by wishes and fantasies current at the time of the experience" (p217). Recovering memories in therapy, he argues, is therefore a by-product ensuing change rather than instigating it.

In art therapy, however, the artwork is central to the therapeutic relationship and process, which raises the question yet again, as before with Plato and Aristotle, if and how art relates to "truth," as revealed or construed, in therapy.

Truth in art therapy

Clients, and maybe art therapists more so, enter therapy with the hope that this work might be helpful in the face of the client's painful or seemingly hopeless situation. As patients are grappling with their problems, they are often somehow aware that these might be rooted in something unknown. In the arts therapies, as in other psychodynamic therapies, we work on the general and traditional premise that a work of art, at least in parts, is an expression of the artist's unconscious. And it is in the unconscious we reckon that somehow and somewhere a key must be found to unlock the patient's arrested development. To do so, we encourage our patients to make art, trusting, as Dannecker (2006) put it, in the transformative power inherent in art therapy. Repressed memories, desires and conflicts can, if all goes well, become embodied and at least temporarily resolved in the creation of a work which it is pleasing and, by its aesthetic, for-mal means, syntonic to the artist's inner experience. This process and its end result are engendered as the artist's ego is eventually drawn into responding to the aesthetic stimuli of the material and his or her unconscious, while continu-ously striving towards the most suitable, most apt form he or she can derive from shaping an initially amorphous material.

However, it would be rather a precarious belief that the resulting artwork therefore is "embodied truth," in the sense that it could be read by the artist and the viewer as an illustration or account of a historic past that is finally revealed. Rather, in art therapy, it may be more fruitful to apply Aristotle's idea that a work of art is a condensation or distillation that, though distinct from historic truth or reality, can reveal something important by its formal and sensory means. In art therapy we are well advised to bear in mind that these aesthetic alterations, emphases or distortions must be understood and viewed in the context of the therapeutic relationship, the present moment and the inevitable limitations of any "objective" understanding that patient and therapist, in their deliberations on past and present experiences, are subjected to.

In other words, this "truth" must remain an ambiguous one, as much as any work of art is determined by ambiguity. A work of art cannot be "read" in a binary way as "true" or "false" or be pinned down to a sharply defined meaning or an indisputable exactness, like a mathematical equation or a chemical formula. Rather on the contrary, art, beyond its silent, phenomenological "being-there," is inexact, uncertain, mercurial and open to manifold meanings that each viewer, as the art-ist, has to create anew on the instant of viewing or re-viewing the work. It is this wavering and ambiguous quality inherent to art that makes it ideally suited to grasp the many dimensions and tones of complex phenomena, especially when it comes to the realm of human feelings and relationships. This implies that our relationship to an artwork, as viewers or as artists, is a highly subjective one. It is subject to, and open for, persistent change. Applying Fonagy's thoughts, i.e. transference not being an "accurate" replay of past relationships and truth not being a state but a process, we may similarly think of a work of art in art therapy as a reworked and autonomous version of the residue of a past experience in the live relationship with the therapist.

When an artist feels she or he succeeded in creating a "genuine" piece of art, the feeling is one of joy about having created something that captures her or his inner state. This may then be felt as a reciprocal understanding: the artist's feeling "understood" by his or her work and therefore understanding it as "true" to him or her, and likewise the art therapist's being able to catch a glimpse of this under-standing or to contribute to it by an appropriate intervention, a nod, a smile, a question, an observation or by simply sharing in the silent gaze at the work. I suggest though that the shared feeling of such a moment as "true" may not be entirely due to the work, its content and form, and to whatever reading one may apply to it, but to the situation as such. In other words, truth is embedded in the connectivity of the moment, coming to patient and therapist as the ever-new revelation and surprise that human understanding, though never absolute and eternally unchanged, is yet momentarily possible.

Such "true" moments, stored and alive in each artwork, may provide us with something to know and simultaneously with suitable means of knowing "it." However "true" something may feel, it is a knowing-for-the-moment that is, and must be, mutable and transforming. Only when ambiguity is left intact in our relationship to art can making art can become a transformative and therefore helpful experience for the patient artist and the art therapist. This transformation is the core hope that patient and therapist harbour when they begin their work. For patients, it is a hope born from hopelessness and this is why they may initially conceive of it only in a very limited way – maybe by hoping to make a small change to the material, or, at best, hoping that they will have produced a "good-enough work" by the end of the session.

Maybe Rebecca, the 16-year-old congenitally blind girl I will describe in the next section, entered art therapy with that hope. This case example is more than two decades old; I chose to revisit it because I had vivid memories of Rebecca's increasing interest in revealing her "true story" and had already written about it (Herrmann, 2011a). I wondered how "true" my memory would hold when returning to these now "historic" case notes, the transcriptions of Rebecca's own comments, and her artwork, and what I would find when critically looking at the material from today's perspective.

Rebecca: changing truths

Revisiting the case material, I noticed that in spite of the time that had elapsed our work was highly alive to me. Rebecca's artwork was as fresh and stunning as it had been in therapy, if not more so, and so was her story. What I saw more clearly now though was that core beliefs stood out in individual phases of Rebecca's process, how important and absolute they had felt to her at the time, only to be replaced by others.

When she started art therapy, Rebecca was 16 years old. She was born three months early and had become blind due to retinopathy of prematurity, caused by excess oxygen in the incubator. Rebecca was an only child whose parents had divorced when she was born, leaving her with no recollection of her natural father. Growing up happily with her grandparents until age six, Rebecca moved in with her mother and stepfather, with whom she reported a tense and often unhappy relationship. Rebecca had been at a boarding school for the blind since she was six. When I met her, she had come to the attention of school staff for suicidal thoughts, low self-esteem, social isolation and panic attacks which led to her referral to the art therapy service I had just developed at the school.

Rebecca had refused verbal psychotherapy, but easily accepted art therapy. She had kind memories of the adaptations to her blindness made by her grandfather, who would build miniature models with her, allowing her to touch and to better understand her environment, and this eased her decision for art therapy as much as it tinged our transference relationship.

Rebecca stayed five-and-a-half years in therapy, amounting to 108 sessions, and created 63 clay sculptures.

What I recalled and also found in my notes was that when first meeting Rebecca, she appeared very insecure, anxious and full of reproach, seemingly directed at herself but, upon inspection, at the world at large, in which, she explained, she had no place as a blind person. She should better be destroyed, she said, and done away with like a box of washing powder. This unusual metaphor would later become significant. I listened and asked questions while Rebecca cried and complained, but eventually asked her if she wanted to do some artwork; she accepted with ease, almost with relief, and, as she became quickly and completely absorbed in modelling, her tears subsided. For the first two years, this order of things – arriving upset and tearful, modelling and leaving more balanced and consoled – became a pattern.

Rebecca's artwork was symbolic and figurative from the start – something which is not a given for the congenitally blind (Herrmann, 2010, 2011b, 2016, 2017). Over the first year, however, her relationship to her sculptures, as her relationship to herself and to me, was mostly void of any personal reference to her past, her biography or her family. To me, our sessions felt impersonal, abstract and somewhat stale; little seemed to change other than Rebecca leaving the session in a much better emotional state, only to return distressed for the next session. In her artwork, every now and then she modelled small figures to which she ascribed magical helpful qualities – animals or fantasy creatures, tending to her every need with their imaginary, science-fiction-like sensory gadgets (Fig. 3.2). Though we could never explore these figures verbally, they seemed hopeful. Rebecca's truth of this first year thus seemed:

FIGURE 3.2 Rebecca: Helpful creature, white stoneware. Uwe Herrmann.

FIGURE 3.3 Rebecca: Self as gyroscopic figure, white stoneware. Uwe Herrmann.

The world is bad. I have no place in it because I am blind and should be destroyed. But sometimes something comes to my aid.

In her second year, Rebecca started modelling figures concerned with change and movement, like this one showing herself as part human, part gyroscope (Fig. 3.3). She said that the gyrating movement meant change to her – which she conceptualised as being in motion and yet securely staying in the same position. Rebecca's truth in her second year of therapy seemed to be: somehow something may change. Change can be frightening. But this change is safe. It sets me into motion and leaves me centred.

Well into her second year, in her 35th session, she modelled a figure which showed herself – for the first time – as a figure standing on top of an enclosed

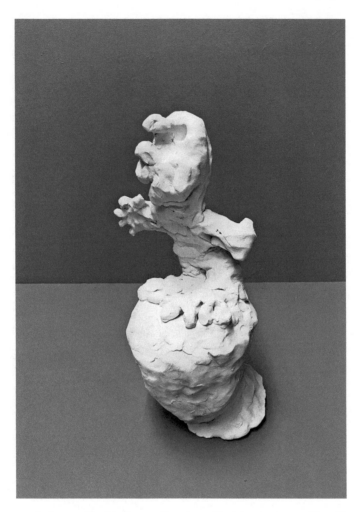

FIGURE 3.4   Rebecca: "Ambivalence of my 'now,'" white stoneware. Uwe Herrmann.

container, making a silencing gesture, as if daring someone not to speak. She said this sculpture was titled "Ambivalence of My Now" and that this closed vessel contained two opposite, unspoken and unknown things better left undisturbed (Fig. 3.4). Six months later, in the 49th session and at the beginning of her third year, Rebecca reported that she had beaten herself in the face after a conflict at school and modelled this scene. Here, she shows two figures of herself, one dealing the blow and the other one receiving it (Fig. 3.5). Looking closely at both figures revealed that each was in possession of body parts that the other was lacking. The aggressive one had a face and eyes but no legs, while the passive, victim one was faceless but in the possession of legs. By the end of this session, Rebecca mused if they might not be two different persons, but two parts of her own self in conflict with each other. When we later looked back at these sculptures, Rebecca

FIGURE 3.5 Rebecca: Self beating, white stoneware. Uwe Herrmann.

would recognise that the conflicting parts of her self, as expressed in the latter sculpture, represented the ambivalent, unspoken and concealed things contained in the previous figure's vessel.

By this time our sessions had notably changed in atmosphere. My initial sense of emptiness in relation to how we were together and how Rebecca used her art had dispersed. Instead, she and I were drawn into, and fascinated by, her sculptures. They now seemed not merely to illustrate something that she held as an intellectual conviction or "truth," but to embody and reveal something of vital, personal importance to her that she had been unaware of.

Subsequently, she modelled several sculptures in which these two conflicting aspects, passive and aggressive, victim and perpetrator, negotiate and finally learn from each other.

FIGURE 3.6   Rebecca: Negotiation between conflicting parts of self, white stoneware. Uwe Herrmann.

In this first figure, the two sit down at a negotiating table, signing a peace contract, with a mediator between them and a seated person by the side functioning as a witness and control (Fig. 3.6). In our retrospective review sessions by the end of therapy, Rebecca would identify the mediator as her own growing capacity to reflect and negotiate her inner conflicts, while she said that she now realised that the figure seated by the side represented me, aiding this process. At the time, though, she had no idea as to their meaning.

These sculptures played an important role in Rebecca's ability to reflect, and from today's perspective I would say: mentalise. In Fonagy's words, these sculptures reveal her growing capacity to develop a varied, multidimensional idea of herself and to include the therapist as a person in this scene.

Truth, in Rebecca's third year, could be this: something is struggling inside me that can be revealed. I have a growing capacity to reconcile this internal struggle and there is an outside person to confirm and witness this function.

Fonagy speaks of mentalising as a process and not a representation; a sculpture, however, as an end result of an artistic process, is capable of representing, while retaining traces of its making process. This is a forte of art therapy, as it abolishes the division between process and representation and encompasses both in a mental, psychological way, and a formative, aesthetic one. Differing from verbal analysis, it often concludes with an enduring, visible or tangible work of art that reminds of the process and comes to a preliminary formal, aesthetic conclusion that can be revisited for future reference in therapy.

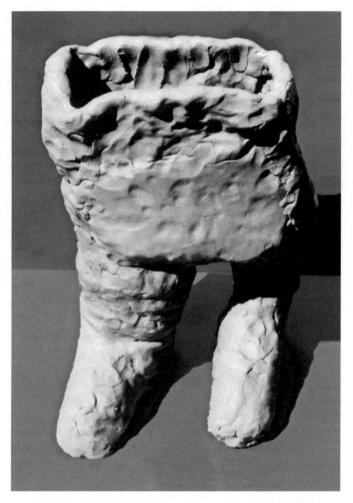

FIGURE 3.7 Rebecca: Unfinished, destroyed and reclaimed self-figure, white stoneware. Uwe Herrmann.

In her fourth and fifth years, Rebecca's work took on a remarkable speed: she
started making a large figure of herself, became dissatisfied with it and eventually
knocked the figure into pieces, reclaimed the clay and returned the fragments to a
soft, amorphous state (Fig. 3.7). This might have been a destructive act, had it not
felt like liberation and a new beginning to her. From this clay, she made all of her
subsequent artwork in which she now headed for a deep exploration of her life story.

Rebecca now remembered her mother's frequent accounts of how her father
had tried to kill Rebecca at birth by interfering, for religious reasons, with her
being placed in the incubator and how he had left her family because she had
become blind at birth. This, it transpired, had fuelled Rebecca's beliefs about
herself: that, somehow, she was not only unworthy because she was blind, but

also dangerous because her blindness had the "power" to oust her father. At this point in therapy, her hatred at her father grew immense. From the reclaimed clay of her self-figure Rebecca started to model her father's face – whom she had never seen or touched – and other figures meant to represent him and to be ritually destroyed.

Rebecca's truth in her fourth year thus seemed: my father wanted to destroy me, and I therefore want to destroy my father.

The mask she modelled, meant to represent her father, unintentionally turned into a self-portrait, which made her realise that for years her mother had told her how bad her father had been, always followed by her remark that physically Rebecca looked "as if cut from his living face" (Fig. 3.8).

FIGURE 3.8 Rebecca: Hybrid portrait of father and Rebecca, white stoneware. Uwe Herrmann.

FIGURE 3.9 Rebecca: Self as puzzled figure with tilted scales, white stoneware. Uwe
Herrmann.

At this point Rebecca started asking questions to her mother about her
natural father and received new information contradicting all previous family
narratives. It transpired that he had not left home because of her blindness,
but because the relationship with her mother had failed and he had left for
another woman. Rebecca was crestfallen and puzzled. She modelled herself
as a figure with empty and yet tilted scales to show how inexplicably "off"
all her convictions suddenly seemed (Fig. 3.9). She said that the truth she had
lived with for two decades was suddenly turned upside down and, confusingly,
had changed into something false. She then set on modelling a final series of
sculptures designed to make peace with her unknown father. To her, she said, he
had turned from a monster into an ordinary person and she no longer needed to

destroy his image but to rescue it. As fuzzy and unclear as his image necessarily had to remain, she concluded, she could now see it was neither fused to nor confused with herself, but a part of her life's story.

Rebecca's fifth and final truth in therapy thus was: my father left for another woman. He is human. He is not me, I am not him. We are related.

Soon afterwards Rebecca was to finish school; upon ending therapy we held two sessions reviewing all her artwork, which were remarkable and moving. She left all her sculptures behind.

Conclusion

The subject of truth is not only an intellectual concern, but one to which our individual and collective welfare is tied. The ability to endure the vexing state of not knowing, until the complicated process of eliciting truth has run its course, is crucial and requires a stable, mature ego. This function seems more needed than ever given the rise of populism in Europe, North America and other parts of the world in the early 21st century. Populism relies on the idea of post-truth, in which facts matter less than slapdash convictions and emotions, and has developed its communication strategies accordingly (Sengul, 2019; Zhang, Afzaal & Liu, 2020). Our ability to reflect and therein our ability to pursue truth as an individual and as a society is key for building resilience against such manipulations.

Therapy and art are therefore not private activities, unrelated to politics or societal change, or even keeping the individual locked within established societal and economic constructions, as Horkheimer and Adorno (1939/85) and Horkheimer (1968/85) once critiqued with respect to psychoanalysis. Rather, they do the opposite, in as much as both, from different ends and with different means, work towards the individual's ability to question and reformulate established beliefs, which includes being wary of past and present *Führers*, of any persuasion, and their intoxicating, simplistic promises.

The case study of Rebecca provided an exemplary view of such a strengthening of an individual ego and the critical evaluation of self and others of which it eventually can be capable. In art therapy, Rebecca was constantly challenged to deconstruct and (re-)construct truth. Her conscious and unconscious internal models of past and present family relationships surfaced in her artwork, and each, over time, needed to be dismantled and replaced by a succeeding one, only to be recast in due course. The most dramatic sculpture illustrating this dance of destruction and reconstruction was her unfinished self-portrait which she destroyed to reclaim the clay and to form new and more apt sculptures. As she was doing this, she was cleansing her idea of herself, and that of her father, of toxic introjects she had been infused with since childhood. In this retrospective light, the metaphor she used in her first session showed itself to be very apt: at the time, she had likened herself to a washing powder that should be dissolved and done away with. Indeed, she had functioned as a container for the unresolved, dirty and ugly story of her parent's separation and had reported feeling guilty,

FIGURE 3.10 Matryoshka dolls, private collection © Claus Dorsch, 2019.

contaminated and worthless as a result. Within these dynamics, she was condemned to serve as a detergent of sorts to wash the family clean. With every new "truth" she brought to light and with every new sculpture she managed to shed some of these unwanted attributions.

From my case notes and my recollections, as much as from my fresh analysis of our process, I gathered that Rebecca and I went through stages of changing truths which made sense only for a given time. As it were, truths were hidden in truths, like Matryoshka dolls of differing sizes and colours nesting in each other (Fig. 3.10). In our sessions, we increasingly experienced moments, then entire sessions which felt "true" and alive, while Rebecca's artwork became increasingly expressive and personal, as she was more and more able to tolerate ambiguity.

With Freud one might argue that this was perhaps more of a construction than a reconstruction of truth. Allison and Fonagy (2016) however caution that when the history of the patient is largely ignored and its construction takes precedence, there is the danger of a folie à deux. With reference to Rebecca's case, I agree. It would have been easy to stop and be content at any of these stages and declare this as the one, final truth. But there was a "felt" sense in both of us that some important parts of the story had not yet been told, which made us carry on with therapy.

In Rebecca's work, we can see how the distortions of her family story were replaced by more objective accounts and approximations. Truth may be elusive when it comes to an overall and indisputable account of an individual or collective history or to an exact analysis of a complicated present. However, it is far less elusive when looking at Rebecca's art process. Rebecca trusted the material enough to delve into the unknown before she could trust our relationship. Her artwork was wavering between construction and reconstruction, but, to speak with Aristotle, it was the distillation and condensation of form from matter that allowed truth to take the shape that Rebecca needed at a given time and that made her question any previous beliefs she had been burdened with. A person who has undertaken such work, I suggest, will, as a private, political and social being, continue to pursue truth – a truth that, as Oscar Wilde said, "is rarely pure and never simple."

References

Allison, E. and Fonagy, P. (2016). When is truth relevant? *The Psychoanalytic Quarterly*, Vol. 85, No. 2, 275–303.

Aristotle (ca. 330 B.C.E.). *Poetics*. Translation and editorial material by Anthony Kenny, 2013. Oxford: Oxford University Press.

Aristotle (ca. 350 B.C.E.). *Metaphysics*. Translated and with an introduction by Hugh Lawson-Tancred, 2004. London: Penguin.

Biro, M. (2003). Representation and event: Anselm Kiefer, Joseph Beuys and the Representation of the Holocaust. *The Yale Journal of Criticism*, Vol. 16, No. 1, 113–146. DOI: 10.1353/yale.2003.0001

Blass, R. (2016). The quest for truth as the foundation of psychoanalytic practice: a traditional Freudian-Kleinian perspective. *The Psychoanalytic Quarterly*, Vol. 85, No. 2, 305–337.

Busch, F. (2016). The search for psychic truths. *The Psychoanalytic Quarterly*, Vol. 85, No. 2, 339–360.

Dannecker, K. (2006). *Psyche und Ästhetik. Die Transformationen der Kunsttherapie*. Berlin: Medizinisch Wissenschaftliche Verlagsanstalt.

Fazio, L.K., Brashier, N.M., Payne, B.K. and Marsh, E.J. (2015). Knowledge does not protect against illusory truth. *Journal of Experimental Psychology*, Vol. 144, No. 5, 993–1002. Online source: https://psycnet.apa.org/doiLanding?doi=10.1037%2Fxge0000098

Fonagy, P. (1999). Memory and therapeutic action (guest editorial). *International Journal of Psychoanalysis*, Vol. 80, 215–223.

Goebbels, J. (1928/1934). *Erkenntnis und Propaganda*. Speech given on 9 January 1928 to an audience of party members at the so-called 'Hochschule für Politik,' a series of training talks for party members in Berlin. Source: *Erkenntnis und Propaganda, Signale der neuen Zeit*. 25 selected speeches by Dr. Joseph Goebbels, Munich: Zentralverlag der NSDAP, 1934, 28–52. Online source: https://research.calvin.edu/german-propaganda-archive/goeb54.htm

Greenberg, J. (2016). Editor's introduction: is truth relevant? *The Psychoanalytic Quarterly*, Vol. 85, No. 2, 269–274.

Hanly, C. (1990). The concept of truth in psychoanalysis. *International Journal of Psychoanalysis*, Vol. 71, No. Pt 3, 375–383.

Heidegger, M. (2008) Basic Writings, 'On the origin of the work of art'. In: Krell, D.F. (ed.). 1st Harper Perennial Modern Thought Edition. New York: HarperCollins, 143–212.

Heidegger, M./Trawny, P. (2014) (ed.): *Überlegungen XII-XV (Schwarze Hefte 1939–1941)*. Gesamtausgabe Band 96. Frankfurt: Klostermann.

Herrmann, U. (2010). Braucht das Selbst ein Bild? In: Wendlandt-Baumeister, M., Bolle, R. & Sinapius, P. (eds.). *Wissenschaftliche Grundlagen der Kunsttherapie, Bd. 3: Bildtheorie und Bildpraxis in der Kunsttherapie*. Bern: Peter Lang.

Herrmann, U. (2011a). The tangible reflection: a single case study investigating body image development in art psychotherapy with a congenitally blind client. In: Gilroy, A. (ed.). *Art therapy research in practice*. Bern: Peter Lang.

Herrmann, U. (2011b). Art psychotherapy and congenital blindness: investigating the gaze. Unpublished PhD Thesis, Goldsmiths University of London.

Herrmann, U. (2016). Touching insights. Visual and tactile cultures in researching art psychotherapy with congenitally blind children. In: Dokter, D. & Hills de Zaraté, M. (eds.). *Intercultural arts therapies research. Issues and methodologies*. ECArTE/ICRA research series. London/New York: Routledge.

Herrmann, U. (2017). Der Blick des blinden Schöpfers: Kunsttherapie mit Geburtsblinden. In: Dannecker, K. & Herrmann, U. (eds.). *Warum Kunst? Über das Bedürfnis, Kunst zu schaffen*. Berlin: Medizinisch-Wissenschaftlicher Verlag.

Horkheimer, M. and Adorno, T.W. (1939). Diskussionen über die Differenz zwischen Positivismus und materialistischer Dialektik. In Horkheimer, M. (ed.), (1985). *Gesammelte Schriften* (Bd. 12). Frankfurt a. M.: Fischer.

Horkheimer, M. (ed.). (1968/85). Die Psychoanalyse aus der Sicht der Soziologie. *Gesammelte Schriften* (Bd. 8). Frankfurt a. M.: Fischer.

Levine, H.B. (2016). Psychoanalysis and the problem of truth. *The Psychoanalytic Quarterly*, Vol. 85, No. 2, 391–409.

Liddell, H.G. and Scott, R. (1887). *A Greek–English Lexicon*. Oxford University Press, 8th edition. New York: American Book Company.

Mills, J. (2017). Challenging relational psychoanalysis: a critique of postmodernism and analyst self-disclosure. *Psychoanalytic Perspectives*, Vol. 14, 313–335.

Nietzsche, F. (1878/1996). *Human, all too human: a book for free spirits. Man alone with himself*, Vol. 483. Cambridge: Cambridge University Press.

Ogden, T.H (2016). On language and truth in psychoanalysis. *The Psychoanalytic Quarterly*, Vol. 85, No. 2, 411–426.

Plato (around 380 B.C.E.). *The Republic*. Translated by Jowett, B. 3rd edition, 1888, Oxford: Clarendon Press. Online source: http://eremita.di.uminho.pt/gutenberg/5/5/2/0/5520 1/55201-h/55201-h.htm#page307

Sengul, K. (2019). Populism, democracy, political style and post-truth: issues for communication research. *Communication Research and Practice*, Vol. 5, No. 1, 88–101. DOI: 10. 1080/22041451.2019.1561399

Steiner, J. (2016). Illusion, disillusion, and irony in psychoanalysis. *The Psychoanalytic Quarterly*, Vol. 85, No. 2, 427–447.

Ulbricht, W. (1961). Press Conference on 15 June 1961, East Berlin. Film footage in German: https://www.youtube.com/watch?v=Yz9DNSTrHBY&t=32s Transcript in German: http://www.chronik-der-mauer.de/material/178773/internationale pressekonferenz-des-staatsrats-vorsitzenden-der-ddr-walter-ulbricht-in-ost-berlin-15-juni-1961

Wilde, O. (1895). *The importance of being earnest*. Online source: https://freeditorial.com/en/books/the-importance-of-being-earnest–3/related-books

Wirtz, J.J. and Godson, R. (2002). *Strategic denial and deception: the twenty-first century challenge*. Piscataway: Transaction Publishers.

Zhang, H., Afzaal, M. and Liu, C. (2020). American populism in digital era: strategies of manipulation in Donald Trump's election tweets. *Revista Argentina de Clínica Psicológica*, Vol. XXIX, No. 3, 1273–1280 DOI: 10.24205/03276716.2020.957

Visual sources:

Kellyanne Conway NBC *Meet the Press* interview on January 22, 2017: https://www.theguardian.com/us-news/video/2017/jan/22/kellyanne-conway-trump-press-secretary-alternative-facts-video

"Alternative facts can be found in our fiction section": https://me.me/i/ist-sta-alternative-facts-can-be-found-in-our-fiction-8728665

Rob Rogers 2018 drawing: https://www.wesa.fm/post/fired-political-cartoonist-fires-back-new-book-exhibit#stream/0

René Magritte: 'La trahison des images': https://collections.lacma.org/node/239578

Ricardo Macarrón: Portrait of Baron Hans Thyssen-Bornemisza, 1987 https://coleccioncar menthyssen.es/work/retrato-del-baron-h-h-thyssen-bornemisza-1987/

Lucian Freud: Portrait of Baron Hans Thyssen-Bornemisza, 1983-85 https://www. pinterest.de/pin/38773246776009418/?amp_client_id=CLIENT_ID(_)&mweb_ unauth_id={{default.session}}&amp_url=https%3A%2F%2Fwww.pinterest. de%2Famp%2Fpin%2F135178426292235873%2F

Anselm Kiefer: https://www.bbc.co.uk/programmes/articles/5WMRLbqJbKC4WDxM- 8mDGWhw/opening-the-wounds-of-history-anselm-kiefer-s-war-on-forgetting

4

DRAMATHERAPY AND MATERIALITY

Richard Hougham, Bryn Jones

Abstract

This chapter revisits and further develops the ideas and working processes of a workshop designed specifically for the 2019 ECArTE conference: *Imagining Windmills: Trust, truth and the unknown in the arts therapies*. The workshop *Is it the trees or is it the wood? The play of projection, materiality and reciprocity in the therapeutic encounter*, was seeking to test and experiment with ideas concerned with the nature of space and the selection and use of physical materials within dramatherapy practice. In developing these areas of interest and in designing and facilitating the workshop, we were struck by several recurring philosophical and theoretical themes. These informed the writing of this chapter and have been further augmented by a productive collaborative process and workshop experience.

The recurring themes include the effect of the materiality of the objects; the nature and elasticity of aesthetic space; the places of play, questions of assemblage and the constellations of people and materials within a performative space. Inspired by the main conference theme, we were also intrigued by how these might induct a sense of "truthfulness", not in a cognitive sense, but more through a *working with* unexpected and unorthodox materials.

Some key theoretical ideas that inspired and underscored the original workshop are returned to, re-examined and expanded through the writing. These include the play theory of British dramatherapist, Peter Slade, and ideas from phenomenology and space as described by French philosopher, Gaston Bachelard. The writing investigates intersections between the interests and ideas of these two practitioners to forge a new dynamic amalgamation. This draws out the aesthetic sensibilities of Slade's work and the playfulness of Bachelard.

DOI: 10.4324/9781003110200-4

Keywords: aesthetics, materiality, personal play, projected play, coalesce, constellation, composition, observation, dramatic encounter

Scenography, social space and a dramatherapeutic aesthetic

Ryan Gander is a British conceptual artist who works with a wide range of materials. In 2011, he made a piece of work, which centres around a strong magnet. The magnet holds in place countless pieces of used metal objects. Gander (and the magnet) then sculpt these in to an apparently perfect sphere. The piece is called *Really Shiny Things That Don't Mean Anything.* Gander declares his work is "just providing the possibility, the condition for things to happen" and that this art work within and of itself "does not mean anything" (Chaillou, 2012). The ideas alive here are signalling the notion that meaning cannot be imposed, it can only be produced through a long process of negotiation. In this Gander is echoing the thoughts of the French philosopher, Henri Lefebvre, and his theories about how social space is produced. According to Lefebvre, social space is one that consists of a net of community relationships which overlap one another like a dense cobweb. Creating a community and creating a space for the community cannot be separated, proving that the process of constructing public space is both a social and a political act (LeFebvre, 1991). This caused us to wonder further: who is in a position to read this space – are certain preconditions necessary? Are there presumptions about space which we are challenging when it comes to the discipline and practice of dramatherapy? This piece also prompts questions about the relationship between meaning and value in materials – shiny doesn't imply meaning, value is not a fixed entity when it comes to materiality. This calls into question the many possible meanings both projected onto and derived from substances and materials, and how these considerations might become an aspect of dramatherapeutic thinking and practice.

In beginning to plan the workshop we considered the conference themes of trust, truth and unknowing. The idea of seeking some kind of truthfulness raised a fitting counterpoint to the post-truth zeitgeist of fake news, clickbait, misinformation and media manipulation. How might a truth be established when so much appears uncertain and unreliable? How might a fresh experiment with unorthodox materials offer a means of inducting moments of truthfulness and meaning between people? Where might we find the truth in a world of unknowing? These questions became our magnet. They began to pull our thinking and talking into some kind of shape and towards the formulation of an unsettling and uncertain workshop experience, which was to research truth in a materialist and aesthetic sense. The element of unsettlement seemed important. A pushing back against several tired and predictable tropes often found in dramatherapy practice. We considered the anaesthetising effect of comforting convention. Kafka came to mind. His axe "breaking the frozen sea within us" (Kafka in Stach, 2017, p301). And Toni Morrison's exhortation that if "You wanna fly, you got to give up the shit that weighs you down" (Morrison, 2016, p258). As part of this intended unsettlement, we chose building materials to work with and found a space more akin to the industrial than the therapeutic – a large asymmetric storage room with two entrance/exits and light sources from either side along the longest walls. Everything about it was of irregular proportion and shape. Its exact centre remained elusive and it offered no natural stage space from which to present and deliver. In place of the usual fare of cloths, juggling balls and pastels, we offered a selection of materials from a construction wholesalers: roughly textured local bricks, breeze block slabs, sheets of insulating felt and corrugated cardboard, lengths of copper piping and rubber tubing, galvanised steel buckets and metal bracing brackets. We also had single A4 sheets of white paper and had placed masking tape across the floor as a means of delineating space.

As people began to arrive, there was a sense of awkwardness. Where to stand? How to respond to the markings on the floor? How to interpret and respond to the building materials and lack of guidance as to where to position themselves? The immediacy of these reactions and responses began to inhabit and shape the space, breathing into it, a rhythm of entrances from different doors, different languages bouncing around and amplifying the acoustic into rumbles and pitches of sound. It gradually became an echo chamber, though of course this is precisely what we were attempting to avoid insofar as we wanted to break free of custom-bound practices and self-referential dramatherapy ideas. That said, we did hope this would become a sense-making place, an experiment where new sense might be made of otherwise no sense. An invitation to produce meaning. To weave these disparate elements together and in so doing to construct our own social space. Our dense cobweb that might catch and hold the fluttering moments of truthfulness that might fly from the work; a series of episodic, improvisational and durational encounters.

To open the session a performative beginning was improvised which brought attention to the disorientation of the space and the place and the collection of people populating it. Individuals mostly from other lands. Travellers, who for their own peculiar reasons had journeyed here and now stood amidst strangers in this evolving strangeness. Before we tell some of the story of how the session unfolded, we first indicate some of the ground from which these initial ideas grew.

Philosophies of space and truth, Gaston Bachelard

The collaborative process between us was key. This had started months before and had slowly been developing in terms of angles on key ideas and research into associations with materiality – artistic, political and personal. This process of allowing time for the workshop ideas to unfold and germinate was important as we worked towards clarity whilst also listening at the edges of what we had planned. This process was in itself conversational, as we threw each other questions, associations, provocations. Part of the nature of both the collaboration and the design of the session was inspired by the question of space. As well as an enquiry into "social space," questions of aesthetic space in dramatherapy emerged. Central to these discussions was the work of the French Philosopher, Gaston Bachelard. Bachelard is perhaps best known for his publication *The Poetics of Space*, which has become a key text in diverse disciplines including architecture, philosophy and psychology. Part of its appeal is the ways in which he manages to reinterpret space in an aesthetic sense, transforming the functional into the artistic. *The Poetics of Space* examines how space and in particular the spaces within a house are a profound metaphor for our psychological experience. He offers a poetic rendition of intimate spaces in relation to psychoanalysis, which can support the therapeutic encounter and generate a methodology more akin to scenography or dramaturgy than to orthodox verbal therapy. However, he does not limit his lexicon of intimate spaces to metaphor. As a phenomenologist, he opens up questions of how we respond to space emotionally and psychologically, citing Jung's dream of the house and its representation of the different levels of the psyche. His work focusses on different spaces in the house – corners, turrets, cellars. The house image he says "would have appeared to have become the topography of our intimate being" (Bachelard, 2014, p20). As Gillian Darley suggests of Bachelard's writing, "the journey into intimacy is neatly evoked by drawers, cupboards, wardrobes and above all locks" (Darley, 2017, p3).

This evokes deep-set feelings of secrets, thresholds to other worlds, magic in the minuscule and memories caught by angles. The *Poetics of Space* not only prompted us to think about the space for the workshop, but also inspired us to think about the objects and materials placed in the space and how these might facilitate a sense of intimacy and encounter. Bachelard tackles the nature of roundness, the value in edges and the dialectic of immensity and the miniature. He examines how these spaces and features speak to us, how they affect us, in rest, in memory, through experience. His is a poetic rendition of intimate space, which comes across almost as a performance, one that invites the reader into the nooks and crannies and cupboards of the psyche and somehow into the introversion of intimate space. His is not a building of empire and castle, but an exquisite attention to detail, to texture, to cracks. It is an elaboration of the housing and space of the psyche, with its shadows as well as its windows. Woven through his book is the poetic image and how, in his words, "The image touches the depths before it stirs the surface" (Bachelard, 2014, p8).

Our conversations dwelt upon such ideas and images and inspired us to try to generate a milieu and working space for the workshop that was inductive rather than prescriptive. In other words, we tried to move away from conscious manipulation of the materials and space and encourage participants to be agents of revelation (hence the lack of direction or instruction at the beginning). As a phenomenologist, Bachelard tries to return "to the things themselves" bringing attention to the reciprocal relationship between the human imagination, materials and space. For example, he talks of how an "Imagination that is material and dynamic enables us to experience a provoked adversity" (Bachelard, 1971, p68). This "provoked adversity," which might be understood as a psychology of opposition, seemed a good phrase to contain our intention to unsettle the space and facilitate process-oriented work. This approach aimed to reveal links between space, matter and meaning. In so doing, it examined the pliability of truth, filters of observation and discrepancies in perception. For example, by way of introducing building materials to a dramatherapeutic process and creating an atmosphere, which allowed process to unfold, we hoped to bring a freshness to these dynamics and invite "adversity."

In terms of reaching towards moments of "truth," two further ideas from Bachelard were particularly useful in guiding our thinking: his notions of the resonance and reverberation of image. Bachelard discusses how images hold meaning both internally and externally: "The resonances are dispersed on the different planes of our life in the world, while the repercussions invite us to give greater depth to our own existence" (Bachelard, 2014, p7). These ideas, which speak to the revelation of truth and meaning through image, acted as a centre ground for the sensibility and meaning-making process of the work. Not only did it offer a philosophical idea of the induction of meaning through image but also one that, in psychoanalytical terms, reflected both internal and external worlds. As we were thinking through the actual exercises, these ideas were our guides. How might we curate and facilitate the work, in ways, which encouraged the material to shape itself? How to guide participants to make a space both within themselves and through the placing and animation of bodies?

Notions of play and proximity and Peter Slade

Peter Slade was a pioneer of children's theatre, educational drama and dramatherapy. In fact his was the first recorded use of the term "dramatherapy," which may mean he might be considered the "first dramatherapist," at least in the context of the discipline's development within the UK. He evolved his unique and innovative approaches via a variety of professional roles which included local authority Drama Advisor and Director of the Educational Drama Association. The development of his work is of further note in that it stands as a direct response to the austere and fragmented landscapes of post-war Britain. He was active from late 1940s, throughout the 1960s and in to the 1970s, practising, speaking and campaigning to evidence "the importance of drama (as opposed to theatre) as a means of personal expression and development of the self" (Slade, 1954, p47). Slade's ideas of projected and personal play indicate the potential for the animation of different objects and materials in the therapeutic space. He spoke of projected play as a process involving the "projecting of a dream out of the mind … into, on to or around objects outside of oneself" (Slade, 1965, p7). He also examined the experience of the "projecting" individual and their state of being within this form of play and towards notions of personal play. He describes those moments when "I can't get a symbol or an object to do this thing. I have to be involved myself. I do it. I create. I am" (Slade, 1965, p8). Slade traces a process which appears composed not of a long and drawn out singular discourse but one fuelled and ignited by "flashes" of truth: "Think of the greatest moments of your life, were they not flashes of experience, great swords crossed? The moment of truth lives but in a second" (Slade, 1965, p11). These processes and the experience of playing and acting out from the heart of the action begin to link with some of Bachelard's conceptions of space and materiality.

In addition, Slade's subtle considerations around the role of observation are indicative of the hitherto overlooked aesthetic distinctions in his work. Slade himself was the consummate observer, the thoughtful, concerned witness of everyday street scenes in post-war urban Britain. He worked with the so-called delinquent children in the halls of Digbeth in Birmingham, bringing them together through drama. Indeed much of his theory and practice draws from and/or is in response to the social interactions of children at play in public places. The core of his writing involves the considered articulation of a sustained narrative, ever respectful and nuanced, in its description of children's play. As we read and share what he is witnessing, we connect with the open and egalitarian spirit which was the life blood of his work and life.

> ...young children when they are concerned with their acting, really have the feeling of the centre of themselves ... in their circular running, they run firstly counter clockwise, with their hearts to the centre and around and sort of outwards from the centre, throw(ing) off energy and creation ...
>
> *(Slade, 1965, p4)*

Slade talks about street play – pavements, levels, drains, footfall, hand claps, stones, running and the mortal threat of the car to the playing "absorbed" child. These observations chimed with the spatial and intricate observations of Bachelard, finding intrigue in the mundane and fascination with the detail and possibility in everyday spaces and objects.

Considering the role and function of observation in dramatherapy, Slade brings attention to the quality of those observations and to an individual's capacity to cultivate an "objective observation without necessarily immediately being involved" (Slade, 1965, p3). This is Slade as phenomenologist. From this held, suspended or *actively inactive* state, he indicates a subtler take on an approach to Projected Play:

> Projecting a dream out of the mind, into, on to or around objects outside of themselves and at that moment something comes alive ... the objects are left, deserted but in a pattern and these objects outside of oneself become significant.
>
> *(Slade, 1965, p7)*

From these insights Slade goes on to consider the transitions towards Personal Play. Here he speaks of there being a journey:

> You start from a place. There is a journey from a place to another place ... not really being concerned with an audience but acting all around myself

from the centre outwards, while being in an I am-ish condition. And then I return to the base, but I make some fascinating shapes while I am on my way with the journey of my footfalls …

(Slade, 1965, p8)

In reflecting on these processes, Slade comments on notions of equidistance and space:

The first sort of relationship between art and drama is in the appearance of equidistance. In child painting you notice tidiness coming like this. Equidistance between shapes and dots … towards something we call composition … mass, weight and colour … in drama the parallel is grouping.

(Slade, 1965, p9)

And finally, the importance of small contributions:

…how important it is for each tiny little person, in each group, each class, each community to give his little bit, his contribution. And out of these very sweet or simple and sometimes slightly irrelevant contributions little stories can be made. And this is our story, utter us-ness …

(Slade, 1965, p11)

In drawing together these examples, there is an attempt to articulate and demonstrate the rich and enlivened aesthetic sense that runs through the work of Slade. These qualities, carefully integrated within his writing and honed through the practices he describes, so as to deliver their subjects towards an experience of truth; a reflexive and numinous encounter with one's being.

The workshop

Having introduced something of our initial interests, subsequent conversations and the thinking behind them (along with our two, perhaps unlikely protagonists, Bachelard and Slade), what follows is a partial account of the workshop itself. This includes specific and generalised information, material fact, insubstantial reflection and imaginings. All of which play some part in the establishment of that thing called truth.

Place

This took us time to find. It seemed key. We began with a process of negation; that which we didn't want. We didn't want a drama studio, a dance space with a sprung floor, a classroom or a lecture hall. We didn't want a space which comforted us or colluded with the easier institutionalised anticipations of our professions. After visiting and standing in a series of increasingly (and pleasingly) random spaces we were shown two adjoining spaces. Asymmetrical and irregular. Peculiar. Odd. Something immediately feeling ill-conceived in their arrangement. Divided and abutted by storage spaces (cupboards). Accessed by two doors at opposite ends of the space. Light sources down one outer facing wall. A dull grey painted concrete floor. A high ceiling with fluorescent tube lights. The space had something of a garage about it, a storage depot or a place where broken things are taken to be disassembled, repaired or cleaned. In any case, it felt right. It was a space easily overlooked, perhaps disliked and even avoided. It presented us with immediate challenges. The acoustics were poor. There was no natural stage from which to present to a group, nor a natural and definable "play space." Everything was a bit off and discordant, one area encroached another before it had really achieved itself. We wandered around a bit, slightly dazed and disconcerted by it before nodding, yep, this will do.

Materials

We travelled to a builders' yard on the edge of town. We selected and bought the following:

× 3 galvanised steel buckets
× 12 building bricks
× 4 aerated concrete blocks
× 7 joist hangers and steel restraint clamps
Lengths of copper piping
Lengths of plastic tubing
Lengths of bamboo
Rolls of corrugated cardboard
Sheets of insulating felt
Sheets of paper
Masking tape
String
Various pieces of ironmongery, plastic cable connectors and trunking

We devised a session plan which aimed to speak to conference themes related to imaginal capacity, trust and truthfulness in light of our ruminations on space and the nature of play. The workshop further picked up on other conference enquiries around paradoxical encounters and consensual reality.

We listed our workshop aims as providing for:

- An experimental enquiry into the use and role of materials and how they might be used to facilitate the building of relationships and the cultivation of intimacy within therapeutic encounters
- The perception and mobilisation of objects as sites of relational encounter, reflecting psychological states and the embodiment of feelings and images
- The malleability of space as it is effected and affected by bodies and materials

The workshop was an immersive and continuous two-hour process. What follows is not a verbatim account of all that happened but rather an episodic re-telling of specific moments which we have been able to recall and which, in some way, seem reflective of the themes under investigation and/or the tone and feel of the time we all spent together.

Preparing

Ahead of the session we prepared the space. The space offered no obvious stage or play-space. We taped out sections on the floor. These we thought might be helpful as the work unfolded, and if the emergent process required defined spectator/performer locations. We placed, leant and grouped the materials along one length of recessed wall. Although we lacked a rationale for so doing, we took care and time to site the objects in the space and in relation to one another. It quickly seemed important. We were attending to and collaborating in an emergent aesthetic process – a ritual marking of the space and materials. In this we were also warming towards a structure for engagement with the materials that we would later direct; to observe, choose, rise, place, return.

Arriving

Gradually participants began to arrive. People entered sequentially via both doors. The room began to fill with people, bags and belongings, movement and voice. The acoustic was immediately noticeable. Echo, resonance, dead spots. Again, perhaps due to no clear stage or centre, groups began to form randomly. We milled around. Dowsing and divining for some common ground of address. Not wanting to shout, we attempted a few half-hearted calls to gather from awkward placings. A singular collective contact could not be achieved; some stirred in response, others remained beyond our reach. We moved to develop a roaming and repetitive mantric refrain of "where have I come to?" Gradually all present came to hear this question and a focus was pulled. This question also held encouragements towards being present and attentive to being here at this time. The vocal incantation developed to notice and acknowledge views from the windows and shapes of the space; seeing *here* in the context of *there*. We had begun.

Flocking

Soon the group were moving as one. Not necessarily mirroring but in some sort of relation to one another, be that concordant or discordant, in synchrony or counter pointed. Individuals took turns to *lead the flock*. Instantly and repeatedly, flock members were put in touch with their own inclinations to work with or against the rhythm, pacing, proximity and texture of what was being suggested. An innate sense of dramatic process emerged, whereby one type of flocking would be followed by its opposite; fast by slow, bound by flowing, light by weighty. The space being worked and warmed. The group forming through these motive ways of doing and being. In motion. In space. The unison and intermingling of all of this was then switched with a move towards solitude. Being alone in the space again. Separate from others. Distanced. The space now in-between self and other. Here and there. And stopping to notice one's own movements; breathe, tremble, perspire. And to notice and be with what occurred, what's just ended and what remains, what now is present?

Emergence

As the process of the work developed through consecutive exercises, we were attempting to encourage a softness of the gaze, a sense of social space and an inductive spirit of play. We had devised and ordered a sequence of exercises to support people in approaching materials and dialoguing with one another in the initial moments of their encounter. There was a ritual sense emerging through the way we were working the space, the exercises, one another. Our hope was that this formed an increasingly tangible and clear convention to provide containment and a sense of safeness (partly by way of consciously embracing unsettlement). One of the exercises included working in pairs and improvising with the materiality of an A4 piece of white paper. As this exercise played out, initial associations and functional attributes of the paper soon seemed to fall away, as participants were offered simple directions which supported a process of revelation rather than manipulation. In turn, each person had the chance to shape, tear, move, fold the paper in what became a three-way conversation involving the other person, the material and oneself. The earlier work exploring the quality of the gaze and the spirit of play seemed to support people in approaching the paper and the dialogue with attention, curiosity and a capacity for surprise. There was a ritual sense to this exercise, with the clear convention of each person receiving the communication from the other through the shaping of the paper. Gradually, the atmosphere in the space changed, as a sense of play and process was given oxygen. Participants appeared to find their way towards those "gateways to the play process," whereby the images reveal themselves naturally through the action. In what seems on the face of it such a simple exercise, a texture, rhythm and depth developed, as the shaping, tearing, sounding and placing of the paper developed into a conversation more of attitude and affect than cognition.

One of our reflections on this exercise was how (by way of the "blank sheet") there was an echo of the notion of the *tabula rasa* in psychoanalytic work, where the psychoanalyst works mainly with the transference as the central dynamic within the psychotherapy. However, the A4 sheet, along with the other various materials located within the "third area," or "potential space," conceivably invited not only the transference but the unconscious process of projection. Further questions as to the extent to which the shaping and dialogue emerged from the materiality of the paper and to what extent was it caused and influenced by the unconscious projections of the persons involved. Some paper was not folded, torn or shaped, but explored kinaesthetically, being lifted, landed and left. Other pieces became smithereens, like snowflakes on the ground. Some objects were used repeatedly. Others remained overlooked, left leaning against the wall, forgotten and abandoned. What resulted, as we walked around and observed the "monuments" created, as they rested on the floor in their unique shapes and states, was a gallery of story, encompassed through angles, corners, shadows and a strange sense of purpose.

Observing, Choosing, Rising, Placing, Returning

Following a brief stopping and gathering moment of meditation, group members were invited to turn their gaze to take in and *observe* the arranged building materials. The materials sat adjacent to one of the previously taped out sections of the room. It was vacant. All group members sat elsewhere. This space was now identified as a place of encounter, play, perhaps performative. The next invitation saw people *choose* a material/object, then *rise* to *place* it somewhere within the demarcated space. This process began very slowly. For a long time no one moved. Like a battery on a slow charge, gradually building until something flickers and the charge is released. One by one, turn taking. One observed, taken in, watched, noticed, drunken up by all. Silence, stillness, charging and again, release. Objects gradually inhabiting the space before us, forming patterns, shapes, polarities and constellations. Being added to, taken away, subverted, balanced, tipped and dropped, hidden and revealed. The next step grew from this. Individuals entering and remaining in the space *with* their object and others bringing themselves and their object to connect, oppose, enact to and with each other. Here there was intimacy, risk, tension. The players beginning to test the edges of the play space. Where am I taking myself… where am I finding myself… where have I come to?

Aerated concrete block

One person lying flat on their back. In their right hand they hold a long length of copper piping. They hold it by their shoulder and most of it extends away from their head down and beyond the length of their own body. They lie there alone being observed for quite some time. Others work in pairs and threes around this person. Most appear oblivious to their prone, horizontal presence. Now another approaches the person lying on the floor. This person holds in their hands a large aerated concrete block. They very gently kneel down at the side of the person prostrate. They lean slightly forwards from the kneeling position to suspend the block above the chest of the person lying down. Immediately the breath of the other is noticed. As their chest rises and falls within the space between themselves and the suspended block. Now very gradually the block is being lowered to rest upon the inhalations and exhalations of the chest and again instantly that movement is transferred and amplified in to and through the rising and falling of the block. The holder of the block takes great care to keep it balanced, to keep it safe in place. Together observing and feeling the rising and falling. The person prone open, vulnerable, receptive to this accentuation of their current state of being. The person kneeling as a supplicant to a holy rite, in observance of the life force; breath.

Balancing buckets

In another moment, one solitary participant stood with eyes closed. Arms slightly away from the sides of their body. Their hands open, fingers splayed as if alert, sensing space, anticipating contact. Another participant is close by and gradually inclines forwards to say something quietly. Having heard those whispered words, the arms of the standing figure appear to soften and come to rest naturally at their side. Hands also relax and the previously splayed fingers release to close and rest. The one who whispered now steps away and moves towards the materials, soon to return, now with a length of bamboo. As they return the length of bamboo is being carefully considered. There is no certainty of intent in what will happen next. The active partner in this formative encounter now raises the bamboo in the space between them and the other participant remains still with eyes closed. They move the bamboo around carefully as if divining, as if inviting, encouraging the bamboo to participate and find its own way. Now it is coming to rest gently along the top of the standing partner's shoulders. The standing figure with eyes still closed, adjusts their stance almost imperceptibly and in so doing acknowledges and receives this light, subtle contact. The active partner now moves the opposite end of the bamboo to rest on their own shoulder and then there it is, suspended in the space between them. Time passes and others draw close, observe and move on to continue with their own playful and curious encounters. Then two others join the original pair. Now the two are four and two are stood still, both with eyes closed. The new pair have added another length of bamboo. The original pair stand facing one another. A single bamboo length is balanced simply and freely between their opposite shoulders. Their other shoulders similarly support a single length of bamboo but this now holds the weight of two galvanised steel buckets, hanging from either end of the bamboo cane. The contrast is startling. The ease of one contrasting with the stress and tension and clattering consequence of the other. The play has grown precarious in nature. There is something striking here around balance and harmony. Testing the tolerance of what can be held between two poles and where the intrusive edge or the tipping point resides.

Glimpse

One final example from the workshop involved some members of the group entering the performative space and working with the objects to create what was to become an echo of the conference theme. Don Quixote, this wandering knight-errant, seemed to make an appearance in the final moments of the drama improvisation. A steel bucket became a helmet, a mop handle a lance as his character emerged. Such a moment of constellation was poignant and unplanned, different interactions and assemblages manifesting this figure which was the original inspiration for the conference theme. By way of the group process, and the combination of the space and the materials, here was our protagonist, shaped by forces which remain curious to this day. On reflection, there was perhaps something in the spirit of Quixote in the collaboration and design of the workshop, which led to this culminating final image. The materials we chose are functional, but just as Quixote encounters the mundane and functional, so his imaginal life is sparked into life. This part of the workshop also seemed to unsettle. In delineating a performative space, the nature of the play seemed to change. It became more self-conscious than the earlier play in small groups, in which the witnessing and observations were glimpsed and momentary. In this shared gaze into the collective performance space, the nature of the play seemed to become more intent on fixing something. Perhaps there was the pull for laughs or a need to develop a shared reference point in the performance. Whatever the influence, this change struck us as notable insofar as it relates to the question of unearthing something truthful in the process of play and improvisation. How to maintain the quality and freedom apparent in the smaller group and pair work in the ensemble? How to avoid performance-led play, and remain true to the emergence of the social space, which tracks and cultivates meaning making?

Resonance and reverberation

Throughout the experience of the workshop, in the shared group work and in the pair work, there was a sense of intrigue and adversity. The materials we introduced, coupled with the space, nature and tone of our instructions seemed to create a sense of revelation through the unfamiliar, through the unsettlement. The strangeness of the placing and manipulation of the materials sculpted in tandem with physical shapes all contributed to the development of an adverse space, one in which the functional and the literal were replaced by a sense of the symbolic and an emergent aesthetic (even if this became self-conscious at times). In these shapings and constellations, it seemed there were flashes of contrast, balance and communication between people, materials and the space.

In discussing the emergence of art forms and dramatic play in childhood, Peter Slade brings attention to notions of equidistance: "The first sort of relationship between art and drama is in the appearance of equidistance" (Slade, 1965, p9). This also appeared as a recurring motif in the experimental encounters between participants and in relation to contact with the working materials. Moments of what we might consider a "truthful communication of affect" seemed to arise in the atmosphere, through the innovation of design, connection and play. We speculate on this, and of course, there is no way of objectively evidencing levels of meaningfulness, but we both felt moments of resonance and reverberance. These "moments of meaning" seemed to happen just under the surface of consciousness, communicated more by virtue of sensibility and atmosphere than cognitive imperative. There was a sense of unfolding and emergence rather than intentional outcome. Some of the examples we have mentioned were a kind of improvised assemblage of materials and bodies, eliciting a meaning that remained just below conscious awareness, but nevertheless was experienced. It was as if something truthful happened through the dissonant and oppositional quality of the materials and spaces. This echoes the innovations of Bachelard and Slade, insofar as they each speak of a truthfulness that is elicited not by manufacture, but more through allowing the spirit of play to guide thought and action. Perhaps this goes some way in articulating an aesthetic sensibility in dramatherapy practice, one which is not restricted to a particular set of materials or objects, but is free to develop as much from the rubble as from the shiny things. In this it speaks to James Joyce's "aesthetic arrest" and of arts therapies reaching beyond a literalised version of knowledge and truth towards one which is imagined through shape, tension, materiality and the balance of opposites.

Over 50 years ago, Peter Brook wrote about the sands shifting in theatre, and a move away from a deadly theatre to new forms and new practices. He was alert to the dangers of comfort and predictability in theatre and argued for a theatre, which was "immediate" and "rough." In this search for the new, he advocated for "experimenting with new forms, new relationships, new places, new buildings" (Brook, 1990, p151). Perhaps dramatherapy sits in a similar moment, in which we re-assess not only the spaces and materials we introduce, but also the manner in which we perceive them.

References

Bachelard, G. (1971) *The Poetics of Reverie*. Boston: Beacon Press.
Bachelard, G. (2014) *The Poetics of Space*. New York: Penguin.
Brook, P. (1990) *The Empty Space*. London: Penguin.
Chaillou, T. (2012) *Interview with Ryan Gander*. The White Review. https://www.thewhitereview. org/feature/interview-with-ryan-gander/ (accessed 07.02.20)
Darley, G. (2017) 'How Gaston Bachelard gave the emotions of home a philosophy'. *Aeon*. https://aeon.co/essays
LeFebvre, H. (1991) *The Production of Space*. (Donald Nicholson-Smith trans.) Oxford: Basil Blackwell.
Morrison, T. (2016) *Song of Solomon*. London: Vintage.
Slade, P. (1954) *Child Drama*. London: University of London Press.
Slade, P. (1965) *Child drama and its educational value in education*. Educational Drama Association: University of Bangor.
Stach, R. (2017) *Kafka: The Early Years*. New Jersey: Princeton University Press.

5

THE DRAMATIC SELF PARADIGM

Human nature from a dramatherapist's perspective

Salvo Pitruzzella

Abstract

I have been growing fond of the "Knight of the sorrowful countenance" in spite not only of the fact that he is a fictional character but also that, even within the literary frame, he is an imaginary person, devised by the "madness" of the lonesome hidalgo of La Mancha, who, in its turn, is influenced by the literary world, including Cervantes' book itself.

To some extent, Don Quixote can be seen as a forerunner of the postmodern identity fragmentation, which has eventually led to the deconstruction of the concept of Self at the beginning of the third millennium: the idea that there is nothing like a "noumenal" Self behind the "phenomenal" manifestations of the person; the Self is considered instead as an illusory construct, which can be either a necessary armour or a dangerous hoax.

But if the Self is a delusion, what about therapy? We have been taught that restoring people's "real" selves is one of the therapy's aims, but what if there is nothing to restore? Where can we find solid ground upon which we can establish a transformative process?

One of the basic tenets of dramatherapy is that the dramatic tendency is an inborn human feature, manifesting itself both in our cultural inheritance, in the forms of theatre and ritual, and in our individual development, in the form of dramatic play. Therefore, its main hypothesis is that the structure of drama itself can provide us with a pattern to understand human nature. Can this pattern give us some useful insights into what we call our Selves?

In my unremitting quest for a comprehensive theory of dramatherapy, I have tried to show how the intimate structure of drama might guide us to a deeper knowledge of who we are and how we function (Pitruzzella 2006, 2016). More recently, I tried to connect the key elements of drama with the new paradigm of human nature

DOI: 10.4324/9781003110200-5

emerging from the recent confluence of studies in various fields: neurosciences, cognitive sciences and philosophy of the mind, psycho-linguistic studies on metaphor, complexity theories, enactivism and intersubjectivity research.

The result is a descriptive model of human development in a world of relationships, which I called the *Dramatic Self Paradigm*: a complex and comprehensive model, which can help us to understand the blocks that can hinder a balanced growth.

The model will be developed at length in my next book: here I present for the first time some of the major lines of inquiry that support it. I hope it can eventually encourage readers to acknowledge that Don Quixote's weakness is precisely his strength.

Keywords: Don Quixote, dramatic metaphor, complexity, Self, intersubjectivity

Abstract in Italian

Col tempo, mi sono sempre di più affezionato al "Cavaliere dalla trista figura," ancorché non solo sia una finzione letteraria, ma sia anche dentro la cornice letteraria un personaggio immaginario, partorito dalla "follia" del solitario hidalgo della Mancia, a sua volta influenzato dal mondo della letteratura, che include lo stesso libro di Cervantes. Per certi versi, Don Chisciotte è il precursore della postmoderna frammentazione dell'identità, che ha infine portato alla decostruzione del concetto di Sé all'inizio del Terzo Millennio: l'idea che non esiste un Sé "noumenico" dietro alle manifestazioni "fenomeniche" della persona; il Sé è piuttosto considerato come un costrutto illusorio, che può diventare una necessaria armatura di protezione, ma anche un pericoloso auto-inganno. Ma se il Sé è un'illusione, quali conseguenza per la terapia? Abbiamo imparato che il rafforzamento del "vero" Sé è uno degli scopi della terapia, ma che cosa succede se non c'è niente da rafforzare? Dove possiamo trovare un terreno solido per attivare un processo trasformativo?

Uno dei principi di base della drammaterapia è che, considerato che la tendenza drammatica è connaturata all'essere umano, e si manifesta sia a livello ontogenetico che a livello filogenetico, la struttura stessa del dramma possa suggerirci uno schema per comprendere la natura umana. L'Ipotesi del Sé Drammatico, alla quale lavoro da diversi anni, è un tentativo di integrare i concetti emergenti di intersoggettività, enazione, percezione ecologica e processi omeostatici – che implicano l'abbandono della tradizionale concezione del Sé – in una versione ampliata e rivista della "metafora drammatica." Sono convinto che il modello che ne risulta possa suggerirci dei nuovi strumenti per comprendere il disagio, e usare i nostri metodi in modo più consapevole ed efficace.

The Knight and the Self

At the end of the first part of Cervantes' novel, Don Quixote comes back home, transported on a wagon drawn by oxen. He has been beaten nearly to death by a hooded penitent carrying a statue of the Virgin Mary, which he mistook for a real damsel in danger. So far, he hadn't defied religion in such a direct manner, and we can expect, as Sancho does, that his bravery had to be sternly punished. However, Don Quixote, as saddened, bruised, wounded, and ashamed as he could be, is still himself, intending to have a pause, in order "to let the malign influence of the stars which now prevails pass off," and then leave again for a new adventure.

At the end of the second part, Don Quixote is defeated by a "real" knight (being actually the second attempt of the bachelor Samson Carrasco of using a "shock therapy" to heal his friend's insanity). This setback has a tremendous impact on the story: Don Quixote falls into a feverish state, and when he recovers, he is no more Don Quixote, the Knight of the sorrowful countenance whose deeds had spellbound the reader for some thousand pages, but someone else. Who? Is he now the same person he was at the beginning of the story, the quiet and dull hidalgo living in some nondescript village in La Mancha? As he has done all the way through the novel, Cervantes once again baffles us: although he mentioned a few of the possible surnames for his character, none of them seems to be the one he chooses now, Alonso Quijano el Bueno, and even of this epithet (the Good) we found no mention so far. Under this name, he will reject his previously beloved books of chivalry, dictate his last will and soon meet death. Unfortunately, he will be remembered as a literary hero neither in this latter role of good and wise Christian, nor in his former role of idle, rather lifeless hidalgo, but in his role of madman, enduring through hunger, thirst, beating, mocking and bodily injury, but still going on.

At the end of the day, we are left with many doubts about our hero's real self.

Doubts crowd in our minds because of our inclination to assume that something like a *real self* must necessarily exist: an entity that is the centre of our individual existence, that can perceive, feel and think, that can store experience in its memory and most of all that can act as a controller of our behaviour. A *real* self that can sometimes be obscured by a *false* one; delusional selves that, like our knight-errant, must be knocked down in order to heal their victims.

This assumption has called into question many times in western culture, but never has it been shaken so deeply as in recent times, since the inquiry into the brain and its functions has thrown a totally different light upon the issue. Asked about where in the body the seat of the soul could be, Descartes, albeit hesitantly, would have answered: in the brain, or, more exactly, in the pineal gland. Unfortunately, leaving aside the pineal gland, a control centre that presides over people's thought, emotions and behaviour has not been found in the brain, even though there have been many attempts at homunculus hunting. Homunculus (little man) is the traditional name given to the agency paradox: if there is an entity that coordinates and commands the manifold aspects of our life, it should be as complex as we are; in this case, it would need a homunculus in its mind to control it, and this mind would need another one, and so on, in a paradoxical *regressus ad infinitum*.

It seems that the brain actually works with parallel processes that are occasionally coordinated in some automatic ways and seldom need the contribution of our conscious will in order to accomplish their tasks (Gazzaniga 2011; Wegner 2003). The renowned experiments on conscious will made by Benjamin Libet have shown beyond doubt that when the conscious decision to perform an action appears, the brain impulse to act has already started; in a nutshell, when we decide to perform an action, our brain has prepared it long before (Libet 2005). So why should we need a conscious self?

Complexity theories may provide us with a useful framework for an understanding of how it came to be that something so unusual, and probably quite useless from an evolutionary point of view, as the feeling of having a conscious self has come into the game.

According to the customary definition, a complex system is a collection of components interconnected in such a way that if you act on one of them, you act on all. It cannot be described just by listing its components, but it is necessary to consider the relationships among them. At the same time, it behaves as a single entity, in constant relationship of mutual influence with other systems at various levels. A complex system's functioning has therefore some specific characteristics, different from those of a simple one (even though in nature systems that lack some degree of complexity are relatively rare). Many of these characteristics have been identified, and I will list some of the most relevant.

Self-organisation

A living organism is neither a machinery always working in the same way nor a state in which elements freely flow creating bonds as they meet each other. It is rather a dynamic yet well-organised system, able to rearrange its internal setting according to the environment and its activity according to the other systems with which it interacts. Each of the elements that are part of such a system have multiple relationships with many others, constantly influencing each other. When the whole of these relationships becomes too large, they tend to organise themselves along hierarchic orders. A complex system is always in contact with other complex systems – on one side with the larger ones of which it is a part; on the other side with the other systems at its level. This continuous interchange triggers fluctuations in the state of the system itself, which in their turn provoke its reorganisation as a whole. The tendency of the system to reorganise itself, maintaining some of the characteristics marking its identity, is called *homeostasis*. The opposite tendency, pushing the system towards collapse, is called *catastrophe*. Usually, living systems are well equipped to find their safe middle ways between these polarities, accepting change but keeping balance.

Emerging properties and structural coupling

When a system organises itself, new properties that were not present in its single parts emerge; these emergent properties can become dominant for the system's behaviour, as they often act at a new hierarchic level. The process through which the encounter of a complex system with an external object (which can be also another complex system) is reworked by the system itself can reach a limit beyond which the impact of the external perturbation cannot be integrated by the system anymore. This can involve moments of fluctuation, when the web of reciprocal relationships that kept the elements together so far is shaken, before a new organisation can appear. Within these fluctuations, new nucleuses can surface, around which the system will model its reorganisation, being the first bases of new emergent properties. When two systems encounter each other, they can have what Varela called a "structural coupling," in which they can form, albeit provisionally, a new system with new emerging properties (Varela, Thompson & Rosch 1991).

Non-linearity and recursivity

What makes all these matters quite interesting is the fact that the complex systems have chaotic aspects. Chaotic is defined as a process of which we cannot predict the outputs, even though we know its initial state and its rules of functioning. This happens because the relationships between the elements are non-linear: a modest input can provoke an unpredictable upshot that will end in a disproportionate output, the so-called butterfly effect. Conversely, massive inputs can be absorbed by the system making no impressive change. Non-linear processes are not sequential, but they spread out in networks. They also tend to be recursive, producing loops that can either self-regulate or self-intensify. Recursivity expresses itself through negative feedbacks, which, coming back to the first link in the chain, carry new information that moderates the effects of inputs, thus stabilising the system. Positive feedbacks, on the contrary, amplify inputs, causing a dangerous instability of the system.

Redundancy and integration of the noise

In order to prevent an uncontrolled series of positive feedbacks causing it to collapse, a complex system has its tools, first of all redundancy, that is the repetition of crucial bits of information upon the system's organisation in fundamental hubs of the system's structure. This allows it to be easily brought back to a default state, averting collapse. At the same time, redundancy decreases the system's flexibility, making it more rigid or brittle, less able to learn and to adapt. An excessive rigidity of the system obstacles the integration of noise. Under this term are to be included all the messages that the system receives both from inside and outside which are not pertinent to its homeostasis. However, these messages can contain important developmental possibilities that a complex system is usually able to integrate, turning them either into factors of order, including them in its organisation, or into factors of transformation, modifying the organisation and increasing its complexity.

From the complexity point of view, the mind is an emergent property arising from the structural couplings of the brain (which, in organisms that have one, is the most complex body organ) with other complex systems.

First, the brain's structural coupling with the other body organs, in particular the sensorial systems, through which it receives information about the internal state of the body and on the external environment. Such information thus forms the basis of mental states, which can produce feedbacks that modify the body state itself. These primary mental states do not imply the presence of a consciousness that refers them to a single aware subject (the Self), but they automatically occur in the homeostatic interaction between the brain and the rest of the body and contain an amount of "biological value," in the sense that they signal an unbalance of the system that urges to be corrected. Antonio Damasio puts them into an evolutionary perspective, and considers them as the expression of an innate tendency to pursue what matches our perseverance to exist: this is what Spinoza called *conatus*. Spinoza maintained that the human *conatus* is regulated by passions, mainly *laetitia* and *tristitia* (joy and sorrow), connected either to the increase or the depletion of our power to act. This tendency has a biochemical counterpart in the brain, manifesting itself as "rewards" or "punishments," which according to Damasio are "feelings," as they are "felt" by the organism; in complexity terms, they become "redundancies," meaningful repetitions of information about the system's organisation that can serve as a blueprint for further reorganisations (Damasio 1994, 2003, 2010). These homeostatic feelings influence our mood and guide our behaviour in an unconscious manner. However, as feeling something implies a feeling subject, they are the first inklings of a potential emergent property, namely consciousness.

The second important structural coupling of the brain is with the others, a plurality of other complex systems, also endowed with brains. Such structural couplings have crucial consequences both at phylogenetic and ontogenetic levels. At phylogenetic level, we can see that as the course of evolution has proceeded from simple organisms to complex ones, the primary relationships with parents or caregivers have become more and more important for survival, with a peak in the *Homo Sapiens,* the most complex organism to have appeared so far (even if not necessarily the best!). Therefore, many mammals have developed a social mind, a coordinated series of functions situated in different parts of the brain that regulate the interactions among the members of the species. The social mind can produce embryonic forms of consciousness (which in animals that have been living with humans for a long time, like dogs, look particularly developed). In these primitive forms, the subjective feeling is not referred only to the experience of a subject with objects (or with itself as an object) but with other subjects: consciousness of ourselves as distinct subjects is enhanced by mirroring ourselves in the others. Besides joy and sorrow, fear and anger and the other basic emotional expressions arising from the relations of the organism with the environment, new emotions appear, the social emotions. They produce the prosocial behaviours visible in all the mammals, and particularly in the primates. The social mind is a crucial feature of human nature (Gazzaniga 1987; Tomasello 2009), and the interpersonal mirroring processes are its foundations. At ontogenetic level, parental care activates each individual's intraspecific relational possibilities (Lewis, Amini & Lannon 2001; Cozolino 2006) and becomes the basis of human communication.

Finally – and this is a unique characteristic of human beings – the structural coupling of the brain with the culture in which the organism is immersed, which is largely mediated by the language. The result is a process in which the primary reality maps guiding our behaviour (derived from the two above mentioned levels – the brain's coupling with the body and with the other organisms) are verified and reworked. Cultural contents can be learnt by observation, imitation or intentional teaching, but they can also influence the mind when it enters into contact with specific fragments of information which, just like the genes, have a strong tendency to replicate themselves, the so-called "memes" (Dawkins 1989; Blackmore 1999). This interaction of the brain with cultural systems provides the tools to recount the world through stories. The specificity of human mind is its narrative dimension: Michael Gazzaniga has called this function "the interpreter" and placed it in the left-brain middle cortex. The narrative function is a fundamental aspect of consciousness: by virtue of this function, consciousness perceives itself as being a proper Self. Daniel Dennett has defined the Self as a "centre of narrative gravity" (Dennett 1992).

In summary: these three processes of the brain's structural coupling produce new emerging properties, the bodily mind, the social mind, and the cultural mind. They present themselves as levels of organisation occurring along the person's development, and each of them encompasses the others. The feeling of Self (my Self) appears gradually, along with the enhancement of consciousness (a Self), from the first felt emotions and their expressions, through the mirroring with the others, and culminating with the narrative ability of the Self to tell stories about itself. Being founded on a large series of interactions among complex systems, which by definition are always changing and constantly reorganising themselves, consciousness is not a constant state of the human condition (a steady attribute of the human mind) but an emergent property of a mind that becomes more and more complex and reorganises itself, adding a provisional hierarchical level that may serve as a decisional centre. Furthermore, quite often consciousness is even absent: in sleep, in hypnosis, in states of trance and in automatic behaviours, as in many damaged brain conditions, consciousness vanishes; someone even said that consciousness is a human characteristic soluble in alcohol. When it is present it does not always have the same level of intensity: sometimes like barely heard background music, sometimes loudly entering centre stage. Often its function is influenced by non-conscious processes; in these cases, the "interpreter" tends to create narratives that justify what apparently seem conscious decisions, but in point of fact are unconscious: we can affirm that the percentage of the mind's work reaching consciousness is definitely minimal. Being the Self, a by-product of the consciousness reflecting on itself, it is subject to the same vicissitudes.

The counter-intuitive conclusion that all these neuroscientific and cognitive studies seem to reach is that the Self is not something stable, a hard-core nucleus implicit in the human condition (which has some similarities with the soul, except for the fact that it is not supposed to survive after death), but a subjective feeling that shifts and fluctuates as consciousness does.

The theatrical metaphor

Theatre is the realm of consciousness. Even when a character acts in a somewhat unconscious manner, like Lady Macbeth's compulsive handwashing in a dream-like state, or when Pirandello's characters act according to deceptive frames of which they are unaware, the audience is always aware of the reasons for their behaviour. Sometimes, they cannot be totally explained and leave the audience with open questions, upon which they are invited to reflect. In any case, as the philosopher Bruce Wilshire claims, theatre puts the world under our inquiry through showing us a compact, concise and comprehensible compendium of it: the "world" of the stage: "Theatre," he wrote,

> is a mode of discovery that explores the threads of what is implicit and buried in the world, and pulls them into a compressed and acknowledgeable pattern before us: the "world."
>
> *(Wilshire 1982, pxiv)*

Let's imagine now being a citizen of Athens in its splendour, going to the Theatre of Dionysus where Sophocles' *Oedipus Rex* is performed. What would you expect to see on stage? Firstly and foremost, a story. The stories of the classical theatre were far from being "original screenplays"; everybody knew them in advance, and there was no risk of spoilers. However, you would be eager to watch it staged, because you would want to renew its message, which is part of your cultural identity. Secondly, the story is staged through characters: they do not just tell the story (as probably the more archaic forms of theatre did), but also enact it in first person. Thirdly, the plot unfolds through the relationships among the characters, which are gradually revealed in the course of the play. Fourthly, after the performance, you will be rewarded with a renewed knowledge. Aristotle ascribed this enhancement of knowledge to the effect of *catharsis*, through which the engulfing emotions are purged (that is, once more, putting them under the rule of consciousness).

Now please let's make a jump of a couple of millennia or so and imagine being an intellectual in Paris not long after World War II, going to the Théâtre de Babylone to see the premiere of Beckett's *Waiting for Godot*. What then would be your expectations? Probably not to hear a story you already know, but a new one, and probably you also expect this story not to have the typical characteristics of the stories told in the theatre you have seen in the past. And you would be right: Beckett's narrative has neither a proper beginning nor a proper end, there is not a clear logic in it, and space, time and reality are fuzzy categories. However, in *Waiting for Godot*, a story advances upon the two main characters and their relationships. And the knowledge you will acquire at the end is a suspended one, full of doubts and questions about life's absurdity.

NARRATIVES, ROLES, RELATIONSHIPS and KNOWLEDGE are the *Dramatic Universals*, the ways in which the "world" of the stage is displayed in front of us, in order to be witnessed and acknowledged. NARRATIVES, ROLES, RELATIONSHIPS and KNOWLEDGE are also the ways each of us interfaces with the world, what I call our *Dramatic Interface System*, or *Dramatic Self*. Even though none of them is entirely under the rule of consciousness, they are at the core of our Self feeling. They reciprocally influence each other, constantly changing and rearranging themselves and their mutual dynamics according to their interactions with the others and with the environment.

NARRATIVES are the stories we tell ourselves about ourselves and about the world, as well as the stories we tell other people about ourselves, about our version of the world, and our version of them. They can be fictional, intentionally or unwittingly; we tell stories of our past in which elements of chronicle are mingled with imagination and also with false memories, which can easily be implanted in our brains (Shaw 2016). They can be told in different ways in different moments, with significant shifts in meaning. We can either strongly believe in them or just accept them suspiciously: whatever they may be, our narratives shape our Self feeling.

ROLES are meaningful and recognisable patterns of behaviour, through which we manifest ourselves in interpersonal situations. We are able to play many of them, and sometimes more than one at once. They can be pre-existent shapes that just need to be filled: roles that are transmitted by tradition or that are implicit in a particular social environment. Conversely, there can be roles that we carefully design: Erving Goffman had described the intentional "presentation of Self" in face-to-face situations as a strategy to influence the others to our advantage (Goffman 1959). Between these two extreme poles – roles to which we mindlessly adhere versus roles we intentionally contrive – there is a vast range of possibilities, which are our potential role repertoire. Our role repertoire affects our Self feeling.

RELATIONSHIPS are the fundamental result of the long evolutionary process that made us social beings. They are based on feelings and modelled by them, either being very intimate or quite shallow; they can engage us totally or just tangentially; they can be satisfactory or conflictual; they can last a whole life or just a few minutes; they can leave a deep mark in our life or remain just as faded memories: in any case, we cannot live without at least a few of them, and the relationships we experience play a crucial part in our Self feeling.

KNOWLEDGE is the sum of the constructs through which we interpret the world and anticipate the events. They are made by what we have learnt about how the world works, by experience or by instruction, and which we presume could be a guide to our behaviour. Whatever its extent and coherence might be, the world version resulting from this process becomes a fundamental piece of our Self feeling.

Following this line of reasoning, one could conclude that we can know what a person is by examining their narratives, roles, relationships and knowledge, but this is not true, for two fundamental reasons. Firstly, because they are all partially non-conscious, informed by many layers of brain-body-mind functions, which cannot be known in first person, even with the most accurate introspection. We can make hypotheses from the outside, but they are extremely hard to validate. However, it is worth trying to investigate the multiple causal patterns that, even before consciousness enters into the game, may contribute to the creation of our interfaces with the world (and this is what we will partly try to do next). Secondly, because a person's narratives, roles, relationships and knowledge are not fixed once and for all, but constantly shifting and rearranging themselves; they influence each other, acting as a complex system which reorganises itself at each fluctuation in ways that are largely unpredictable. What we perceive at any moment as our Self is actually a snapshot of the state of these elements and their connections at that determinate time.

However, the idea of dramatherapy is that playing with these elements in a special space, safe and emotionally warm, may trigger processes of reworking and rearranging them, which can be guided toward a healthy balance. In the planned book, I will provide extensive details on how dramatherapy can achieve these goals.

What I will attempt to show in the next pages is that each of these dramatic modes of interfacing with the world, which compose our Self feeling, is supported by a specific and recognisable body-mind function, which in its turn is shaped by some of our biological endowments.

Let's start with the latter: the inborn roots of what we can call our Nuclear Self.

The Nuclear Self

We have already mentioned Spinoza's notion of *conatus*, the tendency of each organism to persist in its being. Damasio (2018) has reconstrued it in terms of the homeostatic principle, which is the self-regulating capacity of complex learning systems, that Humberto Maturana and Francisco Varela had brilliantly named *autopoiesis* (Maturana & Varela, 1980). A hint of this principle can be seen even in the simplest organisms: bacteria, for instance, obey the "quorum effect," that allows them to exchange information and modify their behaviour according to the size they are grouped. In more sophisticated organisms, homeostasis can be seen as the continuous rebalancing of the body systems according to their changing needs. The recursive mechanisms that regulate blood pressure, heartbeat, metabolism and many other vital functions are of this kind.

We come to the world with many of these mechanisms already working, having been rehearsed, at least partially, in the womb. Our proto-Self is the sum

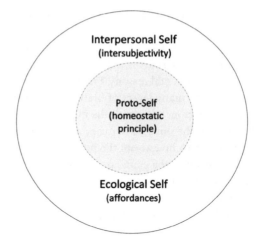

FIGURE 5.1 The nuclear self. S. Pitruzzella.

of these homeostatic processes, in that they, far from being at any rate conscious, are nevertheless related to the life of a single, separate and identifiable organism. Many of these processes are open-ended and require our organism to be coupled with at least another one, by which our first exchanges with the world are mediated, as well as with some aspects of the environment of which we are part. According to the intersubjectivity research, the tendencies to communicate with the others and to act upon objects, distinguishing one kind of interaction from another, are an evolutionary legacy, present at birth, and they define a further level, the Nuclear Self.

The Nuclear Self has two main aspects, for which I like to use Ulric Neisser's concepts of Ecological and Interpersonal Selves: "whereas the Ecological Self is an active agent in a physical environment, the Interpersonal Self is an agent in an actual social exchange" (Neisser 1993, 23). The latter is the feeling of being part of an ongoing communication, manifesting itself in what Colwyn Trevarthen (1979) has described as protoconversations, which establish what Daniel Stern (1985) has called "affect attunement." The former is the function that permits us to discern and select the environment's affordances: in the terms of James J. Gibson's theory of ecological perception, the affordances offered by something are the specific combination of the physical properties both of the object and of the agent (Gibson 1979). We do not perceive first the object's properties and then infer what we can do with it: we straightforwardly perceive their affordances. Both of these aspects of the Nuclear Self are present in many mammals: in most of them, the Ecological Self is more developed, to allow them to understand as quickly as possible the chances and the challenges of the environment, while the Interpersonal Self is developed just enough to establish bonds with the mother and the group, necessary for survival. Conversely, in humans, it is the reverse: while the Ecological Self is quite rudimental and grows in time, as the sensomotory system of the infant is refined and enhanced by learning, the Interpersonal Self is extremely sophisticated. Intersubjectivity studies have revealed the spectacular skills that a newborn baby possesses in order to establish and maintain contacts with an adult. And Giacomo Rizzolatti, in his latest book in which he resumes thirty years of research (Rizzolatti & Sinigaglia 2019), mentions an amazing amount of mirror neurons that have been found in various areas of the human brain, to the point that we cannot talk anymore of mirror neurons, but of a *mirror property* that many neurons can express in some circumstances.

Clearly, this double tendency, for which we are well equipped when we come into this world, has nothing to do with consciousness, but is rather a species-specific expression of the homeostatic principle. I am, however, inclined to construe it according to Martin Buber's dialogical philosophy. For the Jewish philosopher, the world has for us two faces, which are revealed according to the two fundamental words we say to it. One fundamental word is the couple I-It; the other is the couple I-Thou (I-you). When we say I-It, we are concerned with an object; when we say I-Thou, we recognise the other as a subject. "I-It," Buber says, "is the eternal chrysalis; I-Thou is the eternal butterfly." When we say I-It, we are in the world of experience; when we say I-Thou, we step into the sphere of inter-human.

The sphere of inter-human

Our Nuclear Self has some inborn resources through which we start approaching our environment, enter into contact with it and elaborate the results of these contacts in an autopoietic process that allows us to grow up. They are inscribed in our brain, and we share them with our animal relatives. However, in humans,

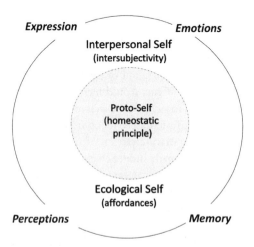

FIGURE 5.2 The nuclear resource system. S. Pitruzzella.

they are also what nudges us into the sphere of inter-human, the space where the special human gift to recognise the others as subjects like themselves is unbounded.

This *Nuclear Resources System* is made by EMOTIONS, EXPRESSION, PERCEPTION and MEMORY. They describe the first circle of the development of our *Dramatic Interface System*.

EMOTIONS. The late Jaak Panksepp (Panksepp & Biven 2012) had found in the mammalian brains (including that of the human) seven distinct emotional circuits, which have been shaped by evolution because of their biological value. They are ready for use from birth, but they must be activated by some external cause, occurring in the course of our growth. Some of them are very archaic and powerful ones, like FEAR/ANXIETY and RAGE/ANGER, which had helped our ancestors to deal with danger, and we have them probably in common not only with other mammals, but with all the vertebrates (including reptiles), or LUST/SEXUALITY, which, activated in due time by hormonal maturation, pushed them towards mating. The circuit of CARE/NURTURANCE offers to the mother or other caregivers the basic tools to establish bonds with the fruits of the consequent sexual reproduction, while through PANIC/SEPARATION, a baby can signal its need to be cared for. Perhaps the most intriguing are the remaining two: SEEKING/EXPECTANCY SYSTEM, and PLAY/JOY. The former directs the exploration behaviour, the latter has a major role in fostering relationship, and both are gratifying in themselves in terms of mood, whatever the result of the search or of the play might be. These primary emotional circuits can be easily classified according to Spinoza's main passions *Laetitia* (which increases our power to act, therefore we actively try to reach it) and *Tristitia,* (which lessens our power to act, and we try to avoid it). As we will see, EMOTIONS are the first nucleus of what will be one of our *Dramatic Interfaces,* namely RELATIONSHIPS.

EXPRESSION. According to Panksepp's theory, these seven primary emotions, which have evolved to produce adaptive behaviours, are part of a more general category of basic-primordial affects, which include also the "homeostatic affects," related to the internal balance of the body (like hunger or thirst), and the "sensorial affects," related to pleasant or unpleasant sensations transmitted by the senses. Such a vast host of affects would have little point in animals that live alone: they have been shaped in order to be shared, so they urge the organisms to produce signals that can be immediately recognised by their kin. These are the expressions, the visible bodily manifestations of an internal state. In humans, it is well known how a baby's first smile induces a chain of reciprocal smiles, which is the beginning of protoconversations. EXPRESSIONS are the first nucleus of ROLES.

EMOTIONS and EXPRESSIONS are strictly related, forming the Interpersonal side of our Nuclear Self, as well as PERCEPTION and MEMORY are, forming its Ecological side.

PERCEPTION is the complex process through which the information transmitted by the senses, including the proprioceptive systems, is conveyed to the brain that reconnects it, reworks it and sends feedback to the body in order to adjust it to the environmental pressures. The brain's reworking of perceptive information is, according to Damasio, largely devoted to the construction of maps and images. They will be stored in our memory, implicit or explicit, and used to interpret the world. Perceptions too can be connotated by what we have called "sensorial affects," implying an inkling of *Laetitia* or *Tristitia,* which makes them more or less appealing, even for a newborn baby: seeing my mommy's face is better than a stranger's one. PERCEPTIONS are the first nucleus of KNOWLEDGE.

MEMORY is even more complex: from the evolutionary point of view, it is the capacity of the organism to store the information reworked by the brain to be retrieved when needed. Keeping records of the experience has an extraordinary survival value. It can help an animal not to walk twice into the same trap; in order to do it, of course, memory doesn't need to be conscious. In humans, memory is inordinately larger and more complex than that of other animals and has played a major role in making cultures: the ancient philosophers used to compare it to a library, constantly growing with new volumes. Such assumption was roughly confirmed by the first studies on human memory at the turn of the 20th century, and is commonly held in folk psychology, seeing our memory as a sort of container in which all our experience (including learning) is safely stored. According to this view, what is not present in our conscious memory must be buried somewhere; as a consequence, ideally it should be always possible to access a *true* version of the facts, which might have been obfuscated by false memories. Research has pointed to the contrary, showing how whimsical memory is in fact. Although the pivotal role of the Hippocampus in the coordination and regulation of memory has been recognised, it is clear that the neural chains that keep the bits of information are almost everywhere in the brain, both at a cortical and subcortical level (Kandel 2006), and that our sensomotory system, through its somatic markers, has its own way to "keep the score" (Van Der Kolk 2014). Memory engrams are the result of a series of filters through which we select incoming perceptual information: sensory filters, which tend to assimilate it to the maps we already have; attention filters, which select information according to its emotional charge; cognitive filters, which endow it with meanings. And each time such bits of information are recollected, they are arranged anew, as our interpreter function needs to fill the gaps among them. Elementary forms of these processes are present in newborn babies, and they will be refined by experience and will have a leap when language enters into the game. MEMORY is the first nucleus of NARRATIVES.

Although these resources are placed in different areas of the brain and proceed in parallel ways, they are related to each other in recursive processes. We have seen how EMOTIONS influence MEMORY, in that they select the relevant bit of information to be stored; in its turn, MEMORY influences PERCEPTION, providing our brain with models to which compare the present reports of the senses; PERCEPTION influences EXPRESSIONS, as the feedbacks we receive from the others help us to refine them; EXPRESSIONS influence

EMOTIONS, as the recursive loop between the motor systems and the emotional circuits has a regulating effect on them. Together, they mark the first relationships our Nuclear Self entertains, not only with the physical environment but also with the others, being our first step into the sphere on inter-human, and they are constantly rearranged by the encounter with other subjects. It is worth repeating that all the systems we have been examining so far do not need consciousness to work, but, being referred to a unique subject, separated from the background but intrinsically connected with it, are the foundations for consciousness to occur when we will move farther towards the world.

The next circle we are going to examine briefly describes the early processes through which our *Nuclear Resources System* dynamically engages with the world, producing at the same time feedbacks that modulate it, and, as emerging properties, new tools to support this engagement, implying an enhanced consciousness and a more structured and aware feeling of Self.

EMOTIONS activate the process of MIRRORING and are modified by it. We know that perceiving another's emotions triggers our mirror systems, producing an *embodied simulation* of that emotion. The first emotional exchanges between infant and caregiver have set this process in motion; as the baby grows, mirrors multiply, and this enlarged experience helps them in fine-tuning their emotional processes according to the social environment. They develop emotional tools to understand the others and the interpersonal frames. At an enhanced consciousness level, the EMOTIONS/MIRRORING process produces what we experience as conscious FEELINGS.

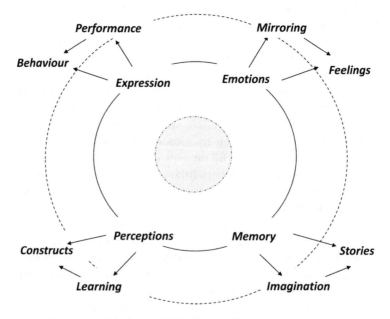

FIGURE 5.3 Engaging with the world. S. Pitruzzella.

EXPRESSIONS, through the continuous feedbacks from other people, as well as through our mimetic tendency, become PERFORMANCES, in which intentionality and direction of the expression are clear, as well as are our expectations of the responses to them. Children become so clever in performing that they use this skill for make-believe play, but they also learn to perform fake expressions, intended to influence the others. At an enhanced consciousness level, the EXPRESSION/PERFORMANCE process produces conscious BEHAVIOUR.

PERCEPTIONS are the bases for LEARNING: all we learn, either by experience, by imitation or by instruction, goes through our sensory receptors. What children learn feeds back on their perceptive systems, modifying their functioning accordingly. Learning influences their system of expectations, that is how they interpret new perceptive inputs according to their previous maps. Eventually, they will start to learn that not all the perceptions should be trusted: in Daniel Dennett's terms, that beyond its "manifest image" the world has a concealed "scientific image," which cannot be appraised by the senses (Dennett 2017). At an enhanced consciousness level, the PERCEPTION/LEARNING process produces conscious CONSTRUCTS.

MEMORY provides the materials upon which IMAGINATION can exert its power. Imagination rearranges, recombines and transforms maps and images that are generated by perceptual elements, either conscious or not, and fills the gaps of

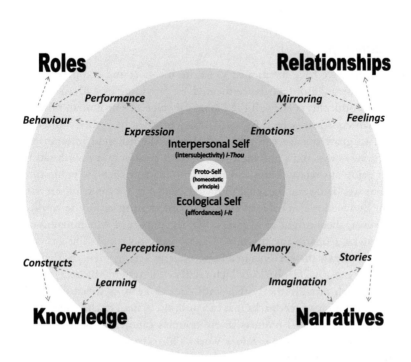

FIGURE 5.4 The dramatic self. S. Pitruzzella.

memory. At an enhanced consciousness level, the MEMORY/IMAGINATION process produces conscious STORIES.

FEELINGS, BEHAVIOUR, CONSTRUCTS and STORIES are under the light of consciousness, but the processes producing them are partially unconscious; this is why they cannot be easily changed by our conscious efforts.

Finally, we step into the third circle of our model, in which these four separate yet interconnected processes mature into what we have called the *Dramatic Interface System*. As we have seen, all the elements composing the system are the outcome of processes that are partly unconscious. ROLES, for example, are partly dictated by conscious behaviour, but are also the product of the homeostatic process of mutual rearrangement of performances and expressions that occur in human interchanges. The same could be said for RELATIONSHIPS, which are apparently ruled by conscious feelings, whereas unconscious emotions, barely regulated by the mirroring process, punctually come up to ruin the party. NARRATIVES seem founded on stories we consciously believe are true (or we consciously know they are consciously contrived), but more than often it can be quite difficult to discern the faithful rendering of the memory from the fancy of imagination. Lastly, KNOWLEDGE seems based upon conscious constructs that establish what we think are the rules of functioning of the world, through which we can foresee the events, but the basic process of perception/learning that produces those very constructs is partly body-based and not-conscious, and, as such, it can be easily distorted, even intentionally, as the many studies on priming effects have showed.

Dramatherapy

The processes we have mentioned so far are life-long and complex. They continuously rearrange and rebalance themselves, providing us with tools to engage with the world: this is after all the biological value of our human minds and of our human conscious selves. As soon as they proceed smoothly enough, we are allowed to grow up: we can play our roles in the different interpersonal and social frameworks, and sometimes we can do it creatively and with satisfaction; we can enjoy our relationships and are able to manage them, keeping those that foster our wellbeing and breaking those that hinder it; we can trust our narratives and our knowledge as reliable compasses to orient ourselves in the world.

However, there might be events in life, the impact of which makes the process go awry, jeopardising the mind's autopoietic potential. The system is not able to encompass these events in a new coherent arrangement, as their effect is of reducing negative feedbacks (which regulate the system's balance) and redundancies (which provide the system with cues to keep its structure), and often they produce positive feedbacks that can push the system to the edge of collapse. These are what we call traumas. Early traumas can affect the ways emotions, expression, perception and memory work. This is particularly visible regarding emotions and their expressions, which can become either confused or extreme and out of control, especially the negative ones, like fear, rage and grief, while some positive ones, like play, care and seeking become out of reach. Traumas can also disrupt the functions of memory, creating false memories and erasing some real ones; they can also provoke dis-perceptions that can border on hallucinations. Furthermore, the effect of trauma upon the *Nuclear Resource System* inhibits the processes that, departing from them, will lead to the emerging of our Self feeling: the processes of mirroring, performance, learning and imagination. The result is often a system closed in itself, stuck in a stiff structure marked by many new redundancies that decrease its flexibility and its capacity to regenerate itself. Finally, in adults, the lasting effects of this process are visible in a poor management of their *Dramatic Interfaces*: roles can become scary masks; relationships gloomy traps; narratives and knowledge fall under the rule of what Spinoza had called *sad passions,* conjuring a gloomy and anguishing image of the world.

Dramatic reality, the "world" of the stage in dramatherapy, can be the place where, gradually and delicately, these stiff structures can be loosened; a safe, warm and joyful place where people's narratives, relationships, roles and knowledge can be brought into play again; we can play with them, disassembling and then reassembling them, and creatively redefining and recombining them. We can let them encounter the others' narratives, relationships, roles and knowledge, building new structural couplings that can temporarily replace the old worn-out ones; we can reactivate and renovate the processes of mirroring, learning, performance and imagination. And eventually this process will feedback on the deeper levels, rebalancing our *Nuclear Dramatic Resources* and establishing a virtuous circle that counteracts the freezing effects of trauma.

Dramatherapy works on this principle: it provides people with a special stage upon which their maps and images of themselves and of the world can play together, transformed by imagination and re-signified by metaphorical shifts; in it, people's *Dramatic Selves* can find the space and the languages for encountering and renovating each other.

Conclusions

At the present point of development, the *Dramatic Self Paradigm,* on which I have been working for a few years, is a descriptive model of individual growth according to the integration of the hypotheses about human nature emerging from current scientific and philosophical research with the theatrical metaphor. I believe it needs further development, in order to become a heuristic resource which can prompt new possible theories about the processes we have explored so far and a practical resource which can suggest strategies to enhance our efficacy as arts therapists. These are my ambitions for the book to come.

In conclusion, I want to express my gratitude to the Knight-errant of La Mancha for strenuously preserving his strong Self feeling for most of the novel. Although this self is fictional (indeed, not so much more fictional than the selves we play with every day), and in spite that, in the eyes of the others, it is just a consequence of madness, he keeps on going – otherwise, there would be no novel at all.

References

Blackmore, S. (1999) *The meme machine*. Oxford: Oxford University Press.

Cozolino, L. (2006) *The neuroscience of human relationships: attachment and the developing social brain*. New York: Norton.

Damasio, A. (1994) *Descartes' error. Emotions, reason and the human brain*. New York: Penguin.

Damasio, A. (2003) *Looking for Spinoza: joy, sorrow, and the feeling brain*. Orlando: Harcourt Brace International.

Damasio, A. (2010) *Self comes to mind: constructing the conscious brain*. New York: Pantheon Books.

Damasio, A. (2018) *The strange order of things: life, feeling, and the making of cultures*. New York: Pantheon Books.

Dawkins, R. (1989) *The selfish gene*. Oxford: Oxford University Press.

Dennett, D. (1992) 'The self as a center of narrative gravity'. In: Kessel, F., Cole, P. & Johnson D. (eds.) (1992) *Self and consciousness: multiple perspectives* Hillsdale NJ.: Erlbaum.

Dennett, D. (2017) *From bacteria to Bach and back*. New York: Norton.

Gazzaniga, M.S. (1987) *Social brain: discovering the networks of the mind*. New York: Basic Books.

Gazzaniga, M.S. (2011) *Who's in charge? Free will and the science of the brain*. New York: Ecco.

Gibson, J.J. (1979) *The ecological approach to visual perception*. London: Psychology Press.

Goffman, E. (1959) *The presentation of self in everyday life*. London: Doubleday.

Kandel, E. (2006) *In search of memory. The emergence of a new science of mind*. New York: Norton.

Lewis, T., Amini, F. & Lannon, R. (2001) *A general theory of love*. New York: Vintage Books.

Libet, B. (2005) *Mind time. The temporal factor in consciousness*. Cambridge, MA.: Harvard University Press.

Maturana, H. & Varela, F. (1980) *Autopoiesi e cognizione*, Venezia: Marsilio (Italian ed. 1985)

Neisser, U. (1993) *La percezione del sé*, Torino: Bollati Boringhieri (Italian ed. 1999).

Panksepp, J. & Biven, L. (2012) *The archaeology of mind: neuroevolutionary origins of human emotions*. New York: Norton.

Pitruzzella, S. (2006) 'Dramatic identity: the challenge of complexity', *Dramatherapy journal*, vol. 28, n.3, London, 2006.

Pitruzzella, S. (2016) *Drama, creativity and intersubjectivity: foundations of change in dramatherapy*. London: Routledge.

Rizzolatti, G. & Sinigaglia, C. (2019) *Specchi nel cervello. Come comprendiamo gli altri dall'interno*. Milano: Cortina.

Shaw, J. (2016) *The memory illusion*. London: Random House.

Stern, D. (1985) *The Interpersonal World of the Infant*. New York: Basic Books.

Tomasello, M. (2009) *Why we cooperate*. Cambridge, MA: MIT Press.

Trevarthen, C. (1979) 'Communication and cooperation in early infancy: a description of primary intersubjectivity'. In: Bullowa, M. (ed.) (1979) *Before speech*. New York: Cambridge University Press.

Van der Kolk, B. (2014) *The body keeps the score. Mind, brain and body in the transformation of trauma*. New York: Penguin.

Varela F., Thompson E. & Rosch E. (1991) *The embodied mind*, Cambridge, MA.: The MIT Press.

Wegner, D. (2003) *The illusion of conscious will*. Cambridge MA.: Bradford Books.

Wilshire, B. (1982) *Role-playing and identity. The limits of theatre as metaphor*. Bloomington: Indiana University Press.

6

AESTHETICS OF CONNECTION IN THE PERFORMANCE OF LIVED EXPERIENCE

Jean-François Jacques

Abstract

This chapter investigates the capacity of aesthetics in the performance of lived experience in dramatherapy to create an ontological connection between the performer and the witnessing spectator. It suggests that aesthetics in performance contributes to the emergence of alternative knowing spaces whereby we are able to understand ourselves in relation to others as performers or witnessing spectators. It explores aesthetics as a relational process that enables access to unknown truths and the unveiling of unsuspected imaginaries.

This investigation of aesthetics in the performance of lived experience is based on the findings of a performance-as-research study that had as its object the production of meaning in autobiographical performance in dramatherapy. This research adopted a relational paradigm through which meaning in performance emerges from the dialogical and embodied relationship between the performer and the witnessing spectator. The findings of the research revealed how aesthetics operates as a regulating mechanism between different lived experiences to create possibilities for renewed awareness, knowledge and change. The chapter offers a discussion of this particular aspect of aesthetics in the performance of lived experience by referring to audio–visual excerpts of the research.

Keywords: aesthetics, aesthetic experience, dramatherapy, autobiographical performance, neuroscience, performance as research, connection, meaning

Abstract in French

Ce chapitre est une étude sur la manière dont l'esthétique dans le théâtre de l'expérience vécue en dramathérapie permet la création d'un lien ontologique entre l'artiste de scène et le spectateur témoin. Il suggère que l'esthétique de la

DOI: 10.4324/9781003110200-6

représentation théâtrale contribue à l'émergence d'espaces de connaissance alternatifs dans lesquels la prise de conscience de soi se développe en relation à d'autres en tant qu'acteurs ou spectateurs. Ce chapitre envisage l'esthétique comme processus relationnel capable de révéler des vérités inconnues et de dévoiler des imaginaires insoupçonnés.

Cette étude sur l'esthétique dans le théâtre de l'expérience vécue est basée sur les résultats d'une recherche par la représentation théâtrale dont l'objet était une enquête sur la production de sens dans le théâtre autobiographique en dramathérapie. Cette recherche adoptait un paradigme relationnel dans lequel le sens de la représentation théâtrale ressort de la relation dialogique et corporelle entre l'artiste de scène at le spectateur témoin. Les résultats de la recherche ont montré comment l'esthétique fonctionne à la manière d'un mécanisme régulateur entre différentes experiences vécues, créant ainsi des possibilités de changement, de renouvelement de prise de conscience et de savoir personnel. Ce chapitre discute cet aspect particulier de l'esthétique dans le théâtre de l'expérience vécue à partir d'extraits audiovisuels de la recherche.

Introduction

The last two decades have been marked by a number of crises that have seriously damaged, torn and in some instances shredded the fabric of a society based on sustainable, fair, safe and caring relationships with others and the ecosystem. The global financial crisis of 2008, the refugee crisis of 2015 onward and the ongoing climate crisis are all examples and reflections of politics and ideologies that place self-interest and gain above collective interest and common destiny. What we have witnessed (and are still witnessing) is a global attack on linking (Bion, 1959) that has found an expression in an increased sense of social fragmentation and in the erosion of the bonds that connect us to others and the wider world.

As I was in the process of writing this chapter, the world entered another crisis of a scale unprecedented for generations. The Covid-19 pandemic has opened a new era that has forced us to re-evaluate the meaning of the emotional, physical and social space that unites and separates us from others. In order to contain the spread of the virus, words such as isolation and distancing became normalised and enforced with psychological consequences that still remain to be fully understood (United Nations, 2020). In addition, the crisis became contemporaneous with a resurgence of racial tension, mainly in the US, a reminder of the structural and systemic inequalities and discrimination at the heart of Western societies.

The real pandemic worldwide seems therefore to be a loss of connection with anything other-than-self (Hari, 2018) and how this is directly reflected in our psychic lives. There is an urgency to think about these issues within our existing paradigms and our different ways of practising as creative arts therapists. As Marianne Hirsch (2014, p.333) wrote, "to survive in vulnerable times, we need to develop connective structures."

This chapter is an invitation to reflect on ways in which the arts therapies can provide and imagine such connective structures, at the time when our disconnections could easily overshadow our inner needs for connection. More specifically, it considers how the performance of lived experience in dramatherapy can be a fertile ground to nurture the connection between self and others and to produce greater mutual understanding. It will particularly examine how aesthetics in performance can regulate such a connection by providing examples from a recent research study.

Aesthetics and the aesthetic experience

Aesthetics is a discipline and construct that defies a simple and one-dimensional definition. Even though it has become associated with the philosophy of art and the theory of beauty within the theory of art, its inception in 18th-century Germany marked a significant deviation from the dominant model of the time to understand reality, the production of knowledge and the uncovering of truth.

The German philosopher, Alexander Gottlieb Baumgartner (1714–1762), introduced the term "aesthetics" to describe "the science of sensible cognition" (Baumgartner cited *in* Guyer, 2016), that is particularly reflected in the work of art and the artistic experience. For Baumgartner, aesthetics refers to "what is sensed and imagined, in contrast to what is known through rational thought" (Carroll, Moore & Seeley, 2012, p.31). With this new term, Baumgartner recognises a different form of perceptual knowledge firmly grounded in sensory experience as opposed to anchored in cognition, reason and logic. He prefigures the role of the living sensing body as creator of knowledge alongside other modes of mental processes. Baumgartner opened up a new field of study that linked the experience of the body to the production of affects, and that was to evolve particularly in the 20th century with the advent of phenomenology (Merleau-Ponty, 2009) and advances in neuroscience (Varela, Thompson & Rosch, 2016; Damasio, 2000). Besides, Baumgartner also associates aesthetics with the capacity of the body to imagine. He introduces the idea that through sensory perceptual experience, the body enters into a realm of possibilities that unlock ways of engaging with ourselves, others and the world around us.

The nature of aesthetic experience and judgement was further developed by Immanuel Kant (1724–1804), most notably in his third Critique, the *Critique of Judgement* (Kant, 2007 originally published 1790). Kant argues that aesthetic experience shapes and structures human experience alongside the exercise of reason and pre-existing concepts, representations and laws. In other words, not all aspects of experience can be objectified. An understanding and account of reality also rests on how it is aesthetically experienced. The idea of aesthetic judgement represents for Kant a particular capacity to engage with the world outside of norms and criteria. As for Baumgartner, it refers to the sensible aspect of our experience and what can be induced from it. It is, for Kant, a type of judgement that is disinterested and ultimately subjective in the sense of operating outside of existing rules of interpretation. Quite interestingly, Kant views aesthetic judgement as "an equally shared capacity in all human beings" (Dikeç, 2016, p.16) that can claim universal validity and communicability. This innate capacity for aesthetic judgement or for sensuous perception creates a space for relationality and connectivity between experiences.

This specific aspect of Kant's philosophy found a particular resonance in the political aesthetic of Hannah Arendt (1906–1975) and the creation of common worlds (Arendt, 1958). Arendt saw in Kant the relational implications of the aesthetic judgement and the basis for the constitution of a plural and shared reality. She understands the capacity for aesthetic judgement as something that deeply connects us to others because of the way in which it places us in direct contact with the perspective of others. As such, aesthetics is viewed as the cornerstone of how to be together as social beings. As Arendt (2006, p.218) wrote, "judging is one, if not the most, important activity in which this sharing-the-world-with-others comes to pass."

Arendt rightly observes that the discussion about aesthetic judgement in Kant is "primarily from the viewpoint of the judging spectator" (Arendt, 2006, p.216). Kant does not consider in any way the object of aesthetic judgement or the source of production of that object, especially in the context of art production. If aesthetic experience is an experience in itself, as suggested by Kant, it is also an experience *of* something (a phenomenon or an object) that can be described in aesthetic terms. Aesthetics does not only reflect a particular mode of experiencing and knowing, it is also a form of expression of experience as lived by the producer of the aesthetic object. If anything, aesthetics stands in-between perceptual experiences.

The philosopher and phenomenologist, Mikel Dufrenne (1910–1995), particularly emphasised this aspect of aesthetics as embracing both the experiences of the creator and the spectator. Hence, he found it necessary, as he wrote (1973, p.xlvii), "to define aesthetic experience by reference to the object being experienced, which we shall call the 'aesthetic object'." Dufrenne suggests that the aesthetic object, although being tied up to perception, is also a *thing-in-itself* outside of it. As he puts it, "the correlation of the object with the act which grasps it does not subordinate the object to that act" (1973, p.li). The aesthetic object is therefore for Dufrenne deprived of any determinism that defines and sets its meaning, and through which it can be explained. It is not, as in classic Freudian theory, the symbolic expression of unconscious and repressed drives and desires that can be decoded. Neither is it a pure reflection of the perceptual and responsive capacities of the beholder. Dufrenne suggests an emancipation of the aesthetic object that has two important implications.

Firstly, the aesthetic object is not envisaged for what it might represent in terms of content, or what particular psychological function it might fulfil. It is grounded in its objective qualities (Hagman, 2005). These qualities reflect five different aesthetic dimensions of the object: sensory (i.e., colour, texture, sound, rhythm, tone), formal (i.e., form, shape, structure, pattern), kinaesthetic (i.e., movement, gesture, sequence), relational (i.e., communicability, interactivity, sociability) and spatial (i.e., setting, distance, volume). Secondly, the aesthetic object can be described as a liminal and transitional phenomenon between different states of being (Winnicott, 1971). As Dufrenne writes (1973, p.l), "one consciousness crosses another as it encounters the object." The meeting with the object enables access to a particular form of knowledge and an expansion of consciousness "anterior to any logos" (p.xlviii). The aesthetic experience reflects a fundamentally relational and qualitative dynamic through which new meanings can emerge.

Recent developments in cognitive neuroscience have provided additional insights into the way in which the perception of an object contributes to the construction of consciousness and the emergence of the sense of self. Although not directly discussed in the context of aesthetic experience, Damasio outlined the physiological and neurological mechanisms through which the relationship and interaction with an object "infuses new knowledge" in the organism (2000, p.25). Damasio describes how the encounter and engagement with an external object (whether this is an image, a phenomenon or anything else that we find ourselves in relation with) produce a particular form of knowledge that remains largely felt and sensed. As such, it can be described in aesthetic terms for the way in which it is engendered through the "sensory portals" (p.9) of the organism. Gallese and Guerra (2020) have provided a detailed analysis of the neurological underpinnings of the intersubjective relationship between the moving image as aesthetic object in the cinematographic experience and the spectator. Drawing on a large number of examples, they examine how the qualities of that particular aesthetic experience translate the activation of sensorimotor processes that are directly linked to the development of cognitive and imaginative functions. In particular, they suggest that the concept of embodied simulation accounts for the way in which the aesthetic experience is received and resonates within the body of the spectator. Not only does this non-representational process explain how we come to understand others, it also foregrounds how we see and understand ourselves through our experience of others, and how the self is inescapably intertwined with the other, as previously suggested by Merleau-Ponty (2009). Aesthetics can therefore be described as intersubjectively enactive because of the way in which it creates experiences and possibilities through this fundamental intercorporeality between the action on screen and the spectator. The neuroscientific basis of the aesthetic experience of the moving image offers an understanding of how the qualities of the aesthetic object modulate the emotional and physiological response of the spectator with ethical implications.

Although most of what Gallese and Guerra (2020) suggest about the cinematographic experience are directly applicable to the theatrical experience, very few scholars have actually integrated the neuroscientific approach into the study of performance as an aesthetic object (Falletti, Sofia & Jacono, 2016; McConachie, 2013). De Marinis (2016), for instance, underlines the role of the body in aesthetic experience specifically from the perspective of the spectator and how their performative capability is released through their embodied presence and engagement with the action played out on stage. And yet, the multimodal sensory perception that characterises aesthetics is not necessarily linked *per se* to how the performance object is experienced by the performer and the spectator alike, and to how they both co-constitute one another (Sofia, 2016).

Aesthetics, healing and transformation in dramatherapy

It is not an overstatement to say that aesthetics has not found or been given a prominent place in dramatherapy theory, practice and research. There may be different reasons for this. One may be that arts therapists in general privilege content over form and process over product. Another one may be that aesthetics is associated with artistic standards, taste or beauty. These may be seen as value judgements that do not belong to the ethical practice of the creative arts therapies. And yet, it can also be argued that dramatherapy, like the other arts therapies, is essentially an aesthetic therapeutic modality by being enactive and privileging somatosensorimotor forms of expression and reflection on the content of our conscious and unconscious worlds. There are grounds to suggest an aesthetic paradigm within dramatherapy (Sajnani, 2016a) that would reflect ways in which we aesthetically experience ourselves and the world and whereby the therapeutic intervention would be envisaged as the creation of new aesthetics.

Only a few authors have actively integrated aesthetics within their conceptualisation of dramatherapy. Amongst those, Landy (1983) refers to *aesthetic distance* to describe the optimum form of aesthetic representation situated at the intersection of emotional and cognitive awareness. In that sense, aesthetics fulfils a particular functionality to facilitate therapeutic change. Pendzik (2013a) argues that aesthetics reflects the quality of the expressive modes and representational forms used by the client, and that as such it is an essential aspect of dramatherapy processes. More recently, Sajnani, Mayor and Tillberg-Webb (2020) have discussed how the use of aesthetics in the education and learning of creative arts therapists fosters openness and connection. They refer to aesthetics as a range of strategies that include symbolic, embodied and multisensory engagement.

The question of aesthetics and aesthetical experience appears to have been discussed most prolifically in the literature on theatre and healing, and performance-oriented dramatherapy. In his discussion about theatre and healing, Grainger describes what he believes constitutes the nature of aesthetic experience in dramatherapy. Grainger (2014; 2006; 2005) argues that the phenomenological experience of theatre is fundamentally characterised by the encounter between actor and spectator. He suggests that this encounter "is not only the subject matter of theatre but also its *modus operandi*" (in italics in the text, Grainger, 2014, p.117). As such, he echoes the words of the philosopher, Bruce Wilshire, who famously stated: "this is the encounter which is theatre" (1982, p.22).

For Grainger, theatre is defined by its inherent relationality which is also where its healing power resides. Furthermore, Grainger suggests that the potential of theatre for change resides in the space between actors and spectators. As he writes (2005, p.8), "theatre crystallises an experience of betweenness that is creative of personhood." It generates a process of "reciprocal self-discovery" (Grainger, 2006, p.79) and "expansion of individual awareness" (Grainger, 2014, p.132) that emerge from the shared experience that defines it.

Grainger does not only provide a description of how the experience of theatre can be life-changing, but also pursues an understanding of "the fundamental healing mechanism of theatre" (2005, p.8). For Grainger, this happens through a process of identification that he frames in terms of "emotional involvement" (2014, p.125). He suggests that healing in theatre is not just the expression of a relationship but more fundamentally of an emotional connection enabled through that relationship. It is as if that connection created an emotional loop whereby the spectators are not only made to experience the emotions of the character played by the actor, but also, in return, to experience and understand themselves differently as individuals.

Grainger describes this process of personal transformation in terms of catharsis (Duggan & Grainger, 1997). For Grainger, catharsis represents an awareness and consciousness of what is revealed through the emotional and embodied experience of others in theatre. It is not so much a discharge of emotions in an Aristotelian sense as it is "an actual experience of life (...) producing understanding of the most authentic and valuable kind" (Grainger, 2014, p.134).

Grainger observes that "catharsis is revealed as a matter of balance" (2005, p.10). He explains how this balance is achieved through the distance provided by the aesthetic of the performance (Duggan & Grainger, 1997). Before Grainger, Scheff (1976) suggested how aesthetic distance in theatre can be described as the optimum balance between the emotional engagement and the capacity for reflection in the experience of audience members. Furman (1988) described it as a balance between the experiencing self and the observing self of the spectator.

More recently, Sajnani (2012) considered the impact of performance-oriented dramatherapy on the experience of the audience. Sajnani is most interested in the dynamics that enable "a progressive change" (2010, p.190) in the experience of the audience as witness, as opposed to that experience per se. Like Grainger, she seeks to understand the mechanisms through which the audience is able to identify and resonate with the staged experience of the performer. Like Grainger, she particularly considers the modulating role of aesthetics in "bridging the gap" between the performer and the witnessing spectator, and in facilitating a process of mutual transformation. Writing about the aesthetic of a performance, she observes that "finding the balance is what allows for both emotional and rational engagement, affords new perspectives, engenders dialogue, and carries the potential for change" (Sajnani, 2012, p.15). She suggests that aesthetic considerations play a key role in the creation of "socially effective and affective performances" (p.6) whereby one finds the capacity to empathise and connect with the stories of others.

From what precedes, it can be concluded that aesthetics not only represents a singular mode of experiencing and responding to our internal and external reality, but also a mechanism and structure that regulate the capacity for connection to ourselves in relation to others.

The research

Research in the field of autobiographical performance in dramatherapy has recently been met with a surge of interest (Wood, 2018; Pendzik, Emunah & Johnson, 2016; Emunah, 2015; Emunah, Raucher & Ramirez-Hernandes, 2014).

The research that I am describing here took as its object of investigation the production of meaning in autobiographical performance, and the way in which it can be described as emerging from relational, embodied and aesthetic processes between the performer and the witnessing spectator (Jacques, 2020). It was carried out as a doctoral research between 2013 and 2019 at Anglia Ruskin University (UK).

Rather than referring to autobiographical performance, I use in what follows the generic terminology of performance of lived experience to define a performance and therapeutic practice whereby the primary material is a specific aspect or moment of lived experience, the performer is the author of the performance, and that performance takes place in front of an audience (Pendzik, 2013b).

Aesthetics in the performance of lived experience

In her seminal work, Emunah (2020; 2016; 2015) identified a number of significant dynamics and processes in the performance of lived experience that are generally considered as contributing to its therapeutic effects in terms of structuring experience, producing self-discoveries, insights, acceptance, personal growth and meaning (Pendzik, Emunah & Johnson, 2016). Amongst these, is the role played by aesthetics in the production and witnessing of a performance.

Emunah, Raucher and Ramirez-Hernandez (2014) describe how aesthetic and therapeutic processes in the performance of lived experience are of equal importance. They explain that not only do those two processes exist alongside one another, they also enhance one another through their mutual interplay. Their intertwining has an impact on the respective experience of the performer and the witnessing spectator.

With regards to the performer, the aesthetic expression of lived experience can result in significant insights and new meanings. As Pendzik (2013b, p.13) writes, "the translation of painful experiences into stage language is not performed only as a means to express their pain, but also in order to allow it to evolve, to transform into something else." The aesthetic of the performance is similar to a soil in which the seeds of change and transformation can grow. Dokter and Gersie (2016) show that the dramatic and expressive forms available to the performer are not only a vehicle for the communication of sensitive issues, but also a prism that reveals unanticipated understandings and discoveries of profound affective meaning.

With regards to the witnessing spectator, Emunah (2015) argues that the capacity for identification and transformation is a function of the aesthetic distance of the performance. Sajnani suggests that aesthetics is the means through which the "relational purpose" of autobiographical performance is actualised (2016b, p.87). She refers to the concept of relational aesthetics (Bourriaud, 2002) to reveal the double quality of aesthetics in autobiographical performance as reflecting and creating social relations in given contexts. As Sajnani (2016b, p.93) writes, "relational aesthetics privilege the relationships that give rise to and result from the aesthetic performance of personal story." Sajnani suggests, like Arendt (2006) did, that aesthetics supports the creation of a shared world for the performer and the witnessing spectators. Pendzik (2016) is also curious about the ways in which autobiographical performance resonates within the witnessing spectators and how it connects with their own stories. Unlike Sajnani, Pendzik does not directly elaborate on the mechanisms of resonance and how they may be linked to the aesthetic of the performance.

The findings of a research study by Wood (2018) confirms Sajnani's argument about the role of aesthetics in autobiographical performance. Wood's research investigates how the witnessing of a performance based on a particular family experience can "initiate a process of transformation and help families with the challenges they are facing" (2018, p.24). The findings of the research show that the resonance of the performance with the witnessing audience results from forms of representation that create opportunities for both affective and reflective responses. The research shows how the connection with the performance is regulated through its aesthetic and how this leads to deeper understanding and meaning for those witnessing it. This research confirms the observations made earlier by Le Clanché du Rand who explained how her choice of aesthetic structures in her own autobiographical work made "the audience care" (1992, p.215), and ultimately "be moved and brought to new perceptions" (p.209).

Aims, methodology and findings

The existing literature in the field of the performance of lived experience in dramatherapy has shown that aesthetics enables a particular type of connection between the staged experience of the performer and the witnessing spectator. Yet, it doesn't provide a detailed description of the nature and quality of that aesthetic experience, and how it informs the production of knowledge and meaning for those involved. Equally, empirical data and qualitative studies on the aesthetic experience in the performance of lived experience remain scarce.

The research aims were therefore identified as follows:

- to investigate, describe and understand how the production of meaning in the performance of lived experience in dramatherapy can be described as emerging from the relational, aesthetic and embodied encounter between performers and witnessing spectators
- to investigate, describe and understand the mutual experience of the performer and the witnessing spectator in the performance of lived experience, and how it informs the meaning making process
- to investigate the implications of the above for dramatherapy theory, practice and research

The methodological framework of the research reflected a multi-methodological approach (Morse, 2003) integrating performance as research (Arlander et al., 2018; Kershaw & Nicholson, 2011; Riley & Hunter, 2009) and relational phenomenological research (Finlay, 2011, 2009; Finlay & Evans, 2009). Both methodologies were chosen for the way in which they focus on aesthetics, relationality and embodiment in the research process.

The research design consisted of three different stages: selection of the research participants, a 20-week performance-based workshop and an evaluation of the research with the research participants. A total of seven participants completed the research.

In the second stage of the research design, each of the research participants created three different autobiographical performances directly inspired by their experience as performer and as witnessing spectator of others in the research group. My role was that of a researcher who led the overall research process without being directly involved in devising.

Data consisted of pre- and post-project individual semi-structured interviews, 21 autobiographical performances (three different performances for each participant), three focus groups, debrief sessions, post-performance discussions with the audience and a post-performance audience questionnaire. It has to be noted that the audience data were primarily collected to help understand how the experience of the research participants were informed by the responses of the audience, as opposed to understanding how the different performances enabled audience members to connect with their own personal lived experiences. The experience of the witnessing spectator in the study therefore mainly refers to the experience of the different research participants as witnesses of others in the research group. This reflects one of the different witnessing perspectives (Jacques, 2016) in the performance of lived experience that will be privileged at the expense of others in the discussion that follows on the connective capacity of aesthetics. A detailed description of the aesthetic experience of audience members constitutes one of the limitations of the research.

The data from the interviews and focus groups were thematically analysed within a relational phenomenological framework (Finlay & Evans, 2009). This initial analysis enabled the identification of six themes that were used as criteria for a cross-performance thematic video analysis of the recording of the twenty-one autobiographical performances. The analysis made use of the particular creative method of the split-screen (Bizzocchi, 2009) to reveal different layers of relationality between the different performances. It weaves together audio-visual and phenomenological data and shows excerpts of the participants' experiences structured around the different themes[1] (Jacques, 2020).

With respect to aesthetics in the performance of lived experience, the research findings show that:

- the process of witnessing enables a deep connection with oneself through an identification with the performed lived experience of others. That personal connection is regulated through the aesthetic object of the performance that creates opportunities for renewed meaning and awareness
- the somatic and sensory experience of the witnessing spectator creates possibilities to develop one's own aesthetic and creative language that results in the production of aesthetic forms of knowledge and meaning
- aesthetics modulates interpersonal relationships and the capacity to connect to others, whilst this intersubjectivity also contributes to the emergence of a particular aesthetic

Aesthetic connections

I now examine the relevance of those findings to the study of aesthetic experience in the performance of lived experience in dramatherapy, with the view of better understanding how aesthetics supports a connection between the lived experience of the performer and the witnessing spectator. I present and discuss three different excerpts of the audio-visual output of the research that reflect the impact of aesthetic processes on the experience of three research participants.

In what follows, all participants' names have been changed although all understood the limits of confidentiality based on the performance component in the research and in the method of dissemination. All excerpts are only accessible to the readers of this chapter. They require the use of passwords provided in the body of the text below.

Excerpt 1

The first excerpt illustrates the experience of Karen, performer 5 in the research.[2] This excerpt of the audio-visual output of the research is accessible through the following link: https://vimeo.com/427464248 (password: excerpt1).

This excerpt shows an extract of Karen's second performance "A E I O U" with voice-over from her post-project individual interview on the thematic category of personal change and meaning. It then reveals a split-screen showing

FIGURE 6.1 Performer 5 cross-performance video analysis. ©J-F Jacques.

Karen's performance alongside the two other performances that contributed to a specific choice of aesthetics.

Karen's second performance depicts her personal experience of dyslexia. It is almost exclusively non-verbal. This performance shows how Karen found renewed aesthetic ways of understanding and communicating what her dyslexia feels like. This directly resulted from the way in which she aesthetically experienced as a witnessing spectator the performances of Jenny (performer 6) and Sophie (performer 3). This aesthetic and corporeal intersubjectivity between performer and spectator created an emotional connection and response that were essential in the development of new cognitive pathways and meaning (Gallese & Guerra, 2020). Karen's sensory perceptual experience of Jenny's performance, particularly, produced ways in which she became able to think aesthetically about her lived experience of dyslexia in sensory terms. It illustrates how aesthetic experience is situated at the interplay between impression and expression (Koch, 2017) by being simultaneously received and enactive. It also shows how the aesthetic object of the performance can be described as transitional by bridging the gap (Sajnani, 2010) between experiences but also by reconnecting fragmented internal self objects. As Hagman wrote (2005, p.40), "the fragments of our inner lives, of our self-experience, are gathered up, coordinated, and held together in and by the aesthetic experience."

The aesthetic qualities of Karen's performance (mainly sensory, kinaesthetic and spatial) provided her with a language that translated and scaffolded affective states as she felt more able to make sense of her own condition. Her performance also leaves the audience with a particular sensory insight of what dyslexia feels like. The audience is made to journey into a disorientating and confusing world out of which emerges a sense of aesthetic empathy in the sense of a connection directly created through aesthetic means. Although data collected from audience members in the research do not allow for a detailed understanding of their sensory perceptual experiences, Karen's performance illustrates how the emotional involvement of the audience is the expression of an aesthetic distance that regulates the capacity to feel and think empathically at once (Grainger, 2014).

Excerpt 2

The second excerpt illustrates the experience of Natalia, performer 1 in the research[3] (accessible through the following link: https://vimeo.com/427700029 – password: excerpt2).

The excerpt shows a split-screen with Natalia's first performance (top window) alongside three other performances that she witnessed as a spectator in the first phase of the performance workshop. It then shows an extract of her second performance with voice over from her post-project individual interview.

In her first performance, Natalia is aesthetically detached from the story enacted on stage. Her somatosensory experience as a witnessing spectator of three other performances gives her access to a different mode of experiencing and relating to others that finds a particular form of expression in her second performance. She is *touched* in a way that does not only reflect a physical proximity and an emotional reaction but also a neurophysiological response. Her phenomenological account as a witnessing spectator illustrates how aesthetic experience creates a neural resonance in the body of the viewer (Falletti, Sofia & Jacono, 2016), and how this induces new knowledge and meaning at a

FIGURE 6.2 Performer 1 cross–performance video analysis. ©J-F Jacques.

pre-reflective and pre-symbolic level. Her experience describes, in the words of Damasio (2000, p.26), a wordless knowledge that emerges from "the feeling of knowing – the feeling of what happens when an organism is engaged with the processing of an object" and its aesthetic qualities. Natalia's response to the three performances that she witnessed opened pathways to further consider how aesthetic experience produces an embodied simulation in the brain of the observer (Freedberg & Gallese, 2007), but also how that reaction can aesthetically inform the lived experience of the latter.

Furthermore, the excerpt shows how Natalia's experience in the research enabled her to connect with her sensory imagination and with the capacity of the body to imagine, as initially suggested by Baumgartner (Carroll, Moore & Seeley, 2012). She became, as she explained, more open to experimentation and to engagement with the unknown. This shows how aesthetics in the performance of lived experience can actualise the creative and restorative capabilities of the imagination and uncover new horizons of meaning.

Excerpt 3

The third excerpt illustrates the experience of Henry, performer 7 in the research[4] (accessible through the following link: https://vimeo.com/426012961 – password: excerpt3).

This excerpt shows an extract of Henry's third performance "ITCH", followed by a moment of Karen's second performance (performer 5) with voice-over from the last focus group.

In his third performance, Henry chose a particular aesthetic to represent the impact of a number of health problems on his life. He found in Karen's

FIGURE 6.3 Performer 7 cross-performance video analysis. ©J-F Jacques.

performance (see also excerpt 1) the aesthetic means and the aesthetic distance (Landy, 1983) to disclose and engage safely with a difficult aspect of his experience. Henry's performance shows how a newly found aesthetic distance that reflects the optimal qualities of the aesthetic object regulates the capacity for emotional and cognitive connection. It illustrates how aesthetics is located at the intersection of the experience of the witnessing spectator with the experience of the performer. It shows a phenomenon of reciprocity in the shared space of performance whereby witness and performer mutually construe meaning through their encounter, and whereby aesthetics translates an experience of betweenness as previously described by Grainger (2005) and also suggested by Dufrenne (1973).

The aesthetic qualities of Karen's performance became a catalyst that enabled Henry to find the representational forms to structure his own experience (Hagman, 2005) and to enter into a different relationship with himself. The aesthetic form of Henry's last performance illustrates the relational quality of aesthetics that creates an interstice (Bourriaud, 2002) through which a new light can shine.

Henry's performance is the culmination of a thread that emerged between different performances in the research (performers 7, 6, 5 and 1), and that showed how the aesthetic object is a container through which diverse experiences can resonate and find new meanings that transcend differences. It illustrates the universal communicability of aesthetics, as claimed by Kant (2007), and its capacity for the creation of common and shared worlds, as suggested by Arendt (1958).

Conclusion

I have suggested and described in this chapter how aesthetics in the performance of lived experience in dramatherapy practice operates as a regulating mechanism that enables a connection between the lived experiences of the performer and the witnessing spectator. That aesthetic of connection opens spaces of imagination for the creation of new relational perspectives within ourselves and with others. The outcomes of the research have shown how aesthetics reflects and creates "a vision of the world that widens our perceptual and cognitive horizons and exercises our imagination" (Gallese & Guerra, 2020, p.49).

Further research is needed to better understand how aesthetics can effectively co-regulate affect and experience in autobiographical performance in dramatherapy and beyond in other therapeutic practices within the arts therapies (Samaritter & Payne, 2016/2017). Interdisciplinary links with cognitive neuroscience will continue to provide important insights into how aesthetic and sensory experiences inform the acquisition of new knowledge and meaning (Pearce et al., 2016). As the research discussed in this chapter has shown, the qualities of the aesthetic object of performance regulate responses that can be described in neurological terms to confirm the interpersonal foundations of the human mind. Finally, aesthetics will remain an important area of research for those interested in cultural and healing practices that seek to recreate the bonds that connect us to others, and to imagine new ways of being together.

Notes

1 The analysis resulted in the creation of an edited film that is accessible through the following web link: https://drive.google.com/file/d/1Wu8YysPLNQEyC9duR vftnK BlsQkMkbVo/view?usp=sharing.The link is only accessible to the readers of this chapter. All research participants consented to such a dissemination method. The film is divided into seven parts that correspond to the experience of the seven research participants.
2 A more detailed description of Karen's experience can be found in the audio-visual output of the research (43'24" into the film). See the link from the previous footnote.
3 A more detailed description of Natalia's experience can be found in the audio-visual output of the research (0'11" into the film).
4 A more detailed description of Henry's experience can be found in the audio-visual output of the research (1 hr 06'27" into the film).

References

Arendt, H. (1958). *The human condition.* Chicago: University of Chicago Press.

Arendt, H. (2006). *Between past and future.* London: Penguin Books.

Arlander, A., Barton, B., Dreyer-Lude, M. & Spatz, B. (Eds.). (2018). *Performance as research: knowledge, methods, impact.* Abingdon: Routledge.

Bion, W. (1959). Attacks on linking. *International Journal of Psycho-Analysis,* 40, pp. 308–315.

Bizzocchi, J. (2009). *The fragmented frame: the poetics of the split-screen.* Retrieved from web.mit. edu/comm-forum/legacy/mit6/papers/Bizzocchi.pdf

Bourriaud, N. (2002). *Relational aesthetics.* Paris: Les Presses du Réel.

Carroll, N., Moore, M. & Seeley, W.P. (2012). The philosophy of art and aesthetics, psychology and neuroscience. In: Shimamura, A.P. & Palmer, S.E. (Eds.). *Aesthetic science: connecting minds, brains and experience* (pp. 31–62). New York: Oxford University Press.

Damasio, A. (2000). *The feeling of what happened: body, emotion and the making of consciousness.* London: Vintage.

De Marinis, M. (2016). Body and corporeity in the theatre. In: Falletti, C., Sofia, G. & Jacono, V. (Eds.). *Theatre and cognitive neuroscience* (pp. 61–73). London: Bloomsbury Methuen Drama.

Dikeç, M. (2016). *Space, politics and aesthetics.* Edinburgh: Edinburgh University Press.

Dokter, D. & Gersie, A. (2016). A retrospective study of autobiographical performance during dramatherapy training. In: Pendzik S., Emunah, R. & Johnson, D.R. (Eds.). *The self in performance: autobiographical, self-revelatory, and autoethnographic forms of therapeutic theatre* (pp. 181–197). New York: Palgrave Macmillan.

Dufrenne, M. (1973). *The phenomenology of aesthetic experience.* Evanston: Northwest University Press.

Duggan, M. & Grainger, R. (1997). *Imagination, identification and catharsis in theatre and therapy.* London: Jessica Kingsley Publishers.

du Rand Le Clanché (1992). Aesthetic and therapeutic interplay in the creation of autobiographical theatre. *The Arts in Psychotherapy,* 19, pp. 209–218.

Emunah, R. (2015). Self-revelatory performance: a form of drama therapy and theatre. *Drama Therapy Review,* 1(1), pp. 71–85.

Emunah, R. (2016). From behind the scenes to facing an audience in self-revelatory perfor-mance. In: Pendzik, S., Emunah, R. & Johnson, D.R. (eds.) *The self in performance: autobi-ographical, self-revelatory, and autoethnographic forms of therapeutic theatre.* New York: Palgrave Macmillan. pp. 37–53.

Emunah, R. (2020). *Acting for real: drama therapy process, technique and performance* (2nd ed.). New York: Routledge.

Emunah, R., Raucher, G. & Ramirez-Hernandez, A. (2014). Self-revelatory performance in mitigating the impact of trauma. In: Sajnani, N. & Johnson, D.R. (Eds.). *Trauma-informed drama therapy* (pp. 93–121). Springfield: Charles C Thomas Publisher.

Falletti, C., Sofia, G. & Jacono, V. (Eds.). (2016). *Theatre and cognitive neuroscience.* London: Bloomsbury Methuen Drama.

Finlay, L. (2009). Ambiguous encounters: a relational approach to phenomenological research. *Indo-Pacific Journal of Phenomenology,* 9(1), pp. 1–17.

Finlay, L. (2011). *Phenomenology for therapists: researching the lived World.* Oxford: Wiley-Blackwell.

Finlay, L. & Evans, K. (2009). *Relational-centred research for psychotherapists: exploring meanings and experience.* Oxford: Wiley-Blackwell.

Freedberg, D. & Gallese, V. (2007). Motion, emotion and empathy in aesthetic experience. *Trends in Cognitive Sciences,* 11(5), pp. 197–203.

Furman. L. (1988). Theatre as therapy: the distancing effect applied to audience. *The Arts in Psychotherapy,* 15, pp. 245–249.

Gallese, V. & Guerra, M. (2020). *The empathic screen: cinema and neuroscience.* Oxford: Oxford University Press.

Grainger, R. (2005). Theatre and encounter part III transforming theatre. *Dramatherapy,* 27(1), pp. 8–12.

Grainger, R. (2006). *Healing theatre: how plays change lives.* Bloomington: Trafford.

Grainger, R. (2014). *Theatre and encounter.* Bloomington: Trafford.

Guyer, P. (2016). *18th Century German aesthetics.* Retrieved from: https://plato.stanford.edu/archives/win2016/entries/aesthetics-18th-german/

Hagman, G. (2005). *Aesthetic experience: beauty, creativity, and the search for the ideal.* Amsterdam: Rodopi.

Hari, J. (2018). *Lost connections.* London: Bloomsbury Publishing.

Hirsch, M. (2014). Connective histories in vulnerable times. *PMLA,* 129(3), pp. 330–348.

Jacques, J.-F. (2016). Intersubjectivity in autobiographical performance in dramatherapy. In: S., Pendzik, S., Emunah, R. & Johnson, D.R. (Eds.). *The self in performance: autobiograph-ical, self-revelatory, and autoethnographic forms of therapeutic theatre* (pp. 97–110). New York: Palgrave Macmillan.

Jacques, J.-F. (2020). Investigation into the production of meaning in autobiographical per-formance in dramatherapy. *The Arts in Psychotherapy,* 69. Retrieved from: https://www.sciencedirect.com/science/article/abs/pii/S0197455620300320

Kant, I. (2007). *Critique of judgement.* Oxford: Oxford University Press.

Koch, S.B. (2017). Arts and health: active factors and a theory framework of embodied aes-thetics. *The Arts in Psychotherapy,* 54, pp. 85–91.

Kershaw, B. & Nicholson, H. (2011). *Research methods in theatre and performance.* Edinburgh: Edinburgh University Press.

Landy, R. (1983). The use of distancing in drama therapy. *The Arts in Psychotherapy,* 10, pp. 175–185.

McConachie, B. (2013). *Theatre & mind.* London: Palgrave MacMillan.

Merleau-Ponty, M. (2009). *Phenomenology of perception.* London: Routledge Classics.

Morse, J.M. (2003). Principles of mixed methods and multimethod research design. In: Tashakorri, A. & Teddlie, C. (Eds.). *Handbook of mixed methods in social and behavioural research* (pp. 189–208). Thousand Oaks: Sage Publications.

Pearce, M.T., Zaidel, D.W., Vartanian, O., Skov, M., Leder, H., Chatterjee, A. & Nadal, M. (2016). Neuroaesthetics: the cognitive neuroscience of aesthetic experience. *Perspectives on Psychological Science*, 11(2), pp. 265–279.

Pendzik, S. (2013a). The 6-key model and the assessment of the aesthetic dimension in dramatherapy. *Dramatherapy*, 35(2), pp. 90–98.

Pendzik, S. (2013b). *The poiesis and praxis of autobiographical therapeutic theatre*. Keynote speech. 13th Summer Academy of the German Association of Theatre-Therapy, unpublished

Pendzik, S. (2016). The dramaturgy of autobiographical therapeutic performance. In: Pendzik, S., Emunah, R. & Johnson, D.R. (Eds.). *The self in performance: autobiographical, self-revelatory, and autoethnographic forms of therapeutic theatre* (pp. 55–69). New York: Palgrave Macmillan.

Pendzik, S., Emunah, R. & Johnson, D.R. (Eds.). (2016). *The self in performance: autobiographical, self-revelatory, and autoethnographic forms of therapeutic theatre*. New York: Palgrave Macmillan.

Riley, S.R. & Hunter, L. (Eds.). (2009). *Mapping landscapes for performance as research*. Basingstoke: Palgrave Macmillan.

Sajnani, N. (2010). Mind the gap: facilitating transformative witnessing amongst audiences. In: Jones, P. (Ed.). *Drama as therapy: clinical work and research into practice* (pp. 189–207). Hove: Routledge.

Sajnani, N. (2012). The implicated witness: towards a relational aesthetic in dramatherapy. *Dramatherapy*, 34(1), pp. 6–21.

Sajnani, N. (2016a). A critical aesthetic paradigm in drama therapy: aesthetic distance, action, and meaning making in the service of diversity and social justice. In: Jennings, S. & Holmwood, C. (Eds.), *Routledge international handbook of dramatherapy* (pp. 145–160). London, UK: Routledge.

Sajnani, N. (2016b). Relational aesthetics in the performance of personal story. In: Pendzik, S., Emunah, R. & Johnson, D.R. (Eds.). *The self in performance: autobiographical, self-revelatory, and autoethnographic forms of therapeutic theatre* (pp. 85–95). New York: Palgrave Macmillan.

Sajnani N., Mayor, C. & Tillberg-Webb, H. (2020). Aesthetic presence: the role of the arts in the education of creative arts therapists in the classroom and online. *The arts in psychotherapy*, 69. Retrieved from: https://www.sciencedirect.com/science/article/pii/S0197455620300411

Samaritter, R. & Payne, H. (2016/2017). Being moved: kinaesthetic reciprocities in psychotherapeutic interaction and the development of enactive intersubjectivity. *European Psychotherapy*, pp. 5–20.

Scheff, T. (1976). Audience awareness and catharsis in drama. *The Psychoanalytic Review*, 63(4), pp. 529–554.

Sofia, G. (2016). Towards an embodied theatrology. In; Falletti, C., Sofia, G. & Jacono, V. (Eds.). *Theatre and cognitive neuroscience* (pp. 49–59). London: Bloomsbury Methuen Drama.

United Nations (2020). *Covid-19 and the need for action on mental health*. Retrieved from: https://unsdg.un.org/resources/policy-brief-covid-19-and-need-action-mental-health

Varela, F.J., Thompson, E. & Rosch, E. (2016). *The embodied mind: cognitive science and human experience* (2nd ed.). Cambridge: The MIT Press.

Wilshire, B. (1982). *Role playing and identity: the limits of theatre as metaphor*. Indianapolis: Indiana University Press.

Winnicott, D. (1971). *Playing and reality*. London: Tavistock Publications.

Wood, S.M. (2018). Transforming families using performance: witnessing performed lived experience. *Drama Therapy Review*, 4(1), pp. 23–37.

7

INTERCULTURAL ART THERAPY – THE SEARCH FOR AN INNER HOME

Irit Belity

Abstract

In Israel, increasing numbers of Arab citizens are voluntarily seeking counselling from Jewish therapists. This is intriguing, in light of the social-cultural and political reality which is affected by struggles, tensions and differences.

Intercultural therapy involves the encounter between two individuals, but at the same time consists of a universal encounter between different traditions, beliefs, cultures and perceptions (Dwairy & Van Sickle, 1996). This raises the issue of the ways in which trust can be established and gaps can be bridged. Art, as the language of images, may assist and function as a bridge between individuals' expressions and forms, thus enabling the creation of an imaginary transitional space (Winnicott, 1996).

This article discusses issues arising from the intercultural encounter between a secular Jewish art therapist and religious Muslim Arab patients. My encounter with Arab patients extends beyond such stereotypical polar opposites as traditional vs. liberal, rural vs. city or the Israeli majority vs. the Arab minority in Israel in the 2000s. In some spaces, each member of the dyad comes with a different assigned or presumed socio-political discourse, such that the encounter could lead to potential role collisions (Benjamin, 2006). On the other hand, encounters can lead to the creation of a "third space" of infinite possibilities for dialogue and growth. Specifically, I examine the tensions arising from the encounter between conservative norms and more liberal norms, social-political aspects of the therapeutic encounter between Jews and Arabs, the perception of the woman-mother role and her status and the perception of the home. All the clinical examples have been modified to protect the patients' privacy.

This article is an expansion of a workshop on *Intercultural and therapeutic encounters – a meeting between the inner home and the environment*, presented at the 15th ECArTE Conference in Alcalá de Henares, Spain, 2019.

DOI: 10.4324/9781003110200-7

Keywords: intercultural therapy, Jewish-Arab encounter, inner home, social third, cultural competence, mutual recognition

Abstract in Hebrew

טיפול בינתרבותי באמצעות אמנות

חיפוש הבית הפנימי במציאות חברתית תרבותית משתנה

אירית בליטי

בישראל, יותר ויותר אזרחים ממוצא ערבי פונים מרוצונם לטיפול אצל מטפלים יהודים. ממצא זה מסקרן ומעניין לאור מציאות חברתית תרבותית פוליטית בצל מאבקים, מתיחויות ושונות.

בטיפול מתקיים מפגש בין שני אינדיווידואלים אולם בה בעת מתקיים מפגש אוניברסלי בין מסורות, אמונות, תרבויות ותפיסות שונות. בין ייצוג של חברה בעלת תפיסה שמרנית לייצוג של חברה בעלת תפיסות מתקדמות אינדיווידואליסטיות (Dwairy & Van Sickle, 1996; Dwairy, 2006). נשאלת השאלה כיצד ניתן לבסס את האמון ולגשר על פערים נרחבים אלו? אני מוצאת שהאמנות כשפה של דימויים, מסייעת ומהווה גשר בעל שפה וצורה ייחודיים המאפשרים יצירת מרחב דמיוני, מעברי (ויניקוט, 1996).

מאמר זה נכתב כהרחבה של סדנא בנושא "מפגשים בין תרבותיים וטיפוליים מפגש בין הבית הפנימי והסביבה", שהוצגה בכנס ה 15 של ECArTE באלקאלה דה הנארס, ספרד, 2019.

במאמר יוצגו נושאים שעולים במפגש הבינתרבותי בין מטפלת יהודיה, חילונית, למטופלות ערביות דתיות מוסלמיות. המפגש ביני לבין המטופלות הערביות, משתרע במרחבי שיח שבין מסורת למודרנה, בין אמונה לבין חופש מאמונה דתית, בין עיר לכפר, וכן בין בת לעם היהודי בעל הרוב וההגמוניה במדינת ישראל לבין הנשים בנות המיעוט הערבי, בישראל של שנות ה 2000. במרחבים אלה כל אחת מאתנו עוצבה על ידי שיח חברתי פוליטי שונה, ומפגש המזמן פוטנציאל להתנגשויות בין תפקידים או,להיווצרות "מרחב שלישי" של אין סוף אפשרויות לדיאלוג וצמיחה (Benjamin, 2006). הנושאים שיבחנו הינם: טיפול בינתרבותי, מפגש בין מטופלת יהודיה ומטופלת ערבייה, חברה שמרנית וחברה ליברלית, היבטים חברתיים פוליטיים במפגש הטיפולי בין יהודיה לערביה, תפיסת תפקיד האישה האם ומעמדה, ותפיסת הבית. כמו כן ,יובאו דוגמאות קליניות בהם הפרטים שונו כדי לשמור על פרטיות המטופלות.

Intercultural therapy

Therapy consists of an encounter between two individuals. But what is the nature of this encounter when these individuals come from different cultures? Waller (2015) suggested that intercultural encounters can foster curiosity, opportunity and excitement on one hand, but also prejudice and social-cultural assumptions on the other. The willingness to help and reconnect, along with the images and metaphors of art, can bridge these gaps within the therapy room.

The term "cultural sensitivity," which emerged in the 1990s, provided an initial platform for therapists to deal with their cultural diversity (Van Den Bergh & Crisp, 2004). Therapists from other cultures who adhere to notions of culture-sensitive intervention acknowledge that therapy involves basic universal approaches that must be made available to all, without cultural differences. At the same time, therapists need to be aware that patients have their own values, norms and perceptions of reality which must be taken into consideration for the intervention to be effective. Accordingly, therapists who apply culturally sensitive interventions are aware of the existence of cultural factors that influence assessment and treatment. However, since they only partially understand the cultural landscape, or the cultural differences between them and their patients, they need to show warmth, empathy, openness, tolerance, flexibility and a desire to appreciate the cultural realities of their patients (Van Den Bergh & Crisp, 2004). Alred (2003) noted that the role of the therapist is to take proper account of the inner worlds of both parties in an intercultural encounter. Therapist and patient alike are empathic, cautious and respectfully curious when approaching the "other" (Alred, 2003, p22). Self-reflexivity is crucial to broadening one's lens because it allows one to pay attention not only to what one experiences across cultures but also how one navigates the cultures internalised within oneself. Art therapists who navigate intertwined cultures think about culture as dynamic, fluid and identity based (Kapitan, 2015).

The term "cultural competence" developed in response to criticism that "cultural sensitivity" was insufficient to gaining a deeper understanding of the patient's culture. The three pillars of "cultural competence" are belief systems, knowledge and skills (Nelson et al., 2015). Belief systems are made up of the self-awareness and the cultural roots of the therapist, awareness of prejudice towards anyone who is culturally different and the decision to refer clients to fellow therapists who share the same culture as the clients. Knowledge refers to an understanding of the social-cultural dynamics involved in intervening with the client, learning about the values, beliefs and norms of the specific cultural group as well as the obstacles that can prevent a client who belongs to a minority group from receiving mental health services. Skills refers to developing abilities to convey and hear a wide variety of verbal and nonverbal messages using an array of cultural approaches.

Israel is a country where intercultural encounters are frequent. The population can be roughly divided into two main groups – Jews and Arabs. Jewish society is composed of individuals who immigrated to Israel from all over the world, at different times and under different circumstances, with different cultures and customs. Arab society can be divided into Christians, Muslims and Druze. This wide range of cultures creates richness and curiosity, along with conflicts and struggles. Intercultural encounters are a part of the fabric of life in Israel and are present in the therapy room as well.

An encounter between a Jewish therapist and an Arab patient

As a Jewish secular art therapist living in an Israeli-Jewish settlement near Israeli-Arab settlements, I experience many intercultural-therapeutic encounters in my clinic, such as this one:

> One hot summer day, an Arab woman entered my clinic. She sat in front of me, in her traditional long religious dress, and started crying. That was how I met Rima, a courageous 65-year-old from a village in the centre of Israel. While crying, she told me about her son who killed himself when he was a teenager in high school, and his memorial that was scheduled for the day after this meeting.

FIGURE 7.1 Painting 1. The grave as an inner home.

Rima cried for a long time, like a dam that burst open. After she calmed down, she explained why she believed that she could only be treated by a Jewish therapist who would keep the sessions confidential and understand her conflicted inner world, saying: "I can only cry for my son with someone who is not part of my society." Rima felt ashamed about her son's suicide. In a culture that condemns people who commit suicide, she felt it was not socially permissible to mourn him, process the feelings of pain over his sudden death, or her guilt for not taking better care of him and preventing his death. In her first painting (FIG 7.1) she drew his grave as though defying the need to hide him. His name was written in Arabic, her language, unlike the language in which the treatment took place.

A few months later on in the treatment, which spanned 5 years, it turned out Rima was torn between her desire to belong to the society she is part of, and her personal needs and the needs of her children, which were sometimes at odds. There was a disparity between her personal motivations and the behaviour and mental norms expected in a traditional society. This caused conflicts and tensions that made her life more difficult.

The socio-cultural platform in which I grew up supported the development of liberal, feminist conceptions within me. As a secular Jewish woman, belonging to the majority of population in the country in which we both live, the encounter with a woman from a different culture and different perceptions was for me a curious encounter, and at the same time raises questions: could I understand her inner world? Would political disagreements enter our meeting? Would the existing tension between Arabs and Jews permeate our relationship?

This treatment, as well as other treatments with Arab clients, provoked tensions arising from differences between the intrapersonal and interpersonal goals and wishes associated with intercultural perceptions. These patients come from a traditional society, some are religious, believe in a different religion to the therapist, speak a language different from the language used in therapy, and are aware of these intercultural differences. Sometimes the cultural distance allows them to engage in reflective discourse, where they can observe from a distance. The therapist's lack of knowledge of the subtleties of their culture, along with her curiosity, can encourage a shared contemplation and examination of their belief systems and viewpoints. This process helps establish self-perception in a culture that dictates ways of thinking and behaving that are sometimes different from the therapist's culture. However, they share this search for their own personal path within the culture to which they belong, although they cannot identify with some of its principles or attitudes. Dwairy and Van-Sickle (1996) described the intercultural therapy encounter as an encounter between different traditions, beliefs, cultures and perceptions, or between a representation of a conservative society and an individualistic-progressive society (Dwairy & Van Sickle, 1996).

Characteristics of Arab culture

Arab culture in Israel is typically described as traditional, patriarchal and collective, despite modernisation processes generated by greater access to education and exposure to the mass media. Religion still plays an important role in preserving harmony between the individual and environment, which manifests in the preservation of family ties, collective behaviour and adherence to religious commandments (Dwairy, 1998, 2006; Chandrakirana, 2009). This traditional collective social structure is reflected in the nature of social ties, which are tighter and more extensive than those of Western culture. These ties provide vital support for people in crisis. Sometimes this network is the only source of support the family can turn to in times of distress, but at the same time, it can impede individuals or families from solving their problems in less accustomed ways (Aloud, 2009; Al-Krenawi, 2002).

The transition to modernity in Arab culture has manifested in different ways, including: 1) a weakening of the Arab clan and the transfer of power to the nuclear family, 2) a decline in the birth rate (Arar & Rigbi, 2009), 3) an increase in the rate of higher education, especially among women (Abu-Asaba, 2007), 4) an increase in the proportion of women in the labour force (Abu-Asba, 2005) and 5) a trend towards more democratic and liberal values (Arar & Rigbi, 2009). It is important to note that the changes taking place in Arab society have also affected the status of women. More women have access to higher education. There is greater empowerment and self-awareness and more of an appreciation of the value of therapy. However, there is still tension and confusion, as shown in the example below.

> Waffa, a young woman, who has a university education, shared the confusion she felt. She studied for her degree in a large central city at a university where many of the students come from Western countries. During her time there, she experienced the personal freedom to speak her mind on different subjects. For the first time in her life, she experienced independence and lived apart from her parents. Her opinions changed during her university days, and she adopted attitudes more liberal than those of her culture of origin. When she graduated and returned to her family, she faced internal tensions between her desire to fulfil her own goals which she discovered when away from her family, her parents' demands, and the expectations of village culture, which she has known since childhood. She described how she felt torn between the desire to belong to her family, to the culture in which she grew up, and her feelings of being diminished by having to abandon her true authentic self. She felt as though she needed to conceal herself, even though all she wanted was to be who she is.

The women, such as Waffa and her friends, are for the most part college graduates who all lived in a mixed city while pursuing their degrees. Away from their parents, they were able to live in a relatively free way, with less traditional family supervision. They were exposed to the lifestyles of Western society, and to patterns of living and thinking that tend to foster independent thinking and liberalism. Most kept their religious identity and the traditional customs of their families, alongside the experiences they absorbed during their education. When they graduated, the single women moved back to live with their parents, and the married women moved in with their husbands in their village. Their return to the village set off a process of finding a balance between those aspects of their identity, which they often experienced as binary and conflicting (Boxbaum, 2018).

Homi Bhabha (1990) described the mixed and transient feeling of existence that emerges from life on the seam line between cultures. These identities merge without one necessarily dominating the other. He emphasised the embodied potential of the interactions created between cultures. This points to the possibilities of a third space, where one form of being is not dissolved entirely into the other form of being, but together create a new form of being, a new identity, undefined by any of its parts.

The new generation of young Arab women, both Muslims and Christians, no longer experiences leaving for the university as a struggle. Nevertheless, their return to the village engenders cognitive dissonance and conflicts between identities. After being exposed to a Western lifestyle, to efforts to achieve more gender equality and independent critical thinking, going back to the village causes these women to feel "stuck between two worlds." As Waffa noted, "I cannot fit into the modern world, and cannot go back to the village and be the same country Waffa as I was before I left." Parts of these women's identity are individualistic and Western whereas parts remain collective and traditional, but both are lived as binary components of their personality. There is little appeal in a solution consisting of detaching the visible personality layers – obeying the family and social demands – from the hidden personality layers feeding on the inner world of private and personal thoughts and feelings. The gender researcher Lilian Abu-Tabich (2009) sees these women as "immigrants within their people." These feelings become even more complex when the or these women marry since they need to face the disparity between perceptions of women's role in Western society and roles in traditional society.

Socio-political aspects of the therapeutic encounter between a Jewish woman and an Arab woman

Intercultural therapy can give space to acknowledge stereotypes, and at times even racism. Jessica Benjamin (2006) describes the human need for mutual recognition and mutual dependence. If the client's political background, such as gender or race for example, is disregarded and excluded from therapeutic treatment, therapy can fail. Disregard of this type on the part of the therapist means s/he is engaging, knowingly or unknowingly, in normalising an oppressive reality. One possible outcome is over-pathologisation, where the patient might be required to adjust to reality even when it is offensive for her. In diagnosis and treatment, she will be held personally responsible even where the social overcomes the personal (Frosh, 2007). Without acknowledgement by the therapist of the client's sociocultural background and without awareness of her values, belief systems and feelings with client empathy and respect for their background, therapy is likely to elicit topics that the therapist is unequipped to handle (Berman, 2003). In Israel, the intercultural encounter between a Jewish therapist and an Arab patient can be more complicated since the ever-present Arab-Jewish conflict may affect the relationship (Baum, 2007), as shown in the following example.

> Sammer used to call me "Bibi," the current Prime Minister's name, whenever she felt angry or helpless. She would say to me: "Your life, like the prime minister, is better than mine. You do not have my worries. The anxieties of my existence." Later on in treatment, the prime minister's name became a code word for us both to symbolize her frustration and the caged-in feelings caused by her marriage. Sammer, like many other Arab women, had an arranged marriage. She accepted the match but says she was young and naïve. She defines her marriage as failing, lacking in love, support, communication, or mutual recognition. She often feels lonely and longs for a close relationship. Her sense of feeling trapped stems from her fantasy of breaking

up with her husband and starting a new and better relationship. However, she realizes that doing so would damage her children's future and their family's reputation. She explained that divorce constitutes a stigma for the family and would ruin her children's chances for future matchmaking. This constitutes an impossible choice between her happiness and the future and happiness of her children. The prime minister's name stood for someone who can take care of himself without thinking of the consequences and underscored her inability to do so. On a deeper level, she used it to address the differences between our groups. In her view, their hegemony offers the Jewish majority greater personal choice than the Arab minority.

I listened to Sammer and thought about her predicament. I wondered whether for her "the pain associated with obedience is better than the pain associated with freedom" (Benjamin, 1988, p13). She chose to obey the social order, which implies she will continue to suffer to ensure that the family unit will not fall apart and expose her difficulties for all to see. As a woman living in an individualistic society, I struggle to accept her choice to remain in a bad marriage but accept her choice with the understanding that her identity as a woman and a wife is part of her self-identity as a woman in her society.

Perception of the woman – the role of the mother and her status

The place of women in traditional Arab society is complex and demanding. Women are expected to comply with traditional norms, raise their children and care for the home and members of the immediate and extended family. Arab researchers describe women in Arab society as being influenced by the restrictions that gender places on them, and their willingness to confront them (Ahmed, 1992; Badran, 1995). Muslim women are particularly vulnerable to harmful traditional practices such as genital mutilation (FGM), dowry-related crimes and honour killings (Chandrakirana, 2009). There is a gender hierarchy in Arab society in which men are superior to women. The roles of the wife and mother, which also associate her with her husband, children and home, are perceived as appropriate (Dwairy, 1998). On the contrary, in the last two decades, many Arab women have acquired a college education and have successful careers. Sometimes they feel torn between their desire to advance personally and professionally and their traditional role as a woman and a mother (Chandrakirana, 2009; Wadud, 2009). Scholars of Arab society describe the evolution towards greater equality between men and women in recent years, when greater numbers of women have pursued higher education and have entered the labour force and contribute to the household income. However, aspects of the traditional perception of their roles as women and mothers subsist. Moreover, in a society that values men, tensions can arise between mothers and daughters. The transmission of family and social "ghosts" (Fraiberg, Adelson & Shapiro, 1975) can revive the trauma of women in a patriarchal society, as can be seen in the following example:

At the beginning of treatment Rima described her relationship to her mother as close. She felt she needed to talk to her several times a day for advice, permission, support, and approval. Her mother, in Rima's words, is a strong ambitious woman, who is rigid and critical. Rima was torn between her need to grieve for her dead son, and her mother's demands to cease. The mother represents an agent of social conservatism and tradition. She transmits the social norms and in so doing preserves the intergenerational transmission of social and family ghosts. Her life is controlled by her husband, and the only opportunity she has to feel powerful is with her daughters. She transfers all the frustration and criticism that she suffered over the course of years of oppression by her brothers, husband, and his family. In this case, the intergenerational transfer between women appears to preserve the repetitive trauma in patriarchal society. This explains why Rima's relationship with her own daughter exhausts her. Her constant needs and dependence cause Rima to hate her. After expressing this she waited for my reaction and said I would probably think she was a terrible mother. I thought about what Winnicott (1949) said about the many reasons a mother has to hate her children, and how she, in all her honesty and power, said so bluntly. I considered her difficulties with her daughter and the mirror her daughter is placing in front of her, reflecting herself as a child in her relationship with her mother. Rima wanted to fix their relationship and felt guilty for her lack of love. She chose to make a change and end the intergenerational transfer that had been forced upon her. This decision was hard for her to carry out and she vacillated from extreme emotions of anger and frustration toward her daughter to sorrow and compassion for her. During therapy, she was able to detach herself from the oppressive influence of her mother and see her for the first time as a woman who had suffered, and even manifested compassion to her. Rima was conflicted about her relations with her daughter. She was trying to be the mother she never had, to accept her, and to give her space to express her array of emotions without criticism or judgment. At the same time, she is trying to educate her in accordance with social norms.

The perception of the home

The concept of the home plays a major role in the patient's and the therapist's mind in intercultural encounters. Winnicott (1971, pp104–110) noted that the place we live in is not outside, and not inside, but in the in-between: the "transitional space." Matri (2005) addresses the emotional experience of home and locates it on a continuum between the concrete-physical and the metaphorical-mental. He claims we carry an inner home within us, which is the product of the internalisation of primary experiences that includes sensorial and emotional dimensions. Manzo (2003) refers to "being in the world" as intertwined within the dimension of human existence, such that "a place" is an inseparable part of our lives. Nevertheless, a home is not just a physical place but also a metaphor.

The individual creates a connection with the concrete and the metaphorical aspect of the home. Manzo defined four variables forming the connection between a person and a place: place attachment, sense of place, place dependence and place identity. These emotional factors can turn a house into a home. In the workshop I led at the conference, a multicultural encounter was created between women from different countries and cultures in which we personally explored the inner home of each participant, and how it changes in the encounter with another inner home, with a different culture. At the end of the process, an image was created of the third space described by Homi Bhabha (1990), which is a combination of the familiar and the new. In the example below, the client who inspired this workshop, and who was also present during the workshop, describes the development of the inner home as part of an identity-building process, in the framework of an intercultural encounter.

> Rima described her changing perception of her inner home during her years of treatment. First, her home was her son's grave (FIG 7.1). It rep-resented her grief for her son but later represented the sum total of events that have hurt her: the loss of her dream of a perfect marriage, the dif-ficulties her children face that represent her worries, and the difficul-ties she experiences in her own life. The grave that was lonely at first became surrounded by nature, clouds, and flowers (FIG 7.2). After a few years of representing her difficulties through the grave symbol, Rima started to paint houses, and accompanied her first house paintings with

FIGURE 7.2 Painting 2. I. Belity.

FIGURE 7.3 Painting 3. I. Belity.

a wish to "strengthen her inner home." By this, she meant a substantial, confident feeling of self. Her house transitioned from a traditional Arab house (FIG 7.3) to a typical house (FIG 7.4), a house with a flowering environment (FIG 7.5 & FIG 7.6), and eventually to a multi-floor house (FIG 7.7), unlike the houses in her village. The home paintings reflected her process of searching and creating her identity. Through these paintings, she searched for her inner home. She asked herself who she is, and what the house reflected about her feelings when she painted it.

Rima's houses depict her way of finding the third space between society's demands and her own personal needs, as well as a search for self-identity. The paintings of the houses began in brown ground, black grave and blue clouds/sky.

FIGURE 7.4 Painting 4. I. Belity.

FIGURE 7.5 Painting 5. I. Belity.

FIGURE 7.6 Painting 6. I. Belity.

Further on, the houses were given different shades of colour according to her feeling, for example: a yellow house and a pink background (FIG 7.5), a purple house symbolising peace and tranquillity (FIG 7.6) and colour combinations in nearby houses in blue, green, brown, yellow (FIG 7.7). Following the transition in parallel with expression of the complexity of her feelings the transition from the grieving home to the growing home, with shape, size, colours and a setting sums up the process she experienced. Manzo (2003) noted that a home can be also linked to loss and functions as a lost paradise or a trap. It is striking that for Rima, the home was transformed from a grieving home to a home with protection, nurture and comfort.

Matri (2005) views people's life as a journey prompted by the decision to continue in the same home we absorbed or to change it. Matri asks in a poetic meaningful way about the mental components in the experience of the home that people wish to relive and to reconstruct into "their own home." He considers the home as a space that enables the self to form and sees the confrontation with the childhood home as a return to the authentic sources of the self, to the individual's primary truth. In his view, the search for a home for the soul is a journey in which a person must separate from what s/he is not and discover his or her self-identity. Individuals know they have a home for their souls when they have the inner space, the authorisation, and the willingness to listen, to be open in the fullest possible way to the essence of their souls and when they can sustain the fullest possible presence in many instances throughout life (Manzo, 2003, p59).

FIGURE 7.7 Painting 7. I. Belity.

Discussion

The encounter between a Jewish secular art therapist and Arab Muslim religious clients generates many questions. This therapy unfolds in a cultural-social-lingual space that differs from the one these patients grew up in, with its values and perceptions. At first, I believed I would be able to help my clients make a radical change in their lives, but after several years of experiencing intercultural therapy, I realised it is more complicated than that. This is not simply because of the external reality, but also because of the components of collective identity that are internalised and have become part of each person's own identity. Some parts of the self-identify with the values of tradition, religion, belonging and being close to the family, and with the expectations and demands they experience as women in Arab society, such as values of family honour, dress and behavioural codes. I learned that these women engage in an exploration of the internal and external, but also of the different aspects of the self that are often experienced as binary and contradictory (Boxbaum, 2018).

As an art therapist, I find that art allows for expression in a language that is unique to each individual. The artwork functions as the "analytic third," a term defined by Ogden that refers to the product of the unique dialect created by the separate subjectivity of the analytic and that of the patient in the analytic framework (Ogden, 2011). The process of creation allows for expression by documenting a transitional space in which it is possible to manipulate their reality and the difficulties they experience, creating a third mental space. In the workshop I led at the conference, the process included individual art making and a transition to testimony and group sharing. There are two witnesses in art therapy, as McNiff suggested: the artwork in itself is a witness, and the therapist, as a viewer engaging in a discourse related to their lives and to their artwork, constitutes the second witness (McNiff, 2014). The artwork forms a bridge connecting our two different worlds, creating the content along with the meaning, in a language we both understand. This witness is characterised by qualities of nurturing (creative materials, creative processes), active and present listening and accompaniment of the process, which Renik (1993) called the "participating viewer." My presence allows clients to be relieved of the lonely experience that surrounds them and to understand what they feel is misunderstood by their surroundings and sometimes even by themselves. The art-making process and the therapist validate their anger and frustration, in a verbal and non-verbal way.

These clients create what Herzog (2010) called a "politics of the everyday life." They are able to undermine the existing and limiting order of their world in oblique and creative ways in their daily lives, in their relations with husbands and families, their families of origin and the community in which they live. They engage in therapy even though it is unaccepted/taboo in traditional society and integrate their internal and external worlds in which they live in an intelligent fashion.

Boxbaum (2018) described Arab patients' stories as having what she calls a "basement quality" of truth emerging into the light for the first time. This involves a flooding of insufferable experiences and life events, secrets related to relationships, sexuality, traumas from the past, without there being a space for processing and observing. The reality in which they live forces itself on them in a way that leaves no freedom or space for the opportunity to think, feel or act. The social structure acts as a prison forcing them to live in real and existential loneliness.

One of the theoretical terms I use as a platform for containing the complexity, contradictions and the tendency towards the binary is the "social third," as formulated in both writings about identity in post-modern society (Bhabha, 1990), and in those who searched for different ways to connect social arenas and the spaces of the soul (Benjamin, 2011; Wiener Levy, 2006). The "third" as a hybrid space provides new opportunities for the possible to unfold. This occurs when there is a readiness to re-examine stances, rethink them, elaborate or mark them in a way that does not tend to one side or the other, both on the subject and in the intersubjective space.

I also find myself in an ongoing process of developing a third space within me, which is different and distinct from the perceptions I have internalised in the society and culture in which I grew up. I distance myself from the values of "independence and separation." I believe and accept patients' choices to stay in a complex reality that does not allow them to make far-reaching changes, such as divorce, externalisation of opinions that contradict existing social perceptions. I understand that letting go and empowerment can lead them to a life of loneliness and deportation. This means providing an option for life where there is no simple choice between modern and tradition, East or West, freedom or oppression, dependence or independence. I take into account that what is considered oppression for me might be interpreted differently by them.

This requires moving between the two spaces of identity – traditional and Western – without having to decide between them, when sometimes they do not belong to either, and sometimes belong to both. Sometimes they exist both here and there, and sometimes neither here nor there (Wiener Levy, 2006). Creating a "social third" requires mourning for what cannot be, for what is beyond our control, for the existence of manmade wrongs causing us to suffer, which are also an integral part of us as members of human society.

References

Abu Asaba, H. (2007). *Arab education in Israel - dilemmas of a national minority.* Jerusalem: Floresheimer Institute for Policy Studies. (in Hebrew). https://www.jstor.org/stable/23690865?seq=1

Abu-Asba, H. (2005). The Arabic educational system in Israel: Development and present picture. In: Haidar, A. (Ed.) *Arab society in Israeli population, society, economy* (pp. 201–221). Van Leer Jerusalem Institute/The Institute of Israeli-Arab Studies/Hakibbutz Hameuchad Publishing House (in Hebrew). http://library.macam.ac.il/study/pdf_files/d10655.pdf

Abu-Tabich, L. (2009). *On collective national rights, civil equality and women's rights: Palestinian women in Israel and denying their right to choose their residence, theory and criticism.* Aviv 34, pp. 43–69 (in Hebrew). file:///C:/Users/user/Downloads/f08709ecec51656fb318b129bbf58d76.pdf

Ahmed, L. (1992). *Women and gender in Islam: Historical roots of a modern debate.* London: Yale University Press.

Aloud, N. (2009). Factors affecting attitudes toward seeking and using formal mental health and psychological services among Arab-Muslims population. *Journal of Muslim Mental Health,* 4(2), 79–103. https://doi.org/10.1080/15564900802487675

Al-Krenawi, A. (2002). Mental health service utilization among the Arabs in Israel. *Social Work in Health Care,* 35(1/2), 577–589. https://doi.org/10.1300/J010v35n01_12

Alred, G. (2003). *Becoming a 'better stranger': A therapeutic perspective on intercultural experience and/as education,* In G. Alred, M. Byram & M. Flemming (Eds.). Intercultural Experiences and/as Education. (pp. 14–29). Clevedon:.Multilingual Matter. https://www.degruyter.com/document/doi/10.21832/9781853596087-005/html

Arar, K.H. & Rigbi, A. (2009). 'To participate or not to participate?'—status and perception of physical education among Muslim Arab-Israeli secondary school pupils. *Sport, Education and Society,* 14(2), 183–202. https://www.tandfonline.com/doi/abs/10.1080/13573320902809088

Badran, M. (1995). *Feminism, Islam, and nation: gender and the making of modern Egypt.* New Jersey: Princeton University Press.

Bhabha, H. (1990). The third space, interview with Homi Bhabha, In: Rutheford, J. (Ed.) *Identity, community, culture difference* (pp. 207–221). London: Lawrence and Wishard. http://s3.amazonaws.com/arena-attachments/90186/444c4a43b13aec92039a31bef35c4945.pdf?1364059011

Baum, N. (2007). It's not only cultural differences: Comparison of Jewish Israeli social work students' thoughts and feelings about treating Jewish Ultra-Orthodox and Palestinian Israeli clients. *International Journal of Intercultural Relations,* 31, 575–589. https://muse.jhu.edu/chapter/1328233

Benjamin, J. (1988). *The bonds of love, psychanalysis, feminism, and the problem of domination.* New York: Random House. https://books.google.co.il/books?hl=iw&lr=&id=-YxV53NgC8AC&oi=fnd&pg=PR7&dq=Benjamin,+J.+(1988).+The+bonds+of+love,+psychanalysis,+feminism,+and+the+problem+of+domination.+Random+House&ots=-HqlMz4ia9&sig=Am2s6zIeqDqdkq23wQO_c-XWJvI&redir_esc=y#v=onepage&q&f=false

Benjamin, J. (2006). *Beyond doer and done to* (pp. 21–48). London & New York: Routledge.

Benjamin, J. (2011). Facing reality together: discussion of "the social third." In: Dimen, M. (Ed.) *With culture in mind: psychoanalytic stories* (pp. 49–63). New York: Routledge. https://books.google.co.il/books?hl=iw&lr=&id=ZzVZBwAAQBAJ&oi=fnd&pg=PR2&dq=Dimen,+M.+(Ed.)+With+culture+in+mind:+psychoanalytic+stories+&ots=KpL_diazBP&sig=-JDJYktBcVkX_TudqrxPaUI3e_I&redir_esc=y#v=onepage&q=Dimen%2C%20M.%20(Ed.)%20With%20culture%20in%20mind%3A%20psychoanalytic%20stories&f=false

Berman, E. (2003). Israeli psychotherapists and the Israeli-Palestinian conflict. *Psychotherapy and Political International,* 1(1), 1–16. https://onlinelibrary.wiley.com/doi/epdf/10.1002/ppi.47

Boxbaum, T. (2018). Jewish therapist Arab patients: land, home, women. [Electronic version]. Posted on 1/9/2018, *Hebrew Psychology Site*: https://www.hebpsy.net/articles.asp?id=3677 (in Hebrew).

Chandrakirana, K. (2009). Women's place and displacement in the Muslim family: realities from the twenty-first century. In: Zainah. A. (Ed.) *Wanted: equality and justice in the Muslim family.* Malaysia: Musawah. http://arabic.musawah.org/sites/default/files/WANTED-EN-2edition_0.pdf#page=249

Dwairy, M. (1998). *Cross-cultural counseling: the Arab-Palestinian case.* New York: Haworth Press. https://www.taylorfrancis.com/books/mono/10.4324/9781315809946/cross-cultural-counseling-marwan-adeeb-dwairy-jane-jagelman

Dwairy, M. (2006). *Counseling and psychotherapy with Arabs and Muslims: A culturally sensitive approach.* New York: Teachers College Press.

Dwairy, M. & Van-Sickle, T.D. (1996). Western psychotherapy in traditional Arabic societies. *Clinical Psychology Review,* 16(3), 231–249. https://www.sciencedirect.com/science/article/abs/pii/S0272735896000116

Fraiberg, S., Adelson, E. & Shapiro, V. (1975). Ghosts in the nursery: a psychoanalytic approach to the problem of impaired infant-mother relationships. *Journal of the American Academy of Child Psychiatry,* 14, 387–421. https://www.sciencedirect.com/science/article/abs/pii/S0002713809614424

Frosh, S. (2007). Facing political truths. *Psychotherapy and Politics International*, 5(1), 29–36.

Herzog, H. (2010). Alternative spaces: the politics of everyday life of Palestinian Israeli citizens in mixed cities. In: Abu-Rabia-Qwider, S. & Winner-Levy, N. (Eds.) *Palestinian women in Israel: identity of power and coping relations*, Van Lir – Hakibbutz Hmeuha, pp. 148–172.

Kapitan, L. (2015). Social action in practice: shifting the ethnocentric lens in cross-cultural art therapy encounters. *Art Therapy: Journal of the American Art Therapy Association*, 32(3), 104–111. https://doi.org/10.1080/07421656.2015.1060403

McNiff, S. (2014). Art speaking for itself: evidence that inspires and convinces. *Journal of Applied Arts and Health*, 5(2), 255–262. https://doi.org/10.1386/jaah.5.2.255_1

Manzo, L.C. (2003). Beyond house and heaven: toward a revisioning of emotional relationships with places. *Journal of Environmental Psychology*, 23, 47–67. https://psycnet.apa.org/record/2003-03653-007

Matri, J. (2005). *Home for the soul*. Modan. (in Hebrew).

Nelson, J.A., Bustamante, R., Sawyer, C. & Sloan E.V. (2015). Cultural competence and school counselor training: a collective case study. *Journal of Multicultural Counseling and Development*, 43, 221–235.

Ogden, T.H. (2011). *On not being able to dream*. Tel Aviv: Am Oved Publishers Ltd.

Popper-Giveon, A. & Weiner-Levy, N. (2010). Traditional healers, higher education, autonomy and hardship: Coping paths of Palestinian women in Israel. Social issues in Israel. Ariel University center (pp. 124–152). https://www.jstor.org/stable/23389205?seq=1&cid=pdf-reference#references_tab_contents. (in Hebrew).

Renik, O. (1993). Analytic interaction: conceptualizing technique in light of the analyst's irreducible subjectivity, *Psychoanalytic Quarterly*, LXII.

Samuels, A. (2006). Working directly with political, social and cultural material in the therapy session. In: Lyton, L., Hollander, N.C. & Gutwill S. (Eds.) *Psychoanalysis, class and politics: encounters in the clinical setting* (pp. 11–28). New York: Routledge.

Van Den Bergh, N. & Crisp, C. (2004). Defining culturally competent practice with sexual minorities: Implications for social work education and practice. *Journal of Social Work Education*, 40(2), 221–238.

Wadud A. (2009). Islam beyond patriarchy through gender inclusive qur'anic analysis. In: Zainah, A. (Ed.) *Wanted: equality and justice in the Muslim family*. Malaysia: Musawah.

Waller, D. (2015). *Group interactive art therapy*. London & New York: Routledge.

Wiener Levy, N. (2006). Higher education as a meeting point with knowledge, society and culture: Changes in the identity of Druze women, pioneers in acquiring higher education. *Social issues in Israel* (pp. 5–30). https://www-jstor-org.ezproxy.smkb.ac.il/stable/23388573?seq=1#metadata_info_tab_contents (in Hebrew).

Winnicott, D.W. (1949). Hate in the countertransference. *International Journal of Psychoanalysis* 30: 69–74. https://www.pep-web.org/document.php?id=IJP.030.0069A

Winnicott, D.W. (1971). 'The place where we live.' *Playing and reality* (pp. 104–110). New York: Basic Books.

8

SAMAGAMA – DIALOGUES ON THE DEVELOPMENT OF PROFESSIONAL CREATIVE ARTS THERAPY PRACTICE, RESEARCH AND TRAINING FROM INDIA

Oihika Chakrabarti, Tripura Kashyap, Maitri Gopalakrishna, Nina Cherla

Abstract

In Indian Sanskrit and Budddhist Pali terms, Samagama means union, meeting, association, concert or simply coming together. In English, the derivative word is Sangam, meaning the confluence of a river with its tributaries. Like the many tributaries of a river, this chapter will bring together creative arts therapy practitioners from the diverse disciplines of dance/movement, art, drama and music – all pioneers in their own right, and document their experiences of contributing to the ebb and flow of arts therapy's evolution in India.

This chapter will seek to unearth current developments in arts therapies practice, research and training that exist on the ground today and present them from the multiple perspectives of the different disciplines. The authors will also attempt to shed light on their own processes of acculturation and their efforts to decolonise and incorporate indigenous processes to make their work culturally relevant to India.

The chapter brings up the ethical challenges and concerns practitioners are faced with in the absence of any formal education, professional training or regulatory bodies and the need for ethical standards and guidelines within the evolutionary domains of professional practice and training of the diverse disciplines in India.

Through the length of these dialogues, we hope to discover our own true path, making visible the unknown in the arts therapies from an Eastern perspective. We hope to build trust and collectively support the creative arts therapies in gaining credibility and recognition, to fulfil the vision of actualising formal education in India. We hope our endeavour will lead to the professionalisation of these fields and motivate future generations of practitioners to enter the mental health ecosystem on a par with other mental health professionals in India and benchmark themselves with global standards.

DOI: 10.4324/9781003110200-8

Keywords: decolonising, arts therapies, India, practice-research, masters-training

Abstract in Bengali

translated by Deepak Mitra

অধ্যায় শিরনামঃ ''সমাগম' - ভারতবর্ষ থেকে সৃজনমূলক শিল্প - চিকিৎসায় চর্চা, গবেষণা এবং অনুশীলনের ওপর কথোপকথন ।

অধ্যায়টির সহ-উদ্ভাবক - ঐহিকা চক্রবর্তী (শিল্প - মনঃসমীক্ষক), ত্রিপুরা কাশ্যপ (নৃত্য-বিচলন মনস্তবিজ্ঞানী), মৈত্রী গোপালকৃষ্ণ (নাট্য মনস্তবিজ্ঞানী), নীনা চেরলা (সংগীত মনস্তবিজ্ঞানী)।

অধ্যায়টির সম্পাদক - ঐহিকা চক্রবর্তী ।

ভারতীয় ভাষা সংস্কৃত'তে এবং বৌদ্ধ-ভাষা পালি'তে 'সমাগম' শব্দটির মানে - মিলন, সমাবেশ, সংঘ, ঐক্য বা সোজা কথায় একত্র হওয়া । ইংরাজীতে প্রকৃতি প্রত্যয়গত শব্দটি হচ্ছে 'সংগম', যার মানে একটি নদীর তার উপনদীগুলির সঙ্গে মিলিত হওয়া । একটি নদীর অনেক উপনদীর মত, এই পরিচ্ছেদটি একত্রে নিয়ে আসবে সৃজনমূলক শিল্প চিকিৎসকদের, তাদের নৃত্য / বিচলন, শিল্প, নাটক, এবং সংগীত প্রভৃতি বিভিন্ন শিল্পক্ষেত্র থেকে, যেখানে তাঁরা স্বাধিকারে প্রবর্তক এবং বহু বছরের অভিজ্ঞতা ভারতের মাটিতে দান করেছেন ।

এই পরিচ্ছেদটি বর্তমানে বিদ্যমান শিল্প চিকিৎসা অনুশীলন, গবেষণা ও শিক্ষার সর্বশেষ অবস্থার সন্ধান করবে এবং সেগুলিকে বিভিন্ন নিয়মানুয় অভ্যাস থেকে যথানুপাতিক ভাবে উপস্থিত করবে । উদ্ভাবকরা অপর সভ্যতা থেকে প্রথা গ্রহণের নিজ প্রণালী মিশ্রণ করে ভারতবর্ষের পক্ষে প্রাসঙ্গিক করে তুলতে চেষ্টা করবেন ।

এই পরিচ্ছেদটি তুলে ধরবে ভারতবর্ষে কোন প্রচলিত শিক্ষাদান, পেশাদারী হাতে-কলমে শিক্ষার এবং নিয়ামক সংস্থার অবর্তমানে সংশ্লিষ্ট অনুশীলনকারীরা যে নৈতিক প্রতিদ্বন্দ্বিতা সমূহের এবং উদ্বেগের সম্মুখীন হচ্ছেন, এবং নৈতিক মান সম্পর্কিত নির্দেশবলী প্রস্তুতির প্রয়োজনে, উভয়ই বিবর্ধনমূলক আয়ত্ত বিষয়ের পেশাদারী অনুশীলনের এবং হাতে-কলমে শিক্ষার এলাকার ভিতর বিবিধ শিক্ষার অনুশীলনে যোগদান করছেন ।

এই সকল কথোপকথনের মাধ্যমে, আমরা আমাদের সঠিক পথ আবিষ্কার করতে পারবো আশা করছি, দেখাতে পারবে সেই অজানাকে যা শিল্প চিকিৎসার ক্ষেত্রে প্রাচের দর্শনানুপাতে অজানা । আমরা আশা করি সেই বিশ্বাস গড়ে তুলতে পারবো যা সমবেতভাবে সৃজনী শিল্প চিকিৎসায় বিশ্বাসযোগ্যতা অর্জন এবং পরিচিতির সহায়ক হবে, এবং ভারতবর্ষে আনুষ্ঠানিক শিক্ষাদানের মানসিক ছবিটিকে বাস্তবে পরিণত করতে পারবে । আমরা আশা করি আমাদের প্রচেষ্টা এই সব ক্ষেত্রগুলিকে পেশাদারীত্বে এগিয়ে নিয়ে যাবে এবং ভবিষ্যত প্রজন্মের অনুশীলনকারীদের প্রেরণা জোগাবে মানসিক স্বাস্থ্যের বাস্তব নিয়মাবলীতে প্রবেশ করতে, অন্যান্য ভারতীয় মানসিক স্বাস্থ্য পেশাকারীদের সমতায় এবং বিশ্বব্যাপী মাপকাঠির অনুভূমিক রেখায় নিজেদের নিয়ে যেতে পারবে ।

Context setting: Creative arts therapies is in a state of evolution in India. Our chapter focuses on the professional development of creative arts therapy via the journey of four professionally trained creative arts therapists in the field of dance movement therapy, art therapy, dramatherapy and music therapy. All of them may be considered pioneers in their own right who have contributed to the development and expansion of their own fields in India, through innovative models of practice, research, pedagogy and training. All of these practitioners trained either in the UK or in the US as to date there is no professional training available in India.

Historically speaking, the first stirrings of arts therapies were felt in the 1990s with the return of early sojourners like Kashyap in the field of dance movement therapy and Chakrabarti in the field of art therapy (Chakrabarti, 2017) constituting the first small wave to bring arts therapies to Indian shores. After a gap of almost a decade, the second bigger wave in the following decade witnessed the return of a number of trained creative arts therapists in different parts of India. A majority of them were dance movement therapists along with a few art, expressive and drama-therapists including Gopalakrishna in the field of dramatherapy. Although traces of music therapy can be found early on in India, with the advent of globalisation, the third decade ushered in a phase of cross-pollination with music therapists like Cherla, who is of Swedish origin but continues to contribute to Indian soil. In the past three decades, arts therapies has traversed a fairly long journey, and despite its many complexities and challenges, seeks to locate itself within the spheres of both clinical practice as well as community care in India today.

The following excerpts illuminate each one's journey as they relate their experiences and perspectives in their own voices of contributing to their individual disciplines and those made by others, in effect shaping the diverse field of creative arts therapies and its myriad possibilities in India today.

Art therapy in its Indian avatar: genesis and development of the field in India

Oihika Chakrabarti (art psychotherapist)

Although the interrelatedness and healing properties of the arts can be traced back to the *Chitrasutra of the Vishnudharmottara Purana*, the world's oldest treatise on art from the 7th century AD (Bajaj and Vohra, 2015), only in the 1990s does evidence emerge of the field of art therapy in India in any formal capacity. I was the first to return to India after the completion of my postgraduate training in art psychotherapy at Goldsmiths in the UK, only made possible by a Commonwealth scholarship awarded by the Ministry of Human Resource Development, Government of India in 1997. I realise it is important to share my trajectory at the outset, and perhaps even my genealogy (Westwood, 2012) to some extent as it might have contributed in shaping the direction art therapy took and the developmental milestones it achieved in its formative years in India. On my return, I found myself in the unique position of a pioneer, in Ibbotson's (2008) terms an "accidental leader," in an India that was yet to become familiar with the term "art therapy."

Although I was grateful for my psychodynamic training, it had not prepared me for the acculturation process I encountered on my return. I was confronted with an India that was familiar and yet changing with the impact of globalisation, when experienced through an acculturation lens (Carlier and Salom, 2012).

Given the urban-rural divide, India remains socially stratified along the lines of gender, class, caste and religion and is multi-cultural with marked diversity in terms of ethnicities, linguistics, customs and rituals. India is full of contradictions, there are many mini Indias within India, one that is moored to its rich ancient traditions, the other much like the concept of culture itself that is not static, is dynamic and constantly changing (Waelde, 2008). Often times I oscillated between the emic and etic perspectives, the former emic or insider perspective that was anchored to my roots and largely Indian schooling and the latter etic or outsider perspective that I owe to my Western higher education in the UK and US. I realised very soon that no Western model should be transplanted as I experienced an unlearning process embracing humanistic traditions, indigenous processes and community arts. This approach was first nurtured during my volunteering years at Mother Teresa's Missionaries of Charity's Shishu Bhavan orphanage in Kolkata and was further enhanced by Tagore's philosophy fostered as a visual artist during my masters years in fine arts (1993–1995) at Kala Bhavan, Visva Bharati University, Santiniketan, and grew to become my foundation as an art historian/research editor at the Lalit Kala Akademi, New Delhi, and art educator at the Delhi College of Art, prior to my journey to the UK.

Therefore, the early years after my return from London, England, were spent in creating awareness about a field that was practically unknown through lectures and workshops at universities, non-profits, and capacity-building training workshops with counselling psychologists, special educators, social workers and school teachers. Working with diverse population groups in creating a new working model of art therapy relevant to the Indian cultural context, whether it was training or community outreach, made me aware that the model that I developed and practised in India needed to be rooted in this country's soil and socio-cultural ethos. Out of these early initiatives, and introductory lectures with masters level students at the Department of Medical Psychiatry and Social Work at the Tata Institute of Social Science (TISS), was born the first Art Psychotherapy service at TISS's Child Guidance Clinic (CGC) at Wadia Children's Hospital in 1999 (Chakrabarti, 2019a). Historically, the CGC was India's first Child Guidance Clinic and art psychotherapy service served children with behavioural and emotional difficulties and special needs. In a collectivist society (Hofstede, 2001), family support structures are an important cornerstone and working with the family is considered valuable and, as I learnt, a necessary and integral part of the therapeutic process (Chadda and Deb, 2013).

To expand the scope of art therapy and take it into community settings, necessitated that the very meaning of art needed to be reassessed, in terms of a culture's own meaning and relevance as a living tradition (Subramaniyan, 1987). In sync with this philosophy, Manahkshetra Foundation, the first non-profit organisation in arts therapy, was spearheaded in 2004 with the aim of using art for social change. Over the past two decades art therapy work expanded to include various indigenous applications of art therapy within clinical, rehabilitative, developmental and training settings in collaboration with non-profit organisations, schools, educational institutes and museums. Innovation has been key in adapting art therapy to serve the diverse needs of marginalised communities such as the use of body maps to work with trafficked young girls, helped increase physical awareness and their emotional sense of self and agency, empowering them to open up dialogue on reproductive health and protection. Other projects included art therapy work with destitute women in shelters, at-risk population groups in an observation home for juvenile offenders for rehabilitation purposes, crisis interventions in times of natural disasters, with street children during Mumbai floods and cross-cultural work post Tsunami (Chakrabarti, 2017). Often art materials used were locally sourced to remain indigenous and site-specific, in order to provide relatedness with the lived environment. For instance, when working at the SOS village in Pune or Gokulam, an orphanage post Tsunami, I discovered that the children found a shared language in using vegetal dyes and floral and animal motifs reminiscent of wall and floor drawings (*Kolams*) in their home surroundings that had eroded and been lost in the natural disaster. When initiated within an art therapy community building initiative, they chose to recreate a mural and discovered a common visual space to dialogue which led them to connect with each other and find a new sense of community.

Within the developmental context, art therapy found applicability in a programme called *Bal Pragati* – Growing up, which essentially looked at exploring puberty issues with school children from various socio-economic backgrounds. One of the highlights of the programme included work with religious minorities such as the Anjuman-i-Islam school which offers education to Muslim boys and girls, to address gender-related issues, body awareness and open up dialogue vis-à-vis equal rights and opportunities. The programme was offered to both vernacular medium schools such as the Marwari Vidyalaya alongside English medium schools to cater to diverse socio-economic strata. To address the needs of the differently abled, an art therapy/education programme called Art Access was created to bring children with visual impairment into museums. The paradox of bringing children with visual impairment into a visual space was resolved by creating a tactile sensory programming, to stimulate a new kind of emotional learning, which was further reinforced through experiential workshops such as sensory exploration of machetes and simulated navigation of anthropological excavation sites, resulting in greater memory recall and retention.

With my relocation to Kolkata from Mumbai in 2009, my clinical work moved to Ahan Mental Health clinic and the focus shifted to training and building the capacity of mental health professionals through Manahkshetra and conducting life-skills workshops through the British Council in Mumbai and Kolkata. Eventually I set up my own art therapy practice. My quest to introduce art therapy to students of psychology, art and social work continued through art therapy courses, training programmes and supervised internships via Manahkshetra at institutes of higher learning such as TISS, the West Bengal State University (WBSU), Kala Bhavan – Visva Bharati University, Santiniketan. Art therapy was included as a distinct discipline to become an integral part of the PG Diploma Expressive Art Therapy programme alongside other disciplines such as dance/movement, drama, music and expressive arts therapies when it was launched at the St. Xavier's College, Mumbai in 2019.

FIGURE 8.1 Facilitating an experiential art therapy training session with the first PG Dip in Expressive Arts Therapy cohort at St. Xavier's College Mumbai 2019. O. Chakrabarti.

After more than a decade, the field began to expand with the return to India of other sojourner art therapists after the completion of their training in the UK, US, Singapore and Israel. The different orientation in training ushered in diverse perspectives and expanded the scope of art therapy further as it began to develop in other regions of India. Although there appears to be only a handful of professionally trained art therapists who are practising in India at present, each with their own unique orientation and training, their contributions are noteworthy as they comprise the second and third generation of art therapists in India. Many returning art therapists have begun to explore their roots and combine them with skills garnered during their training. Amongst them Krupa Zhaveri, an Indo-American and a Master of Professional Studies (art therapy) from the School of Visual Arts, US, is based in Pondicherry, South India. She is a trauma-informed expressive arts therapist who works with communities via her non-profit, Sankalpa Journeys, adapting indigenous Indian art traditions such as *henna, kolams* and *mandalas,* predominantly using art in her therapeutic practice (Zhaveri, 2020). Sruthi Sriram and Disha Dutt completed their masters degrees in art therapy from LASALLE College of Arts and Design in Singapore. While Sriram who is based in Chennai focusses on utilising arts in treatment and assessment of trauma survivors towards their recovery and rehabilitation, the focus of Dutt's art therapy work has mainly been with children with special needs in Bangalore. Saoni Banerjee who received her one-year international masters level training in creative arts therapy, with specialisation in art therapy, from Haifa University, Israel, works in Kolkata and combines her practice with teaching an art therapy course at WBSU. Besides that, she has just completed her doctorate and is also a full-time faculty of the Psychology Department at Loreto College, Kolkata. Arjun Lakshmipathi, who completed his masters in counselling: art therapy from Adler University, US, is based in Bangalore and has experience working with marginalised population groups such as the LGBTQIA+ community.

There are seven recent entrants in the field marking third-generation art therapists in India with Nandini Yadalam, who has a masters in transpersonal art therapy from Tobias School of Art and Therapy, UK. Based in Bangalore, Yadalam has experience working with both children and adults with emotional dysregulation. There are two more who returned after having completed the one-year masters in creative arts therapy with specialisation in art therapy from Haifa University, Israel. Latika Joshi worked in schools in India from 2017 to 2020, before moving to Tanzania for a year and is slated to come back to India this year. A contemporary of Joshi is Meghna Girish, whose work revolves around children on the autism spectrum and adults faced with trauma. The other is Roshni Bhatia who has a masters in art psychotherapy from LASALLE College of the Arts, Singapore. She currently works in private practice in Bangalore and engages in arts-based community projects through her outfit, FoundSpace, which provides a platform for cross-cultural and multi-disciplinary collaboration of the arts and mental illness. Sharmeen Khurana returned to India after completing her masters training in art therapy at the University of Hertfordshire in the UK and started working at Fortis Hospital in New Delhi and is now setting up her own art therapy practice. Another new entrant is Hasika Suresh, who has recently completed her masters in art therapy from Chester University, UK and is currently based in India and despite its challenges using art therapy to work online, given the situation with the worldwide pandemic. The newest entrant to the field is Sanjoli Sakhuja who recently returned to Delhi after completing her masters training in art psychotherapy at Goldsmiths College, University of London, UK. She has completed an internship under supervision with children with special needs and is keen to set up her own practice in tele health.

The return of next generation trained art therapists has been significant and has made it possible to fulfil the vision for a collective, and in 2019, The Art Therapy Association of India (TATAI) was founded with art therapists working on the ground in India. Currently the fledgling association is working on a Code of Ethics, in order to set the standard for ethical practice and required guidelines for training in India. From all of these developments one can therefore celebrate that the field of art therapy is growing further in the able hands of the new generation of art therapists working on the ground in India today. It is imperative that as art therapy develops it embodies its Indian avatar and forms a symbiotic relationship with the culture from which it derives and which it serves, in order to carve a pluralistic cultural identity in India.

Dance movement therapy (DMT) in India with culture-specific focus on the therapeutic dance-in-education (TDIE) model

Tripura Kashyap (dance movement therapist)

At the time I trained in dance movement therapy with Dr Grace Valentine and other dance therapists at the Hancock Centre in the US, there was no awareness of the concept in India. I returned to Bangalore, India, to begin my work in 1990. In the early years of pioneering the discipline, I worked in rehabilitation centres, special schools, half-ways homes and NGOs using dance therapy with groups and individuals. The Ashoka fellowship that I received in 1992 supported me to research into the therapeutic potential of Indian dance forms and spread an awareness of DMT across India through lectures and workshops for special educators. Many mainstream school teachers who attended these workshops requested me to design a DMT course for their neurotypical/normal functioning students. This led me to formulate the Therapeutic Dance-in-Education (TDIE) workshop which later developed into a modular course as discussed below.

FIGURE 8.2 A dance movement therapy training course in action at Artsphere, Pune. O. Chakrabarti.

As I worked towards the acculturation of DMT in the Indian context, I co-founded Creative Movement Therapy Association of India (CMTAI) in 2014 to strengthen the ecosystem of movement therapy, serve as a resource for practitioners and instil professional and ethical standards of practice. Around this time, the Foundation for Expressive and Creative Arts Therapies (FECAT) was set up by Brinda Jacob through her Studio for Movement Arts and Therapies in Bangalore, Anubha Doshi set up Artsphere in Pune and Sohini Chakraborty set up Kolkata Sanved. Although all of them were informally trained, they went on to spearhead organisations that promoted DMT as an important therapeutic modality. Kolkata Sanved set up a PG Diploma in Dance Movement Therapy in collaboration with the Tata Institute of Social Sciences, Mumbai, derived out of Sohini Chakraborty's working model *Sampoornata* – a psycho-social rehabilitation model of DMT with survivors of sexual abuse and trafficking, that culminated in her doctoral study (Chakraborty, 2019). Around the same time, CMTAI set up certificate programmes in DMT in Delhi and Bangalore in 2013–2014. Similarly, in 2017, Artsphere set up another Diploma in DMT in collaboration with CMTAI/The Arts Therapists Colab (TATC) and St. Mira College, Pune. By this time many second-generation Dance Movement Therapists like Preetha Ramasubramanian, Devika Mehta, Rashi Bijlani, Tarana Khatri and RituShree among others trained in the UK and US had returned to India and started working with different populations. In 2019, they set up the Indian Association of Dance Therapy (IADMT) to expand the scope and the ethical practice of the field with a focus on licensing of DMTs and accreditation of courses within India (Zhou et al., 2019).

Within the realm of these developments, I developed a 60-hour certificate course in Therapeutic Dance in Education (TDIE) for educators from across India inspired by the dance-in-education training programmes in the UK and US. I synthesised both disciplines – dance therapy and dance in education into an innovative working model which had two important dimensions. Educators were trained to use dance as a therapeutic tool: firstly, to enhance the personality development of their students (social skills, self-esteem and emotional expression etc.) and secondly, to reinforce academic learning and memory recall with academic subjects like math, science, etc. through movement. Apart from promoting inclusivity, the rationale was that dance engages with the physical, psychological, intellectual, emotional, creative, spiritual, performative and social layers of individuals (Riordan, 1980).

The TDIE model was based on different components related to dance facilitation, starting with the formulation of a movement activity basket combining creative movement with Indian physical traditions alongside movement assessment and evaluation, identifying therapeutic needs of students and the setting up short-term and long-term objectives. Five stages were used to structure and link ongoing sessions. They included: a) movement seeding, b) movement exploration, c) movement expression, d) resolution and

e) integration. Typically, each session is initiated with body preparatory routines, followed by theme development using creative movement or Indian dance techniques, culminating with verbal reflection and cool down. Selection of age-appropriate movement experiences for different age groups of students ranging from grade 1 to 8 is conducted keeping in mind the facilitation styles and approaches for teachers. TDIE was customised for students within mainstream, special needs and inclusive educational settings, with different body types across gender divides, socio-cultural, religious and economic backgrounds in India. The model seeks to foster the creativity, learning potential and well-being of students by guiding them to voice their thoughts and feelings through their bodies and commune with each other on a non-verbal and non-cerebral wavelength. In this daily ritual of self-expression, the body becomes an extension of the self, creating personalised dances (as opposed to mastering a formal dance technique). However, for this to happen, dance needs to be taught in a process-oriented manner rather than with choreography of dance performances as a goal.

For dance-in-education to become culturally effective, adaptations need to be made when applied to Indian schools within a culture-specific dance curriculum (Sharma, 1989). It is therefore necessary that change is advocated in the way dance is created, expressed, taught and perceived. In a bid to indigenise and create further relatedness, TDIE used the *Garba* dance form from Gujarat in which colourful sticks are hit together in unison to create a variety of rhythms around the body space. The dance helped students improve their group coordination, attention span and memory (since it had a series of structured movements in a sequence) but was also cathartic and helped to channel their energy. When movement experiences are based on an Indian theme or dance forms, they can, in fact, have more than one objective. For example, hand gestures from Indian classical dances may be used to express stories, real life incidences, poems or songs in one's vernacular language in accompaniment with the singing of seven notes of Sa, Re, Ga, Ma, Pa, Dha, Ni, Sa (similar to Do, Re, Mi, Fa). This helps students not only to open up their voices, but simultaneously helps them to learn to articulate through their fingers and sharpen their fine motor skills. It is important to keep these sessions interactive and playful between group participants. Similar movement experiences also challenge students to enhance their creativity, emotional expression, movement reflexes and spatial awareness (Kashyap, 2005). The body becomes a learning tool through movement-based internalisation of concepts that get concretised in the students' minds as they begin to understand the textural and movement qualities of what they study in academics. For instance, a grade 4 lesson on the "water cycle" in science was choreographed by students in groups symbolising its different elements using Indian classical dances (facial expressions, foot work and body movements) in grade 4. Expressive and pure dance hand gestures from the traditional text of the Natya Shastra, an ancient Sanskrit treatise for Indian performing arts (Manomohan, 1950), were choreographed by students of grade 6 to depict the life cycle and metamorphosis of a caterpillar into a butterfly.

In many primitive cultures, the dance of medicine men, priests or shamans belonged to the oldest form of medicine and psychotherapy in which the common exaltation and release of tensions were able to change man's physical and mental suffering into a new way of being on health (Levy, 1988). Similarly, as children experience movement activities, they befriend their bodies and work on their rhythm development, body coordination and communication through verbal-physical synchronicity in a "safe" space created by the facilitator. Just as it is important to navigate the new terrain with innovative methodologies, it is also essential to recognise and value our common historical strands as a human race in these times, for movement is our universal language, one that we need to harness for generations to come because movement is what keeps us alive and human!

Dramatherapy in India: a snapshot

Maitri Gopalakrishna (dramatherapist)

The links between drama and healing in India are ancient. For instance, Ayurvedic texts prescribed music, massage and meditation as treatments for depression in addition to herbs and tonics. Ritual story-telling performances using masks formed a part of many community rituals that served psychospiritual functions (Chabukswar and Balsara, 2016). However, dramatherapy as a stand-alone field of practice and research can be traced back to only the early 1990s when Sue Jennings began running training workshops in India (Casson, 1993). Those trained by Jennings began to bring drama to their own fields – social work, education and so on. Practitioners, such as Anand Chabukswar, Pramila Balasundaram, Parasuraman Ramamurthi and many more, set the ground for drama therapeutic work in India, which continues to inspire the field.

The next phase in the development of dramatherapy in India came with people, such as me, going abroad to do masters level training and then returning to India (Gopalakrishna, 2018). Today, we are entering a third phase with a critical mass of about ten professionally trained dramatherapists to add to the organically developing ecosystem of creative/expressive arts therapy and allied practitioners in the country. Dramatherapy in India now also has a space on the world stage through the World Alliance of Dramatherapy and ECArTE.

Our different backgrounds, influences and training make for a diverse and rich field of practice in India today. For example, Pallavi Chander, who trained in dramatherapy at the Royal Central School of Speech and Drama (London), brings her training in visual arts, her passion for community arts and the non-verbal and non-directive and her emphasis of the Sesame approach to work using puppets and story with groups of marginalised communities in Bangalore city. Pallavi is also currently the primary researcher on a project facilitated by the India

Foundation for the Arts and Welcome Trust (UK) to map work in the intersection of arts and mental health in the city. Anshuma Kshetrapal, who also trained at the Central School, brought together her background in psychotherapy and the emphasis on movement and Jungian psychology in the Sesame programme to co-found The Arts Therapists Co-Lab which develops and hosts masterclasses in dramatherapy across India (in addition to a Diploma in Movement Therapy). The masterclasses in 2018–2019 (taught by Armand Volkas, Dr. Nisha Sajnani and Bruce Bailey) were instrumental in bringing together the dramatherapy community in India and sparked collaborations between practitioners. Anupriya Meenakshi Banerjee, trained at New York University, brings together her background in media and journalism with her training in role theory and psychodrama, to develop technology-based interventions (like video games) to make drama therapy more accessible and comprehensible through social media and other virtual platforms. Through Banerjee's efforts, dramatherapists in India have formed a peer group that meets (virtually) monthly. This professional space not only provides a valuable forum for sharing of approaches, contexts and viewpoints but also offers a launch pad for the development of training and holding the field to rigorous ethical standards.

Having been trained at the California Institute of Integral studies, my own practice in dramatherapy is rooted in the Integrative Five Phase Model. However, the influences of intersectional feminism and working in theatre have also added a socio-political lens to my work. I am also part of an ongoing research collaboration with Dr. Nisha Sajnani, investigating theories and practices from the classical Indian performance treatise, the Natyashastra, in therapeutic work (Sajnani and Gopalakrishna, 2017). In 2018, I completed my PhD from the Tata Institute of Social Sciences in Mumbai, which involved looking at dramatherapy as an intervention in working with childhood sexual abuse. The study is significant for a few reasons. Firstly, it is the first doctoral level research in India that studies dramatherapy interventions. Secondly, it offers important insights to both trauma work and the practice of dramatherapy that has been useful to the mental health community at large. Thirdly, it birthed a performance called *Positively Shameless* that weaves together the artistic, therapeutic and socio-political (Gopalakrishna and Rao, 2017). We continue to perform *Positively Shameless* locally and internationally and share the process through publications, presentations and lectures.

It is important to note that the work mentioned here is only a small slice of the work happening in dramatherapy in India. Looking further afield, the creative arts therapies and allied fields in India are vibrant and contribute greatly to our ecosystem. Psychodrama, Theatre of the Oppressed and (more recently) Playback Theatre, have their own lineage, training tracks and practitioners' community of practitioners in India. In some cases, this even includes university affiliated training such as the Diploma in Psychodrama at the Tata Institute of Social Sciences, Mumbai.

My fellow dramatherapists and I have located our work in the intersection of psychotherapy, community building, education, art and media. We have been

FIGURE 8.3 A still from the play: Positively Shameless. O. Chakrabarti.

successful in reaching larger audiences. However, since all of us are based in cities and are from relatively privileged backgrounds, there is the danger of the field being urban-centric and elitist. To intentionally counteract this, many of us have made a concerted effort to work and support work in diverse contexts including rural parts of India. For instance, Kashma Goyal is doing ongoing dramatherapy work with groups of female sex workers in rural Maharashtra (western India). However, the limitations of funding and institutional support make this challenging. It is crucial that individuals from marginalised backgrounds in India can also train to be dramatherapists and other creative arts therapists. To this end, there is work being done to develop culturally relevant curriculum and establish masters level programmes (Chakrabarti, 2019b) in established public academic institutions. By doing this, students can gain access to these programmes at subsidised costs and gain access to state scholarships and other resources that would make training accessible to people from a larger cross section of this country. A third effort to keep our work inclusive is partnering with professionals from allied fields – other creative/expressive arts therapists, applied theatre practitioners, educators, social workers – to be able to support and share tools and resources. It is also important to note that the work of achieving mental health for all cannot be undertaken just by therapists. Therefore, connecting across disciplines/practices/approaches is vitally important. While we need our field to be ethical and regulated, we are cautious of an over professionalised space potentially creating more barriers to access. Hence, our efforts to collectivise have been gradual and intentional.

The importance of decolonising the field of dramatherapy and opening it up to multiplicity in terms of sources cannot be overstated. To this end, along with many of my colleagues and I have been have been looking to our own cultures, traditions and practices. My practice-research work concerning the Natyashastra (mentioned earlier) is one such attempt. An ongoing discussion in our peer group is how working in languages other than English impacts the work itself and constructions of the notions of self, emotions and so on. A caution here is that we must not see India as a monolith and unwittingly subscribe to the idea of a singular Indian culture, thereby reproducing dominant religious and caste ideas. The job of passing the mic and listening is as important in India as it is anywhere else in the world, particularly in the current political climate. As dramatherapists we believe we have tools and a responsibility to do just that. It is an exciting time to be a dramatherapist in India. There is much work to be done and now there is a community with which to do it.

A brief glimpse of music therapy in India and its cross-cultural application in the Indian context

Nina Cherla (music therapist)

India has a population of over a billion people, thousands of diverse communities and cultures, numerous religious sects and over a hundred major linguistic categories (Roy, 2011). As a music therapist trained in the West, India offered a unique set of challenges in terms of cross-cultural music therapy. In this section I will explore music therapy practice in India, its cultural backdrop and the adaptations needed in order to practise cross-cultural music therapy. Coming to India as a music therapist trained in the UK, I was mindful of the fact that India already has a rich history of using music in healthcare with the earliest Indian music healing traditions dating back to roughly 3,500 years ago (Sundar, 2015).

Despite music being of great importance in India, music therapy as a clinical profession is still at a nascent stage. As of 2019, World Federation of Music Therapy (2019) lists approximately 50 professionals practising in India and only a handful of educational programmes offering certification. Some of the early music therapy organisations in India are: 1. Nada Centre for Music Therapy, founded in 2004. The charity organised India's first music therapy conference in 2006 (Sundar and Sairam, 2006) and strives to promote the therapeutic effects of Indian Music. 2. Chennai School of Music Therapy, directed by Dr Sumathy Sundar, offers a postgraduate diploma training programme in collaboration with the IMC University of Applied Sciences in Krems, Austria (Hicks, 2020). 3. Although no longer active, The Music Therapy Trust, founded by Dr Margareth Lobo, promoted awareness of music therapy through educational programmes as well as offering postgraduate diplomas in music therapy (Hicks, 2020). In recent years, there are a couple of trained music therapists who have returned to India after completing their training abroad. Two of them who are working across the spectrum of differently abled populations include Baishali Mukherjee, who trained in the UK and works with the Chennai School of Music Therapy, and Purva Sampat, who returned after her training in the US and practises in Bangalore. Sampat's current work with children includes neurodevelopmental disorders such as autism, CP, ADHD and OCD.

There are a few key differences in the way music therapy is practised in India when compared to the West. Sundar (2006, p1) states:

> The cultural and traditional Indian music has a spiritual and philosophical influence, which expresses one's devotional feelings. This is an integral part of one's religion and is a unique aspect of Indian Music Therapy.

When looking at music therapy research originating in India, one comes across mainly receptive methods (Kaliyaperumal and Subash, 2010; Nizamie and Tikka, 2014; Rohilla et al., 2018), as promoted by the early organisations of music therapy in India. Given the receptive nature of music therapy in India, I observed that the majority of people I met were accustomed to associating it with listening to aesthetically pleasing music performed by the therapist who is almost always a trained classical musician. This is indeed the case, with the therapist ensuring that the music chosen during a therapy session is well-aligned with certain therapeutic goals.

This is in rather stark contrast to the way I practise it as a music therapist trained in the West practise it. My approach is largely grounded in psychodynamic theory and the interventions I adopt have a clear emphasis on the interactive aspects of music. In contrast, my *Clinical Improvisation* (Wigram, 2004) approach was primarily interactive and improvisatory, with the client being encouraged to actively engage with the musical instruments just as much as I, the therapist. This difference in my approach from prevailing notions about music therapy in India initially made it difficult for me to meet expectations by directly applying what I knew as a music therapist. There was, however, the strong belief in the healing power of music among many and an openness to learning about something new. This encouraged me to take a step back, revaluate the reasons and motivations for my methods and make sure to clearly explain these to my clients to align our expectations before commencing therapy.

Adapting my training into practice required taking into consideration family dynamics and confidentiality in the Indian context. Families in India often consist of complex and extended family systems (Chadda and Deb, 2013). I observed that there was a greater involvement of one's family in one's matters that could be regarded in the West as confidential or private. This brings to mind a discourse by Neki (1992, p171) on the role of privacy in Indian society where he states,

> In socio centric organic cultures such concepts of privacy in the sense of separatist living and unshared possessions are alien. Exact synonyms for the term "privacy" may not even obtain in the languages of such cultures. They do not exist in the Indian languages anyway.

Thus, what transpired in the therapy room was not just an isolated matter between me and the client but potentially between me and the entire family.

The tradition of psychotherapy is an import from Western culture, and it is questionable whether a one-to-one therapeutic relationship in the absence of the family or wider community is applicable to Asian cultures (Futamata, 2005). I believe that it is not possible in India, here music therapy must recognise the role of the family in the client's life and by not involving the family I was risking being deemed as cold, distant and even incompetent. It was very common for parents to want to sit in with their children and seek explanation to nearly every musical interaction that took place. There was also an expectation from the families to involve them and direct them in what needed to be done. Often, I was asked what they could do themselves, how they could support what I did in the therapy room at home. Not offering instructions could be interpreted as a sign of unpreparedness (Kim and Whitehead-Pleaux, 2015).

This really highlighted to me the deep connection between therapy and local culture. Wholeheartedly acknowledging and accepting this connection opened up new and interesting therapeutic avenues. I expanded the definition of what I

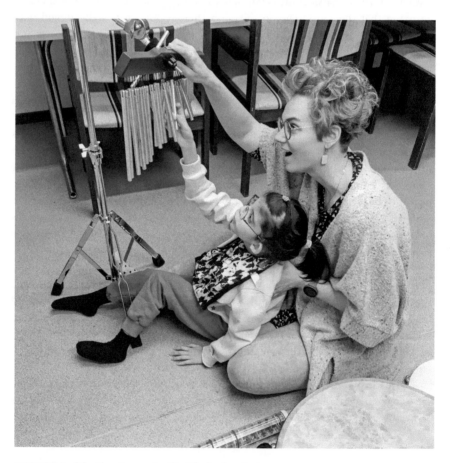

FIGURE 8.4 Meeting in music. O. Chakrabarti.

considered to be therapeutically valuable. It was important to offer parents and caregivers the opportunity to engage in musical interaction with their children at home. To facilitate this, we created the MILNA (**M**eeting in music, **I**nteracting, **L**istening a**N**d **A**dapting) training programme which was specifically designed for this purpose (Konstandinidi and Cherla, 2018), where *milna* is the Hindi word for to meet/connect. MILNA consists of sessions first carried out together with the child, music therapist and caregiver. The musical activities taught in these sessions are tailored to each child. The therapist, who initially leads the sessions, encourages the caregiver gradually to take the lead in order for them eventually to be able to carry out these activities at home. The caregiver also receives a booklet, which contains selected activities from those covered in the programme, with the possibility of adding activities and songs that have taken shape during the sessions.

My training and practice of music therapy led me to perceive the therapeutic process as one between the therapist and the client. This, however, was something that I had to rethink in India's cultural backdrop where caregivers were eager to be actively involved in this process. So, rather than insisting on practising in a certain way, with a fixed idea on what may be therapeutically valuable, I found that, as a music therapist trained in a foreign country, the best way for me to support music therapy interventions in India was not to fixate on what the very definition of music therapy is – but what that definition could be for India. There is a risk that in being too rigid in how we practise music therapy, we might end up isolating ourselves, and that contradicts the very essence of our work which, in my opinion, should value **flexibility, creativity and sensitivity. Flexibility** in seamlessly changing between different interventions, **creativity** in coming up with adaptations in the moment and **sensitivity** in knowing when to do so. We need to look beyond the music itself into all aspects of human interconnection, aesthetics and perspectives on health (Futamata, 2005) and only then can music therapy be fully culture-centred and relevant to the country in which it is practised.

The game changer: decolonising arts therapies and the creation of culturally relevant professional training in India

Oihika Chakrabarti (art psychotherapist)

One significant gap I have observed in more than two decades of pioneering art therapy work in India (Chakrabarti, 2017), since my postgraduate training in art psychotherapy at Goldsmiths, UK, is the complete absence of professional training in the field of art therapy. Till today there is no masters level training (a pre-requisite for practice) available in art therapy anywhere in India. In fact, this very predicament had propelled me to seek training abroad and been my reason for coming back to India after the completion of my training as I wanted to contribute to the setting up of this field in India. As a consequence, those of us who have sought to train or practise art therapy in

India have had to explore training abroad, leading to diverse orientations and the lack of consistency in our standards of practice and our understanding of arts therapies in India.

As the field of creative arts therapies is still in an evolutionary stage in India, a developing interest in the field of arts therapies can be observed to meet growing market demand. However, due to the lack of professional training available in the field, there has been over the years a mushrooming of short-term art-based therapy training promoting the therapeutic use of art, giving rise to title claim by practitioners who have not undertaken professional training in arts therapies. Some are dependent on the sporadic short visits of foreign trainers who, even though well intentioned, are often far removed from the actual psycho-social context of India, be it clinical work or working with communities. These issues have given rise to ethical concerns around upholding the credibility and integrity of the profession, for unethical practice may lead to the misappropriation of arts therapy, and potentially end up "doing more harm than good" (Moon, 2006).

In response to this thought and in recognition of the interconnectedness of the creative arts therapies in India as a whole, the international creative arts therapies conference organised by CMTAI in Pune in 2019 provided the platform for an art therapy workshop, that brought together advanced level arts therapy practitioners, many of whom were pioneers from different parts of India, to co-create a common visionary pathway – *Adarshanapatha* for the field of creative arts therapy in India. There was unanimous agreement that developing formal training would be key to bridging the gap between therapists with professional training and practitioners without professional training, thereby creating inclusiveness and setting ethical standards for practice in India. An important finding of this initiative pointed to the need for an apex body that would become an umbrella organisation for all of the creative arts therapies for regulatory purposes in India (Chakrabarti, 2019c).

One possible explanation for this ethical standpoint in my view relates to Hocoy's (2002) observation that art therapy is culture bound, i.e., culturally situated. This factor plays an invisible role when the culture from which art therapy originates, in this case that of mainstream US or UK, is assumed to be universal and implicit (Hocoy, 2005), leaving India, perhaps, without defined or specific parameters. "Art therapy may be culture bound but it cannot afford to be culture blind" (Hocoy, 2002, p141), perpetuating a colonial view when it migrates to a new culture. Many art therapists have observed the prevalence of ethnocentrism embedded in Western art therapy education (Hocoy 2002; Talwar, Iyer and Dobey-Copeland, 2004). It is therefore important that Western theories and practices are not imposed onto a different cultural context.

In response to this idea, my doctoral research aims to co-create the first culturally relevant home-grown curriculum framework for masters level arts therapy training in India, arrived at via a Delphi consensus-based research study.

A Delphi study in its true essence encapsulates the spirit of the collective, one that is of the people, by the people and for the people as it is ethical, participatory and democratic. The Delphi method is particularly valuable for filling the evidence gap in low-income countries (Minas and Jorm, 2010) where otherwise there would be none. In such times, research relies on expert knowledge from practitioners working on the margins in the field. In this case, trained expert arts therapy practitioners were selected from the diverse modalities of creative arts therapies from a pan-India perspective, wherein they become both knowledge partners and stakeholders in the implementation of the training programme.

The findings of the research study (Chakrabarti, 2019b) helped identify certain gaps, and all research participants agreed that there was a need to draw a distinction between professional arts therapies and other art-based activity that may have therapeutic benefits. Moreover, there was unanimous agreement on the limitations of short-term courses and the need for a formal masters level professional training programme that is locally developed. Certain key findings from the research study point to significant majority thinking that it would be important to develop a creative arts therapy curriculum framework given that the arts are integrated in India (Vatsayan, 2008) along with culture specific pedagogy. In terms of indigenous components of a culturally relevant curriculum framework, respondents placed the highest importance on mental health issues, family/community systems, the use of play, indigenous art forms, Indian cultural expressions, for example, Navarasa, the nine-emotion framework used in Indian art forms and common to dance, drama, music and visual art.

There was emphasis on the need for skill sharing and a professional bridge course to make training accessible to practitioners who have not had the benefit of formal education, and the development of an ethical code of conduct for practising as a creative arts therapist was considered to be of the utmost importance. From these findings, it is evident that in terms of impact, this seminal study demonstrates the potential to transform the current landscape. Culturally developed training would be both an equaliser to creating inclusiveness in the true sense, bringing not-professionally-trained practitioners into the fold, and key to professionalising the field of creative arts therapy. Both would be critical to the development of arts therapies and their own distinct cultural identity in India and the wider global context, and for the overall field to gain professional recognition and acceptance within the Indian mental health ecosystem on a par with Indian and global standards.

I would like to conclude my piece with a powerful reflection by a research participant, envisioning components of the curriculum framework. She claimed,

> When I was painting this, it felt like there were so many patches and layers that needed to be considered. But those bits and parts were so much part of the circle. As these parts were the contributors in its own ways, it was important to hold on to it in a way it does not change its properties.

FIGURE 8.5 The parts that form the whole. O. Chakrabarti.

Although it is important to hold on to global best practices embedded in arts therapy, I believe in order for art therapy to be culturally relevant in India, it must go through a process of indigenisation and decolonisation to seek its own cultural identity. Only then can arts therapies realise its true potential and claim its own position to move from the margins to the centre in its new culture.

The way forward

In the past decade, there has been exponential growth in the developing field of creative arts therapies in India with the emergence of new voices in the field in different parts of the country. From the formation of Creative Movement

Therapy Association of India (2014), the Expressive Arts Therapy Association of India (2017), The Art Therapy Association of India (2019) and more recently the Indian Association of Dance Movement Therapy (2020), it is evident that a collective movement in the creative arts therapies is gathering momentum in India. Moreover, work is now underway to bring the arts therapies within the ambit of the Allied and Health Care Professional Bill in India with the collaborative efforts of TATAI and IADMT.

It is important to recognise that no single template will suffice in defining the arts therapies in a new culture, particularly one that is as diverse as India. The migration of arts therapies to different cultures of the globe also situates sojourners like ourselves at many ethical cross-roads compelling us to question which path we must walk, whether one charted by the founders of our fields or one invented by us as neo-pioneers. Given the VUCA world we currently inhabit, one that is volatile, uncertain, complex and ambiguous, perhaps it is time we embark in search of our own path in creating the future of creative arts therapies in India, one that we arrive upon with conscious thought, reflection and collective wisdom.

References

Art therapy in its Indian avatar: Genesis and development of the field in India - Oihika Chakrabarti (art psychotherapist)

Bajaj, T., & Vohra, S.S. (2015). *Performing arts and therapeutic implications.* India: Routledge.

Carlier, N.G., & Salom, A. (2012). When art therapy migrates: the acculturation challenges of sojourner art therapists. *Art Therapy: Journal of the American Art Therapy Association, 29* (1), pp.4–10. https://doi.org/10.1080/07421656.2012.648083

Chadda, R.K., & Deb, K.S. (2013). Indian family systems, collectivistic society and psychotherapy. *Indian Journal of Psychiatry,* 55 (Suppl 2), p.S299.

Chakrabarti, O. (2017). Genesis of a new cultural model: envisioning the scope for art therapy in India – a pioneering journey. In: Hougham, R., Pitruzella, S. and Scoble, S. (eds.) *Cultural landscapes in the arts therapies.* Plymouth, UK: University of Plymouth Press.

Chakrabarti, O. (2019a). From bystander to engaged witness: drawing the connection between social action and the scope for art therapy within the framework of social work in India. In: Huss, E. and Bos, E. (eds.) *Art in social work practice; theory and practice: international perspectives.* London: Routledge.

Hofstede, G. (2001). *Culture's consequences: comparing values, behaviours, institutions, and organisations across nations.* (2nd ed.). London: Sage Publications.

Ibbotson, P. (2008). *The illusion of leadership: directing creativity in business and the arts.* London: Palgrave Macmillan.

Subramaniyan, K.G. (1987). *The living tradition.* Kolkata, India: Seagull Publishers.

Waelde, M. (2008). *Does culture make a difference.* Kolkata, India: Seagull Publishers.

Westwood, J. (2012). Hybrid creatures: mapping the emerging shape of art therapy education in Australia, including reflections on New Zealand and Singapore. *Australian and New Zealand Journal of Arts Therapy,* 7 (1), pp.15–25.

Zhaveri, K. (2020). Healing roots of indigenous crafts: adapting traditions of India for art therapy practice. In: Leone, L. (ed.) *Craft in art therapy: diverse approaches to the transformative power of crafts materials and methods.* London: Routledge.

Dance movement therapy (DMT) in India with culture-specific focus on the therapeutic dance-in-education (TDIE) model - Tripura Kashyap (dance movement therapist)

Chakraborty, S. (2019). Featured counter-trafficking program: Kolkata Sanved's model *Sampoornata, Child abuse & neglect.* Elsevier. https://doi.org/10.1016/j.chiabu.2019.104169

Kashyap, T. (2005). *My body, my wisdom − a handbook of creative dance therapy,* India: Penguin.

Levy, F.J. (1988). *Dance movement therapy: a healing art.* Reston, Virginia: National Dance Association an association of the American Alliance for Health, Physical Education, Recreation, and Dance.

Manomohan, G, (1950). *The Natyasastra − a treatise on Hindu dramaturgy and histrionics ascribed to Bharata-Muni.* Volume I, Chapters I − XXVII. Royal Asiatic Society Publication.

Riordan, A. (1980). *A conceptual framework for teaching dance to the handicapped.* Reston, Virginia: The American Alliance for Health, Physical Education, Recreation and Dance.

Sharma, B. (1989). *Contemporary dance education in schools.* Paper presented at NCERT seminar to prepare guidelines for dance education in schools. Banglalore, India.

Zhou, T., Kim, N., Machida, S., Sakiyama, Y., Tsai, P.-S., Lee, T., Hung Ho, R., Bijlani, R., Mehta, D., & Bui, M. (2019). Dance movement therapy in Asia: an overview of the profession and its practice. *Creative Arts in Education and Therapy,* 5 (1), pp.40–50. https://caet.inspirees.com/caetojsjournals/index.php/caet/article/view/172

Dramatherapy in India: a snapshot - Maitri Gopalakrishna (dramatherapist)

Casson, J. (1993). Dramatherapy in India. *Dramatherapy,* 15 (3), pp.17–21. http://doi.org/10.1080/02630672.1993-1994.9689361

Chabukswar, A., & Balsara, Z. (2016). Converging lineages: arts-based therapy in contemporary India. In: Jennings, S. & Holmwood, C. (eds.), *The Routledge international handbook of dramatherapy* (pp.19–25). London: Routledge.

Chakrabarti, O., (2019b). *Shilpanjali − A creative arts therapy offering: development of a culturally relevant arts therapy masters level curriculum framework for India.* Paper presented at BAAT & AATA International Art Therapy Practice Research conference, July 11–13, 2019; London, UK.

Gopalakrishna, M. (2018). *Pliable and playable: drama therapy, women's narratives and childhood sexual abuse (unpublished doctoral thesis).* Tata Institute of Social Sciences, Mumbai, India.

Gopalakrishna, M., & Rao, S. (2017). Performance, revelation and resistance: interweaving the artistic and the therapeutic in devised theatre. *Indian Theatre Journal,* 1 (1), 83–90. http://doi.org/10.1386/itj.1.1.83

Sajnani, N., & Gopalakrishna, M. (2017). Rasa: exploring the influence of Indian performance theory in drama therapy. *Drama Therapy Review,* 3 (2), 225–240. http://doi.org/10.1386/dtr.3.2.225

A brief glimpse of music therapy in India and its cross-cultural application in the Indian context - Nina Cherla (music therapist)

Chadda, R.K., & Deb, K.S. (2013). Indian family systems, collectivistic society and psychotherapy. *Indian Journal of Psychiatry,* 55 (Suppl 2), p.S299.

Futamata, I. (2005). Things Asian music therapists should learn. *Voices: A World Forum for Music Therapy,* 5 (1).

Hicks, J. (2020). February. The history, current role, and future of music therapy in India: international interviews with Prof. Dr. Sumathy Sundar and Aastha Luthra. *Voices: A World Forum for Music Therapy,* 20 (1).

Kaliyaperumal, R., & Subash, J.G. (2010). Effect of music therapy for patients with cancer pain. *International Journal of Biological Medicine Research*, 1 (3), pp.79–81.

Kim, S., & Whitehead-Pleaux, A. (2015). Music therapy and cultural diversity. *Music Therapy Handbook*, pp.51–63.

Konstandinidi, E., & Cherla, N. (2018) MILNA – Meeting in Music, Interacting, Listening and Adapting – an intensive music therapy programme for families. Poster presented at: BAMT Conference 2018, Music, Diversity and Wholeness, February 16–18, 2018; London, UK.

Neki, J.S. (1992). Confidentiality, secrecy, and privacy in psychotherapy: sociodynamic considerations. *Indian Journal of Psychiatry*, 34 (3), p.171.

Nizamie, S.H., & Tikka, S.K. (2014). Psychiatry and music. *Indian Journal of Psychiatry*, 56 (2), p.128.

Rohilla, L., Agnihotri, M., Trehan, S.K., Sharma, R.K., & Ghai, S. (2018). Effect of music therapy on pain perception, anxiety, and opioid use during dressing change among patients with burns in India: a quasi-experimental, cross-over pilot study. *Ostomy Wound Manage*, 64 (10), pp.40–46.

Roy, B. (2011). Understanding India's sociological diversity, unity in diversity and caste system in contextualizing a global conservation model. *International Journal of Sociology and Anthropology*, 3 (12), pp.440–451.

Sundar, S. (2006). How to introduce standards for competent music therapy, education and training in countries where music therapy is in an early stage of development. *Voices World Forum Music Therapy*, 6 (2), p.1.

Sundar, S. (2015). Music therapy education in India: developmental perspectives. *International Perspectives in Music Therapy Education and Training: Adapting to a Changing World. Springfield, IL: Charles C Thomas*, pp.202–16.

Sundar, S., & Sairam, T.V. (2006). Therapeutical usefulness of music. Conference proceedings of the 1st international conference, 15 January 2006, Nada Centre for Music Therapy, Chennai, India. *Music Therapy Today*, 7, pp.106–52

Wfmt.info. 2019. [online] Available at: https://www.wfmt.info/wp-content/uploads/2019/01/Fact-Page_India-2019.pdf. [Accessed 1 December 2020].

Wigram, T. (2004) Improvisation: Methods and techniques for music therapy clinicians, educators, and students. London, UK: Jessica Kingsley Publishers.

The game changer: decolonizing arts therapies and the creation of culturally relevant professional training in India - Oihika Chakrabarti (art psychotherapist)

Chakrabarti, O. (2017). Genesis of a new cultural model: envisioning the scope for art therapy in India – a pioneering journey. In: Hougham, R., Pitruzella, S. and Scoble, S. (eds.) *Cultural landscapes in the arts therapies*. Plymouth, UK: University of Plymouth Press.

Chakrabarti, O. (2019b). *Shilpanjali – A Creative Arts Therapy Offering: Development of a Culturally Relevant Arts Therapy Masters Level Curriculum Framework for India*. Paper presented at: BAAT & AATA International Art Therapy Practice Research conference, July 11–13, 2019; London, UK.

Chakrabarti, O. (2019c). *Adarshanapatha – Co-creating a common visionary pathway for creative arts therapy in India*. Advanced workshop session at: CMTAI 6th Annual International conference, November 30th – December 1st, 2019; Pune, India.

Moon, B. (2006). *Ethical issues in art therapy*. 2nd ed. Springfield, IL: Charles C. Thomas Publisher, Ltd..

Hocoy, D. (2002). Cross-cultural issues in art therapy. *Art Therapy*, 19 (4), pp.141–145.

Hocoy, D. (2005). Art therapy and social action: a transpersonal framework. *Art Therapy*, 22 (1), pp.7–16.

Minas, H., & Jorm, A.F. (2010). Where there is no evidence: use of expert consensus methods to fill the evidence gap in low-income countries and cultural minorities. *International Journal of Mental Health Systems*, 4 (1), p.33. https://doi.org/10.1186/1752-4458-4-33

Talwar, S., Iyer, J., & Doby-Copeland, C. (2004). The invisible veil: changing paradigms in the art therapy profession. *Art Therapy*, 21 (1), pp.44–48.

Vatsayan, K. (2008). Retrieving a vision. 52nd (sixth) Ed. New Delhi: Indian Literature, Sahitya Akademi, pp.204–210.

9

TRUST, ART THERAPY AND CARE

An art therapy experience at three community health centres

*Ana Serrano Navarro, Tania Ugena Candel,
Andrea López Iglesias*

Abstract

Reality can be a non-place, where our inner imagined and desired image collapses. In contrast, within a safe place, art therapy helps to co-create, offers a new chance for feeling truly and personally connected to interact with others. In his own particular crusade, Don Quixote's struggles have the sense of justice and longed-for freedom winning through. To do this, his nobility and his true compassion are placed at the service of those whose paths he crosses in his adventures. However, he does not ride alone: he is accompanied by Sancho. Between reality and fantasy, his search, like anyone else's, moves back and forth between the nooks and crannies of reality and the expanse of idealism, which can cast him into the abyss of the impossible. In the balance between the two, life unfolds and health blooms.

This chapter presents the theoretical framework and some of the conclusions of an art therapy programme designed, implemented and evaluated in three Madrid City Council community health centres (Madrid's Municipal Madrid City of Health Care Plan). From 2017 to 2018, 39 workshops targeting the young and adolescent population, groups of women, elderly people, people with autism spectrum disorder, people with functional diversity and mental health groups took place with the participation of 340 people.

Looking at the workshops for women, this programme facilitated art therapy self-care group spaces to promote health through accompanied creative processes and created support networks among participants, institutions and health agents. With the aim of minimising the discomforts of everyday life, confidence-building and mutual care were included in the conceptual basis to evoke and reinforce epistemic trust in the above agents, trying to balance inequalities caused by gender as a social determinant in health.

DOI: 10.4324/9781003110200-9

The methodological design was based on interdisciplinary teamwork with healthcare professionals, as well as reality analysis, continuous assessment, confidentiality and respect. Other conceptual keys were participatory action research, process cross-disciplinarity, the art therapist practitioner as a guide and support worker, the exploration of different techniques and artistic materials and the symbolic and metaphorical value of productions. They are all part of the triple interconnection between art therapist, workshop/artwork and participant/group, underpinned by the museum as a health agent in the incorporation of new methodologies for promoting health and care.

Moods, anxiety, stress and depression, self-esteem, loneliness, general satisfaction, group cohesion and interpersonal relationships were observed and evaluated through mixed research methods, which is in itself an indicator of the lack of specific methodological art therapy tools.

As regards the professional development and establishment of art therapy in Spain, we focused on the implementation process, the identity of art therapists as co-researchers and the methodological design problems (related to both research and art therapy praxis in this context). They highlighted the need to question the foundations of community-based art therapy.

Keywords: care, trust, confidence, community-based art therapy, gender perspective in art therapy, social determinants in health

Abstract in Spanish

La realidad puede ser un no-lugar, en el que nuestra imagen interior, imaginada y deseada, se derrumba. Ese lugar seguro que la arteterapia ayuda a co-crear, ofrece una nueva oportunidad de sentirse verdadera y personalmente conectado para interactuar con los otros. En su particular cruzada, Don Quijote lucha para que triunfe el sentido de la justicia y la ansiada libertad. Para ello, su nobleza y su verdadera compasión se ponen al servicio de aquellos cuyos caminos cruza en sus aventuras. Sin embargo, no cabalga solo: le acompaña Sancho. "Entre la realidad y la fantasía," su búsqueda, como la de cualquier otra persona, va y viene entre los recovecos de la realidad y la extensión del idealismo, lo que puede arrojarle al abismo de lo imposible. En el equilibrio entre ambos, la vida se despliega y la salud florece.

En este capítulo se presenta el marco teórico y algunas conclusiones de un programa de arteterapia diseñado, implementado y evaluado en tres centros de salud comunitaria del Ayuntamiento de Madrid. Entre 2017 y 2018 se llevaron a cabo 39 talleres dirigidos a población joven y adolescente, grupos de mujeres, personas mayores, personas con trastorno del espectro autista, personas con diversidad funcional y grupos de salud mental, con la participación de un total de 340 personas.

En cuanto a los talleres para mujeres, este programa facilitó espacios arteterapéuticos grupales de autocuidado y expresión, para promover la salud a través de procesos creativos acompañados, creando redes de apoyo entre los participantes, las instituciones y los agentes de salud. Con el objetivo de minimizar los malestares de la vida cotidiana, se incluyó en su base conceptual, la construcción de relaciones de confianza y cuidado mutuo para evocar y reforzar la confianza epistémica en los agentes mencionados, tratando de equilibrar las desigualdades causadas por el género como determinante social en la salud.

El diseño metodológico se basó en el trabajo en equipo interdisciplinar con los profesionales sanitarios, así como en el análisis de la realidad, la evaluación continua, la confidencialidad y el respeto. Otras claves conceptuales fueron la investigación-acción participativa, la interdisciplinariedad del proceso, la figura de la arteterapeuta como guía y acompañante, la exploración de diferentes técnicas y materiales artísticos y el valor simbólico y metafórico de las producciones. Todos ellos forman parte de la triple interconexión entre arteterapeuta, taller/obra de arte y grupo/participante, apuntalada por el museo como agente de salud en la incorporación de nuevas metodologías de promoción de la salud y del cuidado a través de la arteterapia.

Los estados de ánimo, la ansiedad, el estrés y la depresión, la autoestima, la soledad, la satisfacción general, la cohesión del grupo y las relaciones interpersonales se observaron y evaluaron a través de métodos de investigación mixtos, lo que es en sí mismo un indicador de la falta de herramientas metodológicas específicas en arteterapia.

En cuanto al desarrollo profesional y la implantación de la arteterapia en España, nos centramos en el proceso de implementación, la identidad de las arteterapeutas como co-investigadoras y los problemas y limitaciones en el diseño metodológico (relacionados tanto con la investigación como con la praxis arteterapéutica en este contexto). Se puso de manifiesto la necesidad de cuestionar los fundamentos de la arteterapia basada en la comunidad.

What is *possible* in a community?

Part of this chapter was written in times of COVID-19, a transnational pandemic that has placed the need for care and attention to human values at the centre of "what is possible" (Fiorini, 2007) in our daily work and lives. Everything has been put on hold so that other values and behaviours can emerge to provide people with a space where they can act to create confidence and well-being.

In its 2019 report (Fancourt and Finn, 2019), the World Health Organisation recognised the importance and the need for art in health over the span of people's lifetimes. It states that "the arts can potentially impact both mental and physical health." Based on a systematic review of over 900 publications, it distinguishes between two major areas: "prevention and promotion, and management and treatment." The findings identify common ideas sustained by this art therapy programme, affirming that the arts can "affect the social determinants of health, support child development, encourage health-promoting behaviours, help to prevent illnesses, support caregiving" (p.7). Without a doubt, art plays a fundamental role at a time when we are facing the inevitable impact of this pandemic.

Our institutions should provide care for us. Artistic practices, like artistic therapies, have a potential for providing integral improvement, personal reconstruction and the search for a profound, vital meaningfulness. While it was necessary
in a pre-COVID times, it is now vital and pressing.

As human beings and art therapists, we realise that reality can be experienced
subjectively as a non-place where one cannot be oneself, where one does not
belong, where the construction of our internal self-image collapses. Feedback
from a young student (a teenager, unconnected with the field of creative therapy, psychotherapy or psychology) reflecting on the meaning of Don Quixote in
this text provided insight that made us connect directly with the essence of our
delicate work as companions: she perceived Don Quixote as a dreamer, someone
who sees life differently to others.

As dreamers and female art therapists, the idea of freedom amplifies the ability
to imagine a life of possibilities as, according to Kieran Egan (1992), "being able
to modify the world around us in the way that we find desirable and satisfying
is certainly an important skill" (p.38). Often, when confronted with reality,
the need to imagine emerges strongly, where pure creation makes life worth
living. Egan establishes a direct relationship between imaginativeness and the
strength to relinquish everything to which we have become accustomed (p.38).
This includes pain, vulnerability, lack of resources and opportunities, gender
aspects and others.

It would, therefore, appear to be essential to bring into play the ability to
imagine our most intimate feelings, our true self, but also what we represent in
the mind of someone else, someone with whom we can connect, within a trustworthy world in which we can show our true face. It would also appear to be
important to be able to dream that such a safe place is possible, however Quixotic
it may seem, and feel capable of creating it from our own health. In art therapy,
this is a team effort involving at least two people who come together to build a
new version of a personal story. And, from an updated, practice-based, ecological
and feminist perspective of attachment theory, this bonding protects.

From this same perspective, the psychiatrist and psychoanalyst, Efrain Bleiberg
(2019),[1] pointed out that the restoration, among people, among ourselves and
within the community, of trust and the desire to care for one another is what
can "save the world." From this relational standpoint, art therapy is effective at
enabling art to provide a new opportunity for us to feel truly interconnected,
to play and create along with others and be a part of the global community.
Likewise, Winnicott (1971) referred to psychotherapy as "that overlapping of two
play areas: that of the patient and that of the therapist," an intermediate area in
which the art therapist nourishes and enriches the person's growth where it may
have been inhibited or blocked. In *Medicina Humana*, Hess and Hess-Cabalzar
(2008) also refer to therapy as the sense experience whereby people:

> Can recognise how they move through the world, how to enter frankly
> into their lives and how to develop within the framework of their particu-
> lar relationships and conditions. This allows self-awareness to develop, a

transfer from invisible to visible, it helps to form a new perception of one's own existence, a new, liberating project for life.

(Hess and Hess-Cabalzar, 2008, p.137)

This text describes the inception of a methodology designed by three art therapists that connects with the essence of art therapy as a space for creation and freedom, of dignity, a place where one can be oneself, look at oneself, confront a subjective change. This should enable people to sketch out a meaningful life project in which they can be active, responsible actors, a life project in which they can open up and join the network of affection and caring represented by others and feel part of that network. It is a space of multiple relationships in which art therapists, as Yalom (2001) predicated, should tell their patients that their principal task is to construct, jointly, a relationship that in itself will become an agent of change (p.52).

The art therapy programme takes place in a context of prevention and promotion of health by Madrid City Council, where there is a profound debate about the need for prevention rather than treatment that contemplates the singularity of feeling ill. This means avoiding medicalisation and restoring people's ability to make decisions about their lives (Del Cura and López García-Franco, 2008, p.10). At this point, we should ask ourselves as community art therapists how we can accompany our patients (Dannecker, 2017) in that context and in a differentiated way. Dannecker, a German art therapist, subtly refers to the concept a "third hand," first identified by Edith Kramer in 1982 as the best way to name the specific competences of an art therapist, reaffirming the methodological basis of the discipline, three decades after it was formulated. It alludes to artistic accompaniment with the appropriate measure of empathy and aesthetic-artistic resonance, underpinned by psychoanalytic theories and the transference-countertransference relationship, which creation alone does not reach.

Over and above the methodological limitations of this study, 340 persons attended 39 workshops over a two-year period, including all ages from children to the elderly. They presented a variety of life circumstances in accordance with this wide spectrum. Women proved to be the most vulnerable population in an urban and productive setting, from which they feel systematically alienated either by their origin, their professional status, the absence of development opportunities, maternity, diseases, their jobs as informal caregivers and many other traumatic experiences associated with their sexual or gender identity. Gender is thus identified as a *social determinant of health* insofar as, according to Hogan (2016), "individuals are shaped by their social context" (p.108) which generates illness in their own relationships and structures. She refers to it as "socioeconomic determinants" (Hogan, 2013, p.417) as well as gender as those aspects that generates progressive discrimination.

This was the reason why the art therapy groups involving women were constituted as self-help, caring and healthy spaces via an accompanied creative process, generating interpersonal and inter-institutional joint-task networks that restored within the subjects self-confidence and confidence in the institutions offering care.

They were systematically told to explore the materials and the techniques, to pay attention to the symbolic value of their productions and to listen to the metaphors. They were asked to explore the three-way dynamic interconnection between the person, their creation and the art therapists within the group interrelationship. Communal spaces and art galleries were integrated as agents of health. They were encouraged to reconsider, beyond the previous symptoms or pathologies, their own experiences as a new creative project, thus recovering their silenced voices as a dreamer would do, as a window open to personal change.

Against this backdrop, subjectivity permeates the questioning of the personal-professional relationship, inviting professionals to ask what stand they should take, as art therapists in the field of health and community, with regard to this panorama and consolidate our field to gain recognition for art therapy as a professional discipline in Spain.

Convergence of community-based art therapy and gender perspective

This convergence is present from the start, although there are two different layers: the direct experience with people, as a field from which to gather relevant data, and the clear establishment of a professional identity in a health context inhabited by other disciplines, unfamiliar with the theory and methods of art therapy. "The incorporation of a feminist framework" (Hahna, 2013) implies, in practice, the adoption standpoint. However, we must work to visualise and understand any emerging inequality narratives in the awareness of differences related to personal identity, privilege or oppression conditions or race issues. The medical system has inherited a patriarchal theoretical model that requires revision from an art therapy standpoint. Art therapist, Susan Hogan, adopts a critical and feminist viewpoint in her work that directly influences ours. She stated that "Art therapy must develop a culturally-aware practice which will maintain a critical relationship to the discipline of psychology in order to avoid oppressing women with misogynistic discourses which are embedded in theories and practices" (Hogan, 2013, p.415). In this sense, not only should female art therapists consider these significant (social, political and so on) differences but also issues arising from women's discourses in art therapy groups.

This implies seeing the group as a subjective space (Aguiló and Losada, 2015, p.2). The working group model, on which the methodology of this research is based, goes beyond its instrumental conception (as developed by Kurt Lewin) towards a social space (as developed by Pichon Rivière). Esteban and Távora (2010) delve into this device from a gender perspective in which new relationships make "members feel that they have more autonomy, embarking on a process to discover what you are like, what you like, what you want and what you do not want, and placing themselves in the central role" (p.13). From there, they can review the network of emotional connections that is at the root of the inequality and subordination around which their life work evolves.

In an attempt to overcome this welfare and individualistic approach, what is said, what is thought, the discontent and the silences in these groups are heard by engaging various professionals, the subject, the group as a symbolic and dynamic space, and the community as a space for its development. The dynamic space is determined by the way in which possible difficulties, resistances or anxieties are faced together, based on the principle of combined directionality of the work or task. Although both feminist authors see the therapeutic group as a turning point and engine for change, they salvage the value of "networks of friends" (p.17) as "privileged spaces of sociability, reciprocal love and momentum for change." It is not unusual to find in the testimonies of the programme participants the feeling of having found a group like this through community art therapy.

As community art therapists, it is not easy to establish a balanced position in this situation, since overlapping objectives make it difficult to find the individual, group and community change indicators, given that the work in the Municipal of Community Health Centres (MCHC) is essentially group-oriented.

Reflections on the differences between group art therapy or the art therapy community device are not uncommon. This is largely due to the research position taken in this project that led the professionals to understand human relationships and attachments as a metaphor of society, and its potential for self-creation and self-recreation, turning the artistic productions into something more than the created products, where belonging, affection, care and meaning emerge as key elements within the art therapy workshop. The group becomes the field of action where the human being brings his or her relational needs into play. From there, the community expands its scope, affecting the prospects of establishing and building a kind of relationship based on care. There is also the issue of what Gysin and Sorin refers to as "how transgressive and dangerous" (2011, p.63) the community group can be in these times because it questions the institutional model of individualistic relations. In her words:

> The group space – according to the devices used for its deployment – introduces doubts about invisible certainties; as they are so stunning; the creative versus the conformist; there you learn to contain and to be contained; to open your ears; to challenge and to be challenged, in a permanent spiral of interrogation and self-interrogation.
>
> *(p.63)*

Therefore, the investigation of how transformative the affection and care that art therapy spaces promote can be a complex task in which we are co-producers of meanings and senses without ceasing to pay attention to ourselves. As López Fernández-Cao (2018) points out, "by joining the group, art separates itself from those collective experiences that alienate individuality and make us no different from the rest" (p.31).

Corral et al. (2017) discuss the difficulty of community work with the strength of the coordinating team supporting the action research, and which is only maintained based on "principles, values and shared reflection" (p.4). Accordingly, as art therapists in a community, we must take special care of own beliefs, values and emotions. It became necessary to think deeply about what Kapitan (2010) defined as the *worldview* of art therapists, their "looking glasses," and to define what they pay attention to, what determines the aspects that differentiate the benefits inherent to this discipline. The accompanied creative process and the structural role of art are what seem to define our concept of the therapy. But we work with people within a community that they intend to transform with their resilient resources, inviting us to be a part of it. We should also think about what we understand by research when we are working with people. Kapitan suggests that the researcher role may be a tinted lens through which we view and understand what we see and how this relates to the cultural context from which it emerges (Kapitan, 2010, p.35) for validation. From this viewpoint, which is tolerant of cultural difference, research is a creative process that emerges from a multiple, diverse and group experience. The wealth contributed by women in discussion groups and interviews as qualitative data, provided us with a better insight into what Holmes and Meyerhoff (1999) called "the relationship between language and gender" (p.174). A similar thing applies to the work team inter-views understood as community of practice, where these authors point out three main dimensions (from a sociolinguist's perspective): mutual engagement, joint enterprise and shared repertoire. These three aspects lead groups of women and interdisciplinary teams, which they think of as formal structures, to find evidence of a gender bias as the main path to meaningful learning.

Based on collective experiments that generate knowledge and social change, Kapitan et al. (2011) refer to the capacity demonstrated by people to see, reflect and convert themselves into the artifices of their own development becoming co-researchers, and strengthening their own personal, spiritual and social development, with an impact on the community.

Our link with the Aletheia: Art, Art Therapy, Trauma and Emotional Memory research project, directed by Marian López Fernández Cao at the Complutense University of Madrid, expanded this viewpoint by delving into the gender and feminist perspective and including an interpretation of the traumatic imprint found in especially painful experiences.

Community art therapy based on a model of preventive health

Given the lack of national references, it was necessary to look at international authors who have conceptualised the notion of community art therapy. The literature describes the increasing expansion of this practice in inclusive settings, centred on well-being and on non-traditional community services that expand the application of this discipline beyond the limits of clinical practice (Kapitan et al., 2011; Ottemiller and Awais, 2016; Timm-Bottos, 2011; Slayton, 2012; Feen-Calligan, Moreno and Buzzard, 2018; Miranda et al., 2019).

Community-based art therapy emphasises the empowerment of the community, rather than the traditional individual psycho-dynamic focus, providing a vehicle for community needs and strengths. It represents a growing tendency towards a preventive service, inclusive and centred on the arts, that increases the scope of the practice and requires professionals with a significant understanding of the needs and knowledge inherent to these environments (Ottemiller and Awais, 2016; Feen-Calligan, Moreno and Buzzard, 2018).

The aim is to attend communities as well as individuals, while serving to redefine and adjust the practice of art therapy (Golub, 2005; Kapitan et al., 2011; Kaplan, 2007; Timm-Bottos, 2017; Feen-Calligan, Moreno and Buzzard, 2018). Art is identified as a form of personal transformation, community development and political expression (Kaplan, 2007).

This is a relevant vision in the art therapy programme. Although it was conducted using art therapy group interventions to develop a stable relationship, the programme maintained individual-group-community interaction that allowed many people who would not normally fit into the centre intervention designs to reconnect. Recruitment was patchy and involved knocking on the doors of healthcare resources for women, child associations and family labour, public educational centres, mental health services, specific social guarantee programmes, etc. But it was also spread by word of mouth, working from within the neighbourhood and with the people to design made-to-measure care and safe spaces.

As stated by Kapitan, a community-based approach may attract people who live outside the mainstream, who have little contact with the formal mental health services or who are not satisfied with the way they are treated when they try to use them (Kapitan, 2008 cited in Gray, 2012). Timm-Bottos (2011. p.63) states that "Community art therapy acknowledges that the fabric of culture provides the necessary healing context for individual healing, therapeutic art making, and transformative community dialogue."

Additionally, Slayton (2012) refers to the same individual-group-community continuum, indicating that, in these spaces, individuals who rarely express their internal worlds succeed in doing so in the workspace of group art therapy. In view of some individual indicators evaluated in this programme, the literature provides evidence that artistic creation promotes independence, competence and belonging, three key components of well-being. Thus, social justice and individual well-being enter into an organic dialogue in the generation of safe, inclusive spaces for relational transformation and significant action (Timm-Bottos, 2011).

Art therapy in a Madrid City Council community setting

There are precedents for the incorporation of art therapists in Madrid City Council that link the arts to the field of health. The CurArte R&D: Favouring the Improvement of Health project commenced in 2003 as a collaboration between the Complutense University and the University of Salamanca (Valdés, 2013).

Valdés (2013) based her design on international references such as the Centre for Arts and Humanities in Health and Medicine (CAHHM), at Durham University Multidisciplinary School of Health and the National Network for the Arts in Health, both based in the United Kingdom. This is a position in which art is a mediator of personal and collective creation processes, a generator of meaningful experiences led by artists and artistic mediators with a special sensitivity to understanding the underlying narratives in groups. These are likely to be approached from art and its languages, from the knowledge that artists provide to promote health; but they are not subjective change processes as we understand them in the art therapy framework.

In 2017, art therapy was included in Madrid Salud programme. This implied questioning and redefining the traditional art therapy concepts (Rubin, 2016) to find an ethical and flexible way to give a sufficiently consistent response based on accompanied creation. That "third hand" comes into play in order to understand the difference in the art therapist's perspective of art, in which creative processes seek to recover everything that is still healthy in the being. This necessary and special triangular relationship, pervaded by the imprint of our previous experiences of relationships and affections, takes on body and voice, giving people a glimpse of previously unimagined or undreamed of opportunity.

Héctor Fiorini[2] points out that traditional psychoanalytic theoretical development (based on authors such as Freud and Klein) was still mainly based on psychopathology, which was highlighted with respect to people's health. People were regarded as being unable to transform their discontent, which was one of the reasons that led him to develop his cliché of the creative psyche. According to Fiorini, Sartre and existential philosophy retrieved the idea of a life project that would lead the subject out of his or her vital pain and to find the "overcoming forces" (as Bachelard worded it) that would allow him to do so.

Art therapy can be community-based as both approaches (art therapy and community development) share a salutogenic position on the understanding of the human being and its potential for improvement and development, enhancing people's control over their own health-disease processes. The understanding of how and where they appear is broadened and underpinned by social determinants of health, in particular gender. This salutogenic understanding of the direction of the work to be carried out in collaboration with the person is structural for art therapy, and implies a distinguishing feature of the discipline in care institutions.

Art therapy experiences involving women

As mentioned above, guided by the social determinants in health theory, women in especially vulnerable situations were selected as the target population. Eighty-four women participated in the art therapy programme carried out in the three MCHCs (located in three districts of Madrid) in 2017 and 2018, with ages ranging from 14 to 81. Processes included visits to art museums as a part of a community perspective model that can be used by women as social, political and participatory spaces. At the same time, as community (and relational) art therapists, we adopted an active position. Gerlitza, Regeva and Snirb (2020) described this position as:

> Being active partners: asking questions, sharing thoughts and feelings, assisting in the selection of materials, demonstrating artistic techniques,

being involved in the art-making or participating as an art maker were mentioned by all as a way to help clients to express themselves.

(p.3)

The groups in the three districts differed widely. Nevertheless, all women perceived art therapy as a real and symbolic safe space. They could listen and communicate through the art prism: drawing themselves, generating personal narratives from paintings or breaking down and reconstructing pieces of art-works to symbolise their inner energy. This way, they were encouraged to and were able to see themselves in a new light. This is what Esteban and Távora (2010) meant by the fact that placement locates the person in the central role, as an object of their own work and creation.

The women managed a transition from the individual to the group setting and were able to share their experiences of abuse, illness, loneliness, break-ups, migrations, motherhood or infertility, etc. They found new meanings and recon-structed their life projects, positively integrating into their narrative emotions that caused them distress or feelings of guilt or loneliness. There, where words were useless, art symbols through creative processes, helped their hands and souls express their repressed emotional and internal conflicts. They finally recognised the need for a new space that would enable them to speak for themselves in a community from which they somehow felt excluded.

The possibility of working with a wide range of age groups allowed us to capture an intergenerational variable among groups that clearly highlighted gen-der and oppressive discourses. Women repeat behavioural patterns that artistic reflection makes visible. In sessions with young women, based on sensorimotor psychotherapy (Odgen et al., 2009; 2016), participants created self-portraits using mirrors to help them look at things from different angles and spy the possibility for change.

Physical workouts were included in art therapy sessions to help create aware-ness of the influence of the body on emotions and exercise fundamental internal resources: alignment, self-orientation, bonding, establishing roots, breathing and safe corporal limits. This emotional and physical knowledge of their own self, along with art creation (self-portraits) amplifies self-perception and identity.

Older women were able to regard care as a personal and political search, as a social construction of the role of women. Personal identity emerged in their creations: painting maternity or abuse served to name a silenced image of them-selves and played an emancipatory role. Migrant women were able to tend to unhealed wounds by drawing their truncated expectations, showing deep grief and suffering in a distant reality.

Using each participant's personal resources as a starting point, group creations emerged as memory landscapes. It included puppets to fix and symbolise a pres-ent and new position, juxtaposing present and future perspectives.

The ages in the life continuum were represented across the three centres, which reinforced how gender can still be considered a social determinant for health, due to a systematic neglect of health, social, educational policies, etc., in Spain and, presumably, globally. Thus, recent research in Spain indicates that:

> the highest prevalence of poor mental health [is] in women of all ages and of all social groups, and there is also a multiplier effect due to the accumulation of experiences of inequality.
>
> *(Bacigalupe et al., 2020, p.6)*

The impact of this therapy is greater, due to counter-transference dynamics, where mostly female art therapists are in charge of developing therapies for the health of everyone, delving into the socio-political roots of women's suffering. Supervision and personal therapy is essential, as is the solid support of interdisciplinary work teams that understand and share the rationale and methodologies to be developed.

Some testimonials from the results of the intervention based on an interdisciplinary model

The art therapy programme adheres to Madrid City Council Healthy District's ethical code of conduct. The experience appears to show that the qualitative method is the most suitable for retrieving non-quantifiable elements that nevertheless validate the intervention. In line with the fundamental theoretical principles, the outcomes differentiate the art therapy intervention from others in which art, its languages and processes are also present.

The cosmogony referred to in the theoretical framework appeared in the responses of the professionals interviewed to the question: "What does an art therapist practitioner contribute to the team and to the services provided in the Community Health Improvement Centres?" We identified the category of team collaboration and integration: "The art therapist is an indispensable and primary practitioner within the centre's project as regards both group and community activities, as well as with regard to contributions to the team that are inspired from a totally different viewpoint compared to the professional profile that the health centres used up until now."

In relation to the changes seen in the application of quantitative scales to measure states of mind, meaning of life, etc., the short term of some of the interventions promoted a significant change towards more depressive positions that could not be accompanied throughout their development. However, they were directly related to better personal awareness, more self-knowledge and understanding of the resource-difficulties binomial, as well as the medium-term possibilities for their transformation, with the idea of the community as a space devoted to care still in the early stages of development.

With regard to networks of women woven into art therapy groups and their potential for change, they also recognised the contributions of the art therapy process in the group setting: "Uncovering ourselves through art, through the painting and the group sessions, we have revealed many things that were hidden there in a corner of our hearts"; "Role changing, knowing someone in a different way to how they normally appear... growing individually inside the group, we can change, above all when the group accepts us as we are."

With reference to the need to place women at the centre of community work as health assets and resilient (as well as vulnerable) agents, we can perceive, as a result of the art therapy process used, an increased focus on themselves: "we can use [art therapy] to analyse ourselves and to propose solutions"; a greater acceptance of their life history: "in the works, I expel the ugly things that I had, things that have happened to me"; and improved comprehension: "finding out that I can do things that I thought I never could [...], leaving behind my fear, being able to look at myself."

Concerning the model of community-based interdisciplinary teams and the possibility of art therapist integration, an analysis of the narrative of the team's responses concludes that acceptance was enormous: art therapy has proved to be a "renewing and stimulating approach," while, at the same time, professionals recognised "the importance of consolidating the art therapists as another practitioner within the MCHCs." These considerations are crucial, since they corroborate the value of a largely unknown profession within the area of public health in Spain, as well as its transversal functionality and multiple applications across work teams.

Conclusions

From this significant experience, it can be said that part of the task was to juggle with the problems with regard to the differences that we found between the real needs and demands of MCHC users, the recruitment process to set up the groups and coordination with the district's network of resources. Often women came to groups with the desire to be somewhere else where they could calmly connect and were able to listen to others and to themselves. Beyond that, there were unresolved grieving processes, situations of long periods of traumatic experiences and of deprivation, possible situations of parental abuse and neglect, and many other circumstances that had apparently not been the driving force behind their seeking out art therapy spaces. There is a need for qualified professional art therapists who can embrace sensitivity and support, accompanying women in their genuine desire to be who they want to be in their lives. From a feminist and anthropological approach, Hogan reminds us that humans everywhere "employ their bodies in expressing complicated, contradictory or hostile sentiments" (Scheper-Hughes, 1991, p.6. cited in Hogan, 2013, p.419).

Although the need for emotional support and sympathy of women with traumatic life experiences was evident in all three districts, this necessity had to be adjusted in a way that did not always accommodate demand, since many of these women were so psychologically damaged that they refused professional help. The very circumstances behind their need for these spaces of care and transformation prevented them from advancing further in their personal work. This increased the spiral of vulnerability in which they are embedded. Parallel work with institutions is necessary to detect possible gender intersections that are holding back the power of community networking, as well as perpetuating hegemonic inequalities among professionals, as well as between professionals and users.

On multiple occasions, it was evident that the assistance and care resources, as well as the lack of family support, did not favour their continued attendance either. This widens the gap that separates their real needs from access to spaces where they can transform them into resilient resources and self-care.

Consequently, we also found that it was easier to work with groups set up in collaboration with other organisations as regards attendance, adherence and regularity with respect to the art therapy process. When recruitment was carried out at the centre, life experiences made it harder, if not impossible, for participants to commit to attending, participating and not dropping out of the group. These difficulties, which led some of the group to regularly attend the workshops while others did so only sporadically, have methodological implications that highlighted the group as a symbolic space.

Regarding the development of community art therapy in our country, the absence of systematised national references that have been shared within the scientific literature is an obstacle to the necessary trial-and-error process through which any methodology passes in its early stages. Instead, the groups and the community itself generate and co-construct knowledge from their own experience. Therefore, it is especially encouraging to note that, globally, the fundamental group and community relational and bonding concepts and theories emerging from participatory reflection and action are shared.

Studying and implementing community art therapy experiences allows us to address and nurture the extensive discussion and clarification of the existing limits between the different art and health practices. It is necessary to make a distinction between artistic practices, artistic mediation and art therapy; it is evident that, with regard to art therapy, the clinical training of art therapists is different, and there is a narrow understanding of the potential of art for subjective change. This cannot be addressed from the other professional profiles.

Thinking, designing and sharing with each other and working, as female art therapists, with a high percentage of women in both the professional teams at health and care institutions and in art therapy groups has determined the gender perspective as obligatory from the very start. It will be present in any future action, intervention and research design to be implemented in the field of community art therapy. Failure to do so would not only denote a poor analysis of reality and needs detection, but would also lead to lax professional practice, lack of ethics and social responsibility. At the same time, it would make nuclear aspects invisible for understanding the health-disease continuum, and therefore the possibilities of development of artistic therapies in the community environment.

We should also focus on the stimulating horizontality that gender promotes in terms of the loving, affective and caring attitude that women promote among themselves. It implies an improvement of overall health, which does not mean less capacity for the management and the control of our own vital narratives. Preventive health practices, including community art therapy, will be balanced in roles and responsibilities (from the perspective of professional ethics) and will therefore be emancipatory. They will therefore understand the structural and systematic inequality that gender imposes on women working for equity, freedom, well-being and creation.

Finally, we stress that this pilot programme favoured a basic and necessary dialogue for the advancement and consolidation of art therapy based on scientific principles that integrate knowledge from a mixed/multi-modal, multidisciplinary and evidence-based perspective. However, the process of reviewing the literature and the creation of the evaluation instrument shows the importance of creating specific, sensitive tools suitable for the research task and defines a specific professional profile for community art therapy.

The testimony of the people who participated in the workshops and the reflections shared with the professionals in the three districts and other institutions show that the art therapy process offers an opportunity for emotional and symbolic expression and communication that allows people to run their lives in a different way, to be more active and constructive and capable of critical judgement and change.

Concerning the professional profile and identity of art therapists in community health, we have identified important elements that must be taken into account in the design of a specific professional profile that can be integrated into the workforce. This should reinforce their professional advancement with equal rights and duties. The programmes should be interdisciplinary and cross-disciplinary. They should strengthen disciplines and profiles and minimise the insecurity and risks that stem from interdisciplinary coexistence.

The development of community art therapy is not straightforward. The ambiguity of its approaches can act as a brake. Professionals should maintain a somewhat "reckless" attitude that, while steering a sensible course, allows human growth beyond the point at which the social environment currently slows it down. It requires Don Quixote's determination and faith.

Reality is perceived as complex, changing and dehumanised. Only from time to time are barriers broken down to allow a glimmer of hope that another world and another way of inhabiting it are still possible. In this world of possibilities, people who belong together and exercise mutual care can devise their crucial potential. This makes old cracks repairable. Therefore, people have the opportunity to see themselves as they might become in the future. We are not talking about heroes, we are referring to people capable of dreaming of and imagining how to transform their reality.

Notes

1 Presentation. Conference "Bond and human ecology in working with families." Comillas Pontifical University. November 06, 2019.
2 Presentation. Cycle "The butterfly effect." Professional Association of Art Therapists, Ate. October 4, 2020.

References

Aguiló, E., and Losada, A. (2015). Los grupos y la intervención comunitaria. www.procc.org

Bacigalupe, A., Cabezas, A., Bueno, M.B., and Martín, U. (2020). El género como determinante de la salud mental y su medicalización. Informe SESPAS 2020. *Gaceta Sanitaria.*

Efrain Bleiberg (2019) Conference "Bond and human ecology in the work with families". Madrid: Universidad Pontificia de Comillas.

Corral, R., Fernández, R., García, M., and González, V. (2017). Una nueva forma de trabajo: de transmitir a construer conocimiento. Sobre el Proyecto "Cambiando en salud juntos". *Revista Área 3: Cuadernos de temas grupales e institucionales,* 21.

Dannecker, K. (2017). Edith Kramer's third hand: intervention. In: Gerity, L., and Ainlay, S. (eds.). *The legacy of Edith Kramer, a multifaceted view.* (pp.141–147). Londres: Routledge.

Del Cura, I., and López García-Franco, A. (2008). La medicalización de la vida: una mirada desde la atención primaria. *Átopos, Salud Mental, comunidad y cultura. Psicopatología de lo Cotidiano.* pp.4–12.

Egan, K. (1992). *La imaginación en la enseñanza y el aprendizaje.* Buenos Aires: Amorrortu editores.

Esteban, M.L., and Távora, A. (2010). El amor romántico y la subordinación social de las mujeres: revisiones y propuestas. *Revista Área 3: Cuadernos de temas grupales e institucionales,* 14.

Fancourt, D., and Finn, S. (2019). What is the evidence on the role of the arts in improving health and well-being?. WHO: Regional Office for Europe. *A scoping review. Health Evidence Network synthesis report,* 67.

Feen-Calligan, H., Moreno, J., and Buzzard, E. (2018). Art therapy, community building, activism, and outcomes. *Frontiers in Psychology,* 9, p.1548.

Fiorini, H. (2007). *El psiquismo creador.* Colección Música, Arte y proceso. Vitoria-Gasteiz: AgrupArte ediciones.

Gerlitza, Y., Regeva, D., and Snirb, S. (2020). A relational approach to art therapy. *The Arts in Psychotherapy.* 68, p.101644.

Golub, D. (2005). Social action art therapy. *Art Therapy,* 22(1), pp.17–23.

Gray, B.L. (2012). The Babushka project: mediating between the margins and wider community through public art creation. *Art Therapy,* 29(3), pp.113–119.

Gysin, M., and Sorín, M. (2011). *El arte y la persona. Arteterapia: esa hierbita verde.* Barcelona: ISPA Edicions.

Hahna, N. (2013). Towards an emancipatory practice: incorporating feminist pedagogy in the creative arts therapies. *The Arts in Psychotherapy,* 40(4), pp.436–440.

Hess, C., and Hess-Cabalzar, A. (2008). *Medicina humana: un arte inteligente de curar.* Barcelona: ISPA Ediciones.

Hogan, S. (2016). *Art therapy theories. A critical introduction.* Londres: Routledge.

Hogan, S. (2013). Your body is a battleground: Art therapy with women. *The Arts in Psychotherapy,* 40(4), pp.415–419.

Holmes, J., and Meyerhoff, M. (1999). The community of practice: theories and methodologies in language and gender research. *Language in Society*, 28, pp. 173–183.

Kapitan, L. (2010). *Introduction to art therapy research*. Londres: Routledge.

Kapitan, L., Litell, M., and Torres, A. (2011). Creative art therapy in a community's participatory research and social transformation. *Art Therapy*, 28(2), pp. 64–73.

Kaplan, F. (2007). *Art therapy and social action*. London: Jessica Kingsley Publishers.

López Fernández-Cao, M. (2018). *Arte, memoria y trauma: Aletheia, dar forma al dolor*. Madrid: Fundamentos.

Miranda, D., Garcia-Ramirez, M., Balcazar, F., and Suarez-Balcazar, Y. (2019). A community-based participatory action research for Roma health justice in a deprived district in Spain. *International Journal of Environmental Research and Public Health*, 16(19), p. 3722.

Ogden, P., and Fisher. J. (2016). *Psicoterapia sensoriomotriz. Intervenciones para el trauma y el apego*. Bilbao: Desclée de Brouwer.

Ogden, P., Minton, K., and Pain, C. (2009). *El trauma y el cuerpo: un modelo sensoriomotriz de psicoterapia*. Bilbao: Desclée de Brouwer.

Ottemiller, D., and Awais, Y. (2016). A model for art therapists in community-based practice. *Art Therapy*, 33(3), pp. 144–150.

Rubin, J. (2016). *Approaches to art therapy, theory and technique*. Londres: Routledge.

Slayton, S. (2012). Building community as social action: an art therapy group with adolescent males. *The Arts in Psychotherapy*, 39(3), pp. 179–185.

Timm-Bottos, J. (2011). Endangered threads: socially committed community art action. *Art Therapy*, 28(2), pp. 57–63.

Timm-Bottos, J. (2017). Public practice art therapy: enabling spaces across North America. *Canadian Art Therapy Association Journal*, 30(2), pp. 94–99.

Valdés, N. (2013). Un modelo de integración de arte y salud en España: el proyecto curArte I+ D. *Revista Hacia la Promoción de la Salud*, 18(1), pp. 120–137.

Winnicott, D. (1971). *Realidad y juego*. Barcelona: Gedisa.

Yalom, I.D. (2001). *El don de la terapia, Carta abierta a una nueva generación de terapeutas y a sus pacientes*. Barcelona: Destino.

10

DANCE MOVEMENT THERAPY FOR COUPLES

Disclosing multiple truths
in the relationship

Einat Shuper Engelhard, Maya Vulcan

Abstract

Couples engaged in psychotherapy often perceive and describe the issues that come up in their relationship as linked to the diverse "truths" held by the partners and their respective positions with regard to the primary causes of conflict, wherein the claims of the other are sometimes perceived by each partner as "imaginative windmills." In these situations, dance/movement therapy for couples (DMT-C) serves as a mediator and a bridge to unconscious contents, aiming to bring forth seminal yet unknown truths in the couple relationship through joint dance, to offer a somatic translation of these unknowns in and through movement and to follow these bodily insights by symbolic and verbal processing in the analytic session.

This chapter presents a qualitative study of nine heterosexual couples who took part in twelve sessions of DMT-C, designed to understand the partners' perceptions of different subjective truths in the relationship. The research findings show that the joint movement experience elicited the articulation of the subjective truth of each partner and also highlighted some significant shared truths, which were all somatically embodied and expressed. Moreover, the "here and now" encounter with emotional contents through the body created a safe space for the acceptance and internalisation of unconscious and previously unrecognised roles and needs, which only came to the fore through the couple's movement. The combination of movement and subsequent verbal processing thus enables the formulation of latent knowledge, which resides in the body and cannot be consciously reached through spoken language alone.

Keywords: bodily experiences, couples, dance movement therapy, embodied stories

DOI: 10.4324/9781003110200-10

Abstract in Hebrew

זוגות הפונים לפסיכותרפיה זוגית, לעיתים קרובות, מתארים "אמיתות" מגוונות ביחס לתכנים שונים בזוגיות שלהם, וביחס לתפקידים בקשר, לסיבות לסכסוך ולקונפליקטים ביחסים, כאשר העשנות של בן הזוג לעיתים נתפסת כ-"טחנות רוח דמיוניות." במצבים אלה, טיפול בתנועה ומחול לזוגות (DMT-C) משמש כמתווך וכגשר לתכנים לא מודעים ומגולמים בגוף במערכת היחסים הזוגית, במטרה להעלותם למודע באמצעות ריקוד משותף. הטיפול בתנועה ומחול מזמין לביטוי סומטי וקינסטטי לאלמנטים רגשיים בזוגיות, ולעיבוד סמלי ומילולי של הביטויים מגוף.

פרק זה מציג מחקר איכותני בהשתתפות של תשעה זוגות שלקחו חלק בשניים-עשר מפגשים של טיפול בתנועה ומחול לזוגות. ממצאי המחקר מראים כי חווית התנועה המשותפת הציפה את האמת הסובייקטיבית של כל אחד מבני הזוג, והדגישה מספר אמיתות משותפות לכלל הזוגות. המפגש ב-"כאן ועכשיו" עם תכנים רגשיים דרך הגוף, יצר מרחב בטוח לקבלה והפגנה של תפקידים וצרכים לא מודעים ובלתי מוכרים בזוגיות, אלו באו לידי ביטוי בתנועה של הזוג. הפרק מבהיר כי שילוב של תנועה ועיבוד מילולי מאפשר גיבוש של ידע סמוי ומגולם בגוף אשר לא ניתן להגיע אליו באופן מודע באמצעות שפה מילולית בלבד.

Before you start reading this chapter, we invite you to take a deep full breath and try to remember a time when you danced with your partner, be it your current partner, or a partner from your past, or – if you wish – an imaginary one. Now, just take your time and observe this dance. Watch the movement, the intensity of the movement, the distance between you, your eye contact, the dominant pace and rhythms. Try to identify a certain feeling, a sensation, an image, or an emotion connected with this dance. Now let these insights accompany you while you read.

A paradigmatic case for couple relationship may be that of Cervantes's Sancho Panza and Don Quixote, who embark on an intimate journey. Their respective psychological mindsets are inscribed, first and foremost, in their bodies – the former is squat and big-bellied and the latter is tall and lean. And while Sancho Panza is anchored in the real, concrete and material world, Don Quixote lives in an entirely spiritual and imaginary realm. They are, thus, opposite representations, which may either complement each other during their journey or, alternatively, suffer conflicts and pain due to their mismatch. As a couple their personal relationship is put to the test, as Sancho yearns for home and Quixote presses onwards. Their adventures and ordeals along the journey would constitute a test of their relationship, involving unconscious truths regarding their dreams, their perceptions of friendship and heroism and the challenges they face together. In dance movement therapy for couples, we use dance and movement for getting acquainted with unknown themes that are inaccessible through verbal language, primary issues that were experienced in the body, but have not yet been verbally processed or expressed. The importance of integrating body and movement in couple therapy has gained recognition in recent years, as evidenced in case studies involving a combination of movement experiences during the couple therapy session (Hawkes, 2003; Wagner & Hurst, 2018). Thus, for example, sex therapy sometimes uses mindfulness techniques to increase the couple's awareness of their bodily experiences and of the somatic origins of emotional processes (Kimmesa, Mallory, Cameron, & Kose, 2015), and the Imago approach integrates deep breathing exercises and techniques as well as eye contact experiences for assisting couples in attaining greater relaxation and a better regulation in situations of conflict (Hendrix, 1988).

Research shows that the integration of ballroom dancing into therapy can facilitate numerous unconscious issues of relating such as elements of leadership, trust, boundaries and dependency (Hawkes, 2003). Moreover, experiences of expressive movement, synchronisation and mutual attunement through movement produce a positive impact on the perceived couple relationship, increase kinaesthetic empathy and improve individuals' ability to attune emotionally in relation to their partners (Kim, Kang, Chung, & Park, 2013). Recent qualitative research with couples diagnosed with borderline personality disorders has indicated that the imitation of a personal choreography, movement synchronisation and collaboration in resolving incidents of non-synchronisation of movement has resulted in greater marital satisfaction, more secure attachment and increased empathy in the relationship (Pietrzak, Hauke, & Lohr, 2017). The results of these studies show that dance movement therapy can elicit intimacy, trust and productive dialogue, and bring to the fore multiple truths that may be integrated into the couple's conscious shared vocabulary. It should be noted that since dance movement therapy has only recently been introduced as a clinical approach for couples' therapy, literature and research in the field are still at a preliminary stage. Current research findings on couple therapy focus primarily on measurable outcomes of the process, and most studies involve only small samples and cover singular or few sessions, whereas this type of therapeutic process involves a significant time period in order to evolve. Moreover, few studies have so far focused either on discovering the subjective "truths" of the partner, or on the establishment of trust, which would allow access to unconscious contents during the therapeutic process.

With this in mind, the study presented in this chapter, compatible with recent studies indicating that embodied knowledge affects each one of our actions in social situations (McNulty, Olson, Meltzer, & Shaffer, 2013; Smith & Semin, 2004), aims to address the way in which movement can highlight the significance of explicit behaviours. The origins and meaning of these behaviours are either unknown or only partially understood by the partners themselves, inasmuch as the partners' unconscious manifests itself through movement and dance. The movements of the body with respect to another's movements and gestures spontaneously and unconsciously express how we perceive and interpret the other (Damasio, 2011; Young, 2005). These reactions are based on embodied experience from previous relationships, culture and environment. Further support for this approach may be found in extensive clinical literature in the field of dance movement therapy, indicating that motor experiences in the body lay the ground for evoking memories experienced in the body in previous relationships (e.g., Meekums, 2002; Chaiklin & Wengrower, 2015).

This chapter thus focuses on the way in which the therapist uses movement to clarify unconscious, embodied content that influences daily experiences in the relationship. These experiences may support or undermine trust between the partners and reflect different truths in the relationship. We will refer to key relationship issues such as: the need to be seen and known by the other, the need to lead and be led, the wish to be supported by and support another, interpersonal communication characteristics, expressions of strength and power within the relationship, touch and intimacy.

Movement therapy for couples – a comprehensive qualitative research

In order to examine the meaning of nonverbal expressions within couple relationship and the couples' perceptions of different subjective truths, we conducted a large-scale qualitative study (Shuper Engelhard, 2018; 2019ab; Shuper Engelhard & Vulcan, 2018; Vulcan & Shuper Engelhard, 2019). The participants in the research were nine heterosexual couples, who have been living together and sharing the same household for at least three years, and who come from a variety of backgrounds in terms of religious affiliation and country of origin. All of the participants took part in twelve sessions of couple therapy, combining body-movement work. The findings in this study highlighted the understanding that working through body and movement can serve as a potential bridge towards genuine multiculturalism emphasising that the language of the body is also constituted by differences of religion, culture and gender. As the language of the body is always idiosyncratic, personal and subjective, this understanding is just as relevant to couples who share the same native tongue, and every two moving bodies need to learn each other's movement vocabulary in order to communicate through movement. The subjective nature of this language stems from the individual differences of genetic attributes, internalised object relations, different bodily patterns and needs. Getting acquainted with this language and acquiring bodily literacy will generate greater sensitivity to individual differences that need to be addressed in relationship and in couple therapy. The rationale for the selection of heterosexual couples is, in this case, purely coincidental and is related to the nature of the population that responded to the call for participation in the study. Further research should continue to examine the contribution of movement therapy in the treatment of relationships of different couples. It should also be noted that using the protocol and adopting this approach for couple therapy requires training in both movement and dance therapy and specifically in couple therapy, as well as supervision and guidance by an expert in the field. The transition to working with couples on issues of intimacy and sexuality requires the therapist to be connected to his/her own emotions, conflicts, wishes and desires related to these issues. Moreover, when the therapy involves the body and its movement, the therapist must feel comfortable in his/her body and recognise the meanings of experiences in the body as well as the processes taking place in the mind.

The sessions were all similarly structured:

1. Each session began with an invitation to attend to the somatic, physical experience with which each of the partners arrived at the meeting. The goal here was to relax and let go of daily experience in order to attain availability for the therapeutic process, practise somatic listening and deepen the awareness of feelings associated with the sensory experience. This introduction was designed to build up and support the couple's trust in the process and in each other.

2. Following this, the therapy session continued by working through dynamic contents of the relationship through movement and dance. The couple was invited to attend to their individual and interpersonal experiences involved in different qualities of movement. They were asked to take note of sensations, emotions, images, memories and associations that come up from their unconscious during movement.

3. Each joint movement session consisted of three elements:

   • Observing the body's stories – the partners were invited to become familiar with their own spontaneous movement in the relationship, the movement discovered in the body, which takes place without any external instructions. They were asked to observe the manner in which each of them expresses him/herself in the joint dance, including parameters like rhythm, use of eye contact, use of strength, touch, personal space, contraction and relaxation, volume of movement, etc.

   • Invitation to new experiences – after identifying the characteristics of the spontaneous movement, the couple was invited to try out new or less familiar movements. For example, increasing or decreasing their pace of walking.

   • Somatic mirroring – the partners were invited to explore the focal topic of the session from the spouse's perspective by exchanging roles and engaging in movement "like" that of the other. The goal here was to induce the participants to get familiarised with the partner's body stories through kinaesthetic empathy.

4. Each therapy session ended with an invitation to translate the movement into words and the partners were asked to articulate and verbalise the embodied knowledge that came up through the session.

Following this, and in order to allow unknown and unconscious materials to come up through movement, Shuper Engelhard (2019c) established a working protocol for DMT for couples, which provides the contents and specific guidelines for each session as well as the proposed questions the therapist can offer for reflection and insight.

We will describe the movement guidelines and the questions designed to support the reflective process of each partner with regard to interpersonal and personal contents in the relationship. Each subchapter will address a major issue raised in the study.

To see and be seen

The wish to be seen by the other is a fundamental need in couple relationship. In order to become familiarised with the spontaneous psychosomatic expressions relating to this issue, the therapist begins his/her intervention by inviting the couple to start with spontaneous joint dancing. Following this, in order to induce awareness of the way each partner uses eye contact, the couple is asked to continue dancing, with no eye contact at all, and after several moments to find a comfortable way of meeting each other's gaze. Throughout the movement experience the therapist invites each partner to reflect on the following topics: do you make eye contact during the dance? Which distance feels comfortable for you to position yourself vis-à-vis your partner? Can you note the factors which allow you to make eye contact and those which make you avoid eye contact?

In order to enhance the partners' awareness of their feelings when being looked at or away from by the other, the movement experience continues and one of the partners is invited to move freely while the other partner alternately observes or does not look at her/his partner. The therapist invites the couple to observe and share with each other: do you feel your partner's presence near you, even without eye contact between you? Is it easy for you to look and observe your partner? Do you feel comfortable when your partner observes you while you move? What does your partner's gaze allow you to do or prevent you from doing whilst moving?

Furthermore, in order to experience witnessing each other through movement, one partner dances while the other "learns" the movement's qualities and joins the dance while mirroring these qualities. During the experience the therapist invites each partner to observe: what changes in your movement while you are observed? How would you like your partner to look at you? How do you express your wish to be seen by your partner? And what type of gaze does your partner need from you?

Leading and being led

The need for attunement, adjustment and synchronisation in couple relationship is another key issue, which brings to the fore contents related to the ability or the wish to lead or be led by the other. In order to become familiarised with the psychosomatic expressions relating to this issue, the therapist begins his/her intervention by inviting the couple for a joint walk in the space (without any further instruction). Throughout the movement experience the therapist invites each partner to reflect on the following topics: what characterises your pace?

What characterises your partner's pace? Who leads the pace, the direction of movement, the movement intensity, the distance from one another?

Following this, the therapist invites the couple to experiment with different styles of pacing together, for example, walking together as slowly/quickly as possible. During the experience, the therapist suggests that each partner should try to observe whose pace is more dominant, and which movement qualities are pleasant when walking together. In order for the partners to experience and share the other's pace, the therapist asks one of the partners to dance, using a rhythm comfortable for him/her, while the other partner joins using the same rhythm. During the experience, the therapist calls on each partner to observe: which rhythm would you like your partner to use when joining you in your dance? What does your partner need from you? What changed in your movement after your partner joined your dance?

The therapist then invites one of the partners to take the lead and choose the quality of movement during their walk, while observing the way he/she communicates change in direction and pace: do I surprise or prepare my partner before making changes in movement? This experience is later repeated while dancing together, starting out with spontaneous dancing and later as the partners experiment with leading the dance. This part of the session is designed to enable the couple to encounter contents related to the way they listen to their partner's needs whilst leading or being led, to help them understand which role is more familiar/comfortable for them and how they can make their partner feel more comfortable in a less familiar role.

Supporting and being supported

The need to feel supported and the wish to support in couple relationship raises embodied contents from early relationships (Shuper Engelhard, 2019d). In order to become familiarised with the spontaneous psychosomatic expressions relating to this issue, the therapist begins his/her intervention by inviting the couple to sit back-to-back and pay attention to the degree of weight they each shift on to their partner.

Throughout the movement experience, the therapist invites each partner to reflect on the following topics: does the shifting of weight lead to relaxation/tension? What emotional content emerges?

Following this, each partner searches separately for the degree to which she/he can lean on the other's back, shift weight and relax. The therapist encourages the couple to explore through their bodies and in verbal conversation the way through which the transitions between leaning on and supporting take place, to find out what makes each position comfortable for them. Drawing on this part of the session, both partners search for options to lean on/be supported by the other, whilst trying to respond to the following questions: how do I arrange my body so that I can support my partner? Am I attentive to his/her needs and to my own at the same time? In order for the partners to become familiarised with each other's psychosomatic experience of leaning, the couple is invited to stand up back-to-back as one partner transfers weight on to the other to the degree which is pleasant for the individual who is leaning. The partner receiving the weight learns the degree of leaning which is pleasant for his/her partner and mirrors it with her/his own body. Then, through conversation, the therapist encourages the partners to examine and share with one another: What was familiar/strange/comfortable/burdensome about the experience of leaning? What kind of support does he/she need from their partner? How does one ask for it? Is there a difference between my need to be supported and my partner's need?

In another movement experience, designed to examine the way the body reacts when one puts his/her weight on to the other, the partners stand face-to-face with their hands touching, palm to palm. The partners are asked by the therapist to let go and relax their weight against one another, whilst looking for a point where they both feel they can support and be supported by the other. Following this, the partners are invited to hold a sponge ball between them using different body parts (without holding on to the ball with their hands). By transferring weight, they are then asked to move the ball between different parts of their bodies, and finally to repeat the same experience while walking around the room. The therapist invites the couple to observe and share with each other the way each of them feels whilst supporting, for example, when I support my partner can I also support myself? Can I ask my partner for something that would make it easier for me support him/her? How do we signal our needs to one another?

Communication through movement

Interpersonal communication characteristics affect nonverbal content (Goldberg & Allen, 2015). In order to become familiarised with the spontaneous psychosomatic expressions relating to this issue, the therapist begins the intervention by inviting the couple to take turns in "movement conversation." One partner begins a movement, and the other observes, "listens," and chooses when to join in. This continues as the second partner takes the leading role in order to continue the movement conversation.

Throughout the movement experience, the therapist invites each partner to reflect on the following topics: how do I arrange and organise my body so that I can speak and listen to my partner? Do I feel that I'm being listened to? Using my body, how do I signal to my partner that I heard what she/he said and that I want to switch roles from being the "speaker" to being the "listener" and vice versa?

Strength and intensity

The right to use assertiveness, or rather the fear of using power and strength in relationships, often provokes conflicts and power struggles (Knudson-Martin et al., 2015). In order to become familiarised with the spontaneous psychosomatic expressions relating to this issue, the therapist begins his/her intervention by inviting the couple to hold hands while maintaining an arm's length distance and begin moving, while trying to relax the body's muscles. After a few minutes, one partner takes the lead and increases intensity in his/her limbs, taking charge of the tempo and the direction of movement in the space. This experience is repeated as both partners use high muscle intensity for moving and, once more, when only the partner being led moves with high intensity.

Throughout the movement experience, the therapist invites each partner to reflect on the following topics: as I am being led, am I passive or active? Which role is more comfortable for me? What do I feel towards my spouse when she/he leads? Do I initiate sudden, or gradual changes in the quality and direction of movement?

In order to examine if the presence of the partner in space enables a full expression of intensities, each partner is invited to support his/her partner's back with the palms of the hands. The leaning partner is invited to increase and decease intensity through her/his body in the space. The supporting partner adjusts the degree of support with regard to the other's intensity of the movement.

In another movement experience, the partners stand opposite each other, at a distance that does not allow for bodily injury, holding a large pillow at chest-height, as far as possible from the body, while one of the partners kicks it with his/her feet or hits it with his/her hands. The therapist invites the couple to observe and share with each other their feelings about the relation of this experience to the way they express, or do not express, aggression and anger in the relationship. The couple is also invited to reflect on whether this experience is related to how aggression was expressed, or not expressed, in their parents' home during their childhood. In order to become familiarised with the spontaneous psychosomatic expressions relating to this issue, one partner chooses one of the experiences and mirrors his/her partner's movement intensity. Following this, the other partner shows how he/she would want to express intensities in their relationship.

Touch and intimacy

The issues of intimacy and touch are related to primary needs and unconscious materials through which one interprets the experiences related to these issues (Seikkula et al., 2015). In order to become familiarised with the spontaneous psychosomatic expressions relating to these issues, the therapist begins the intervention by inviting the couple for a spontaneous joint dance which includes touch. The therapist then guides the couple to investigate different kinds of touch: touch that is respectful, fearful, hesitant, admiring. At first, both partners initiate the touch, and later one initiates while the other is passive. Throughout the movement experience, the therapist invites each partner to reflect on the following topics: what are the images that come to mind when I touch my partner? What are the images that come to mind when my partner touches me? What is the difference, if any, between the characteristics of my touching him/her and the way she/he touches me? How do I feel towards my partner's need for touch?

The exploration of touch continues as the therapist invites one of the partners to investigate and demonstrate which type of touch is pleasant for him/her through examining and exploring different intensity levels of self-touch, while the other partner mirrors the observed different characteristics of touch, using her/his own body. Finally, the observing partner touches his/her own body in the way he/she thinks his/her partner would like to be touched. The therapist invites the couple to observe and share with each other: which kind of touch relaxes me/is pleasant to me/is threatening to me? How do I share my need with my partner? Is there a difference between the way in which I perceive my partner's need and the way she/he expressed it in touching her/his own body?

Another movement experience offered by the therapist guides the couple to dance alongside one another at first without touching. This is later followed by creating one, two and finally three points of contact (the contact "wanders" each time to another area of the body). Gradually the areas of contact decrease until the couple returns to joint dancing without physical contact. In the last movement experience, one of the partners chooses a distance that will enable him/her to feel intimacy during joint dancing without touching. The couple dance at the chosen distance. The therapist invites the couple to observe which body parts are used to make contact? What is the intensity of touch? What characterises the duration of the touch? Is touch accompanied by eye contact? Does an increase of contact enable me to feel greater or lesser intimacy? How do I feel about the different types of touch? When does the closing of my eyes add or detract from the experience? Is there a difference between my need and my partner's need? At what distance do I sense intimacy? Did the distance between us change when eye contact was/was not present? How do I share my need for closeness or distance with my partner?

Dance movement therapy as a means to discover the couple's unconscious

In the course of the project, we have found that diverse experiences in movement introduced the couples to misconceptions about their relationships and elicited individual subjective truths of each partner alongside significant shared truths, which were all somatically embodied and expressed. In the following section, the couple's experiences in the dance movement sessions are shared and rendered throughout the research. All the participants gave their consent to the use of the research materials for publication. In order to preserve their anonymity, pseudonyms are used for quoting.

DMP-C as a meeting ground for unconscious emotional layers

The couples who took part in the therapeutic sessions spoke of the ways that movement illuminated the role of the body as a means for retrieving past experiences, which had been partly unconscious until the moment they were experienced through movement. For example, John, one of the participants, said, "I felt that working through movement, we brought the base of our relationship up to the surface. I encountered things that I had long been unable to see about ourselves." Additionally, couples shared that movement enabled an encounter with new qualities of the relationship and allowed both of the partners to get acquainted with new personality attributes. As John's partner put it, "I saw other sides of him through the movement," and "[Movement] enabled a different point of view on the relationship."

Ora, another participant, came to therapy to resolve a difficulty she felt when trying to communicate in an emotional register with her partner. She spoke of an additional therapeutic aspect of the movement experience, which enabled not only an encounter with day-to-day materials, but also offered her additional ways of coping with them: "The daily turbulence was evident in the session and I could check out or sense another way of dealing with it rather than 'exploding', as I usually do." These processes are related to the trust built in the course of the movement experience between the couple.

Numerous couples spoke about the language of movement as enabling some emotional "suspension" better than verbal language, more immediate, and hence more conducive to intimacy. Michael said, "Even when troubling things come up, it's without the background noises of speech. You face the thing itself. When we move, we don't speak *about* things, we experience them." His partner, referred to a "clarity" she felt through the body and its movement: "There were things we had discussed a lot, but in movement I felt that I could be more nuanced, understand what it was that I wanted to say, because the body speaks closer to feelings, with no defences." Following this, Michael continued:

> I began to take note of my body in the process of communication. The body expressed what words could not express. We found a new mode of communication...I understood that during the session I needed not only to speak but also to do something, to experience something concrete. There are things I know in my body, but there are no words for these things.

DMP-C as a gateway to a rethinking of the diverse truths in the relationship

The "here and now" encounter with emotional contents through the body created a safe space for acceptance and internalisation of unconscious roles and needs, which only came to the fore through the couple's movement. Nathan, who came to therapy following difficulties with intimacy in his relationship, identified various modes of compensation through movement: "It was hard to lean on each other and make eye contact. I understood that when we found it difficult to make eye contact, we held hands. That's how we compensated."

Natanela, Nathan's partner, linked the difficulties experienced during an encounter of aggressive movement with a felt disconnection between body and psyche in her relationship with her partner: "I didn't feel free to express aggression in movement. It's actually the same with my sexuality. I understood that I disconnect both when it comes to sexuality and when it comes to aggression." Here, both of them recognised the ways in which they avoid being intimate with each other.

Another aspect of the sessions, perceived as significant by the couples, was the distinction between emotion, behaviour and sensation. A concept such as being either alone or together can be re-formulated when it is expressed in the body through individual and joint movement. Through the movement experience on this issue, the couple first felt and then understood and conceptualised their sense of space and understood how much of it each partner needed in the relationship. For example, Assaf spoke of understanding the sort of space he and his partner needed in order to feel a sense of togetherness: "During the sessions I felt through the body that I needed a physical space with fewer stimulants so that we could focus more on each other, and it was better for me."

Gill, who entered therapy with a great deal of frustration regarding the toll of "maintaining the pulse" in the relationships, spoke of the movement which enabled her to connect childhood memories with patterns in the relationship:

> The movement led me to open up and reveal myself emotionally, and to connect my childhood to the relationship. For instance, when I was a child, I was not supported or held up, and here [in the sessions] it was nice for me to be leant on... At home we fight about the issue of 'leading', and here I understood that I do not let go. Silly arguments suddenly acquired meaning. I am offended when I have to take the initiative, but at the same time, I am not comfortable when I am led.

Verbal processing as a gateway to embodied, yet unformulated knowledge of the relationship

Alongside the singularity of the body, words and insights have a significant role in DMT-C, as emotional experience attained through movement is in danger of fading away and getting lost without verbal processing. John emphasised this, saying, "The longer we had to digest the movement [experience] through words, the more significant it felt." Similar experiences through movement raised in each partner different feelings and insights, and it was through the verbal processing of these issues that the partners found new ways of learning about each other and continuing their dialogue. For example, Shawn, who came to therapy with a complaint regarding the insufficiency of intimacy with his partner said,

"When she touched me it felt like a slap. I wanted to make it possible for her to do it, but the slightest touch felt like a kick." Dana described her feelings towards her partner's movement:

> He did not find it easy to move in front of me, and this made me wonder how open and liberated we were with each other. I saw him embarrassed. I used to think that he found it easy to move, but it was actually my own movement which allowed him to open up. All of a sudden, I saw the dynamics of our relationship as opposite to what I had previously thought. This opened up my heart.

Dance movement therapy for couples: objectives, uniqueness and innovation

The experience of moving together and the knowledge that resides in the body influences and facilitates the relationship. Movement experience in couple therapy serves as a tool for increased creativity, playfulness and intimacy in the relationship. It seems that the benefit of working through bodily movement enables an encounter not only with issues of exhaustion and detachment, but also with the strengths of the relationship.

Following the sessions, the participants referred to the "language of the body" as having "its own syntax," acquired in the early stages of life. This syntax is idiosyncratic and unverbalised and may be tagged as the somatic native tongue of individuals, being intensely subjective. The idiosyncratic and subjective nature of this language stems from the individual differences of internalised object relations and genetic attributes.

As indicated in several studies, the ability for emotional expression of children and of individuals from non-Western cultures is different from that of adults from Western culture (Kim & Sherman, 2007). Each individual has different bodily patterns and needs, and the language of the body is also constituted by differences of culture, religion and gender. We would like to emphasise that working with couples who come from different cultures shows that they share a fantasy that movement will bridge their cultural gaps, but soon they discover that moving together does not mean that they can truly communicate. Connecting truthfully and deeply requires some learning of the other's movement vocabulary. Getting acquainted with this language and acquiring bodily literacy will generate greater sensitivity to individual differences that need to be addressed in relationship and in couple therapy. The participants felt that movement was a means by which emotional experience can be expressed in a deeper and clearer way, as if the language of movement enables emotional "suspension" better than verbal language. This study indicates that when verbal communication between the partners was already charged with negative feelings, the communication through movement allowed them to feel trust and closeness to each other even in conflictual situations. Couple therapy through movement offers additional ways of coping with forbidden aspects or difficult areas in the relationship, and of legitimising them without hurting or damaging the relationship.

The verbalisation of embodied unknown stories was key in the therapeutic process. It became apparent that without the verbal/symbolic processing of the body-movement experience, the vocabulary of the body could easily dissolve and disappear, or remain incomprehensible, unknown and meaningless for the participants. The emotional contents that emerged through movement required both verbal processing and meaning-making in order to be understood and internalised. In this sense, the concrete experience of in-session movement serves as a bridge to an emotional experience as it illustrates different aspects in the relationship and reveals issues that were only accessible through the body. The participants' insights imply that movement offers a new awareness and understanding of the role of each partner in the relationship. Becoming more literate their own and their partner's somatic native tongue in the course of the sessions enabled the participants to attain a more nuanced understanding of the nonverbal aspects of their relationship.

Movement is a third language, a discourse that forms a bridge between two native tongues, and one that is inherent in the relationship. This language is the optimal register of the couple's communication, their ability to reflect upon their own and their partner's somatic experiences.

Conclusions and implications

Movement-integrated couple therapy enables an encounter with the strengths and joys of the relationship, as well as an understanding of conflicts and discrepancies which emerge from the experience of movement. It offers a framework for exploring and attaining insights into intimacy and communication, allowing these aspects to become accessible to the partners following verbal processing. The therapeutic mediation enables the partners to become familiar with the personal and bodily syntax that each of them brings into the relationship, both when the partners share the same native language and culture and also when each of them comes from different verbal linguistic and cultural backgrounds.

Movement-integrated couple therapy thus involves polyphonic discourse, inasmuch as each partner speaks a different language of the body, inextricably related to early individual bodily experiences. The therapist highlights this polyphonic bodily discourse and works as a mediator between the three registers of communication – verbal language, somatic language and emotional language.

> *Now, after reading this chapter we invite you to take a deep breath and go back to the dance you imagined with your partner. How do you feel about that dance now? What can you learn through this dance about yourself and your relationship at that time?*

References

Chaiklin, S., & Wengrower, H. (Eds.). (2015). *The art and science of dance movement therapy: Life is dance.* London: Routledge.

Damasio, A. (2011). Neural basis of emotions. *Scholarpedia, 6,* 1804. doi:10.4249/scholarpedia

Goldberg, A. E., & Allen, K. R. (2015). Communicating qualitative research: Some practical guideposts for scholars. *Journal of Marriage and Family, 77,* 3–22. https://doi.org/10.1111/jomf.12153.

Hawkes, L. (2003). The tango of therapy: A dancing group. *Transactional Analysis Journal, 33,* 288–301. https://doi.org/10.1177/03621 53703 03300 404.

Hendrix, H. (1988). *Getting the love you want: A guide for couples.* New York: Holt.

Kim, S. Y., Kang, H. W., Chung, Y. C., & Park, S. (2013). Empirical application of empathy enhancing program based on movement concept for married couples in conflict. *Journal of Exercise Rehabilitation, 9,* 426–431.

Kim, H. S., & Sherman, D. K. (2007). "Express yourself": culture and the effect of self-expression on choice. *Journal of Personality and Social Psychology, 92*(1), 1.

Kimmesa, J. G., Mallory, A. B., Cameron, C., & Kose, O. (2015). A treatment model for anxiety-related sexual dysfunctions using mindfulness meditation within a sex-positive framework. *Sexual and Relationship Therapy, 30,* 286–296. https://doi.org/10.1080/14681 994.

Knudson-Martin, C., Huenergardt, D., Lafontant, K., Bishop, L., Schaepper, J., & Wells, M. (2015). Competencies for addressing gender and power in couple therapy: A socioemotional approach. *Journal of Marital and Family Therapy, 41,* 205–220. https://doi.org/10.1111/jmft.12068.

McNulty, J. K., Olson, M. A., Meltzer, A. L., & Shaffer, M. J. (2013). Though they may be unaware, newlyweds implicitly know whether their marriage will be satisfying. *Science, 342,* 1119–1120. doi:10.1126/science.12431 40.

Meekums, B. (2002). *Dance movement therapy: A creative psychotherapeutic approach.* London: Sage.

Pietrzak, T., Hauke, G., & Lohr, G. (2017). Connecting couples intervention: Improving couples' empathy and emotional regulation using embodied empathy. *European Journal Psychotherapy, 13,* 66–98.

Seikkula, J., Karvonen, A., Kykyri, V. L., Kaartinen, J., & Penttonen, M. (2015). The embodied attunement of therapists and a couple within dialogical psychotherapy: An introduction to the relational mind research project. *Family Process, 54,* 703–715. doi:10.1111/famp.12152

Shuper Engelhard, E. (2018). Being together in time: Body synchrony in couples' psychotherapy. *The Art in Psychotherapy, 60,* 41–47. https://doi.org/10.1016/j.aip.2018.06.003.

Shuper Engelhard, E. (2019a). Embodying the couple relationship: kinesthetic empathy and somatic mirroring in couples' therapy. *Journal of Couple & Relationship Therapy.* https://doi.org/10.1080/15332691.2018.1481801.

Shuper-Engelhard, E. (2019b). Ghosts in the bedroom - embodiment wishes in couple sexuality: qualitative research and practical application. *American Journal of Dance Therapy,* 1–16. https://doi.org/10.1007/s10465-019-09302-w.

Shuper Engelhard, E. (2019c). Dance movement psychotherapy for couples (DMP -C): systematic treatment guidelines based on a wide -ranging study. *Body, Movement and Dance in Psychotherapy.* https://doi.org/10.1080/17432979.2019.1653373.

Shuper Engelhard, E. (2019d). Dancing to projective identification in couples' therapy. *Arts in Psychotherapy.* 1–12. doi:10.1016/j.aip.2019.101614

Shuper Engelhard, E., & Vulcan, M. (2018). Introducing movement into couple therapy: clients' expectations and perceptions. *Contemporary Family Therapy*. https://doi.org/10.1007/s10591-018-9474-x.

Smith, E. R., & Semin, G. R. (2004). Socially situated cognition: Cognition in its social context. *Advances in Experimental Social Psychology, 36*, 53–117. Doi.org/10.1016/S0065-2601

Vulcan, M. & Shuper Engelhard, E. (2019). Body and movement in couple intake. *Arts in Psychotherapy*. 49–58. doi:10.1016/j.aip.2019.02.001

Wagner, D., & Hurst, S. M. (2018). Couples dance/movement therapy: Bringing a theoretical framework into practice. *American Journal of Dance Therapy*, 1–26. https://doi.org/10.1007/s10465-018-9271-y.

Young, I. M. (2005). Breasted experience: The look and the feeling. In: Young, I. M. (Ed.) *On female body experience: "Throwing like a girl" and other essays* (pp.75–96). New York: Oxford University Press. doi:10.1093/0195161920.003.0006.

11

WORKING PSYCHOANALYTICALLY WITH CLIENTS WITH LEARNING DISABILITY: THE REAL GIANTS WE FACE

A long-term music therapy with an adopted girl with significant multiple disabilities

Joy Gravestock

Abstract

In this chapter, the author argues that adopted children described as having significant or profound learning disabilities benefit from psychoanalytic music therapy.
Often with such clients, music therapy might be viewed by other professionals
as a distraction activity, or something "fun." However, the author asserts that
all adopted children retain an internal, embodied, unconscious memory of their
early felt sense of being relinquished and separation trauma. Working with this
is the territory of music therapy. It had been thought that adopted children, but
especially those with significant intellectual impairment, could not really know
about such early life experience. The author argues that it is our wish to believe
these adoptees are not-knowing because it is already potentially overwhelming
to acknowledge the pain involved in the birth of a disabled child and the subsequent removal for adoption without also considering the difficulty experienced
by the child. Defence mechanisms come into play when others deride value in
a music therapy that attempts to provide adopted children with an opportunity
to work with unconscious embodied memory or their internalised truth. The
author might therefore be "tilting at windmills" in her belief in doing therapy with such. As a music therapist specialising in adoption/learning disability,
she has to trust the unknown, embarking upon relationships within needs-led
free musical improvisations. She draws heavily on the work of Winnicott and
Stern suggesting that their concepts of holding and attunement are applicable to
musical relational experiences. She cites a range of authors to form her theoretical approach which she describes as a contemporary approach to music therapy

DOI: 10.4324/9781003110200-11

informed by psychoanalytic sources and with a focus on relationship, attachment and trauma. Theory is illustrated with a case study. She concludes that engaging in necessarily long-term therapeutic relationships is essential in order for adoptees with learning disabilities to be enabled first to express their trauma, and have it held and witnessed, before embarking on new ways of relating which sustain their adoptive placements.

Keywords: adoption, attunement, learning disability, psychoanalytic, relational

Introduction

I am a music psychotherapist specialising in practice with adoption for over ten years. During this time, I have evolved an approach for working with adoptees who often are referred with the most challenging of issues, not least of these sometimes being profound physical and learning difficulties. In this chapter, I will describe the body of theory undergirding my premise that it is not "tilting at windmills" to say people with learning difficulties who are adopted should have access to a non-verbal therapy modality. I will illustrate my theoretical approach with a single case study of a six-year long music therapy with a little girl with Down syndrome and associated complexities.

Psychoanalysis had not been considered as appropriate or useful for working with people with learning disabilities who had experienced emotional trauma before the work of the analyst, Valerie Sinasson (2000). She challenged the orthodoxy that learning-disabled people could not engage in psychotherapy because of a lack of intellect (cognitive). Instead, she suggested that the truth about people with learning disabilities may be too painful for us to confront and we therefore shut out any knowledge of their emotional intelligence. As Niedecken (2003) argues, "No-one wants to face in himself the attributes which are collectively projected onto Downs children." Perhaps this is why some professionals have struggled to understand the value in my work, as it was difficult for them to think that clients could know of themselves as learning disabled, let alone have any understanding of their adoption narratives. Was my work then just "tilting at windmills?" Was there really music psychotherapy to be done here and real "giants" to take on? This chapter proposes that the child in the case study (like many other children I have worked with) most certainly knew her early traumatic rejection experiences, though these remained unprocessed and unconscious and therefore presented in enactments and behaviour.

But first I want to tell the reader a story of a birth. I ask you to enter this story with your imagination and to begin to think about the early beginnings of my client, Lily, who was born with disabilities and subsequently relinquished to adoption. What might her very earliest experiences have felt like, and how have such experiences informed my work?

Being born

> "Nine months I have grown here. I am rocked in the rhythms of my mother's breathing. I am soothed by the melody of her voice, still far off, but known exclusively as hers. My mother feels my movements, cradles her hands around her belly to sing to me. I am held. Safe. But then. Screaming. Rushing. Chaos. And in a floodtide, I am pushed out into blinding light and noise…and I am dropped. I fall down and down and down, falling forever. No hands hold me, no voice soothes me, no eyes gaze into mine. My mother's voice screams NOOOOOO! Take it away! I cannot bear it."

This is how I imagined Lily being born, unexpectedly disabled, and rejected immediately because of this. Her mother, unable to bear the shock of unanticipated disability, could not look at her, touch or hold her. Her sister was told the new baby had died. Her father visited her in hospital until deciding she would be relinquished for adoption. Is it any wonder that children who experienced such early loss of the first attachments describe (in Winnicott's 1965 terms) feeling that they are dropped and "falling forever"?

Why psychoanalytic music therapy for adoptees with learning disabilities?

The psychoanalyst, Valerie Sinasson, was a pioneer in using psychoanalysis with adults with profound learning disability/impairment, making therapy accessible to people previously thought unable to access it. In her chapter on music therapy in *Music-Psychoanalysis-Musicology* (2018), Darnley-Smith cites the music therapist, Mary Priestly, a pioneer in psychoanalytic music therapy, stating that patients who lacked a capacity for symbolising could "…explore new pathways symbolically in the world of the imagination but with the bodily expressed emotion in sound" (p.139). Darnley-Smith describes music therapist Tessa Watson's work with clients with learning disabilities, who states music "…communicates something of the client's internal experience" (p.142). The therapist's role is to "…enable, receive and digest these communications, and to help the client find and explore their meaning…through musical, verbal and thinking processes and interventions…She works to enable meaning to emerge and be understood and patterns of relating to be recognised and modulated, thus change and progress may be possible."

Winnicott (1965) has described the enduring impact the earliest days of life have on a developing baby. This informs my premise that early trauma, which remains unconscious, still reverberates through life. Winnicott also felt play was valuable in healing the impact of early life deficits. In music therapy for adoptees with learning disability, there is value in musically playing together, but also a need to consider not only what is being played in a session (such as tempo, melody, etc.), but also how that music is played; the embodiment of the player, and the way in which both music and relationship develop. From such consideration, I suggest the music played in the therapeutic relationship of music therapy with adoptees is similar to the musical non-verbal interactions of early life, providing an audible shape to emotional experience which can reveal unconscious trauma and internalised patterns of relating. Ogden (1989) writes about the psychological "third" being something existent in the space between therapist and client which is fed into by both, but which can also impact upon and feed back to both. Music exists similarly in a transient temporal form, becoming an attentional, acoustic safe space between therapist and client. I argue that music can do something very Winnicottian for learning-disabled clients, by opening up a less threatening space for relational play. A non-verbal therapeutic modality is essential for people who have significant learning difficulties, language difficulties and difficulties with symbolisation, and therefore are denied access to verbal therapy.

Introduction to Lily

Lily was referred to music therapy because of the complex interplay of her emotional trauma with her organic disabilities. Her psychological distress was inseparable from her identity as a disabled child because her disability was the very reason for her relinquishment. Her adopted mother had stated that Lily was impossible to get close to, and she imagined that Lily feared the repetition of the rejection which she remembered from her birth. Together she and I hoped that music therapy could be a modality for articulating Lily's trauma, thereby lessening any need to re-enact early emotional states that remained unconscious but influential.

In the first months of our relating, it quickly became apparent that Lily most definitely could make use of a non-verbal therapeutic modality. She seemed to take ownership of the music therapy room from the outset, and my early video recordings show her confidently taking possession of instruments, singing and vocalising, and dancing in incredibly rhythmic and embodied ways. However, these same sessions also revealed how difficult it was to truly make contact with her, as she resisted any of my attempts to play with her and asserted an independence and control I found painful to observe in such a young child.

Lily's adoptive mother was encouraged that I could see the value of using this modality and she began from the outset to give me insights into the functioning of Lily's internal world. An early email I received from adopted mother stated: "I thought you might like to know Lily asks me to 'sing' to her now. It's like music already provides a way she can initiate interaction and risk relationship."

Adoption loss as an experience of not being held

It used to be thought that the pre-verbal baby was lacking in emotional intelligence, but we understand now that babies know things through their embodied experience. Adult adoptees who experienced the pre-verbal trauma of being removed from their birth mothers as tiny babies describe an enduring tremendous sensation of loss and separation. Such pre-linguistic experience may be expressed behaviourally because the experience came before language. The beginnings of human living and functioning lie much deeper, beyond language. Similarly, music is wordless and connects with inner sensations, evoking pre-linguistic stirring and expression of feeling that is incapable of being put into words. Therefore, the involvement of two human embodied people actually playing music together, which is also wordless self-expression, can potentially reveal to both a level of pre-verbal unconscious material not previously known, which may be impacting here and now. This is especially significant when working with a child who has limited verbal skill in uncovering their emotional truth.

Winnicott's (1960) concept of holding describes an incredibly subtle process occurring between mother and infant. He views holding as a maternal function that originates not just in the mother's physical holding of her baby but also her capacity to stay emotionally with the baby's raw feeling experiences. To feel psychologically held, babies need to have their emotional world carefully regulated by the mother, which happens literally through her physical care but also through her mental communications. If a mother cannot adapt to her baby (or, in the case of adoption, the baby loses the possibility of the mother being able to do so), then Winnicott says the baby's capacity for creative action will be diminished or impaired.

I hypothesised that Lily had absorbed sensations related to the absence of holding from her birth mother right from birth. The impact of the specific adoption trauma of the loss of the mother as the first attachment figure causes an infant to erect defences. Then, once relinquished by her birth family, Lily experienced overwhelming feelings of rejection, which she did not yet possess mental resources to process and assimilate. Verrier (1993) describes this as the emotional wounding underlying all adoption. Developments in neuroscience evidence that traumatised children carry within them an internalised embodied knowledge of early trauma (such as loss of the birth mother and family) which is stored in the amygdala (Schore 1994, 2012), and this applies to those with learning disability too. Adoptees who do not experience holding are not enabled to understand and manage their early mental states. Lily knew in her deepest cell memory what had happened to her. She had not possessed resources to process and assimilate her feelings, which, though unavailable to conscious recall, governed her relational repertoire. The analyst, Margaret Wilkinson (2010), describes this beautifully as "the old present," being alive still in a child's internal world. Accessing this internal world, and modifying its impacts, are core aspects of attachment and trauma-informed relational music therapy that I have evolved within adoption.

Theoretical basis

My approach currently incorporates this combination of theoretical approaches which together I describe as contemporary psychoanalytic, relational, trauma and attachment informed music therapy:

- Contemporary attachment theories
- Trauma related theories
- Intersubjectivity theory
- Relational psychoanalysis
- Developmental neuroscience and neuropsychology

Evolving an adoption-specific approach to music therapy with learning disabled clients

The two main theorists who have influenced my approach to music therapy are D.W. Winnicott and Daniel Stern. I adapt their theories (evolved through their working with infants and adult patients) to my own work with often complex, fragile adoptees. Fundamentally, my approach values the musical relationship between therapist and client because of the way it might replicate the rhythms, forms and affective qualities of early mother-infant communication. Research on early communication demonstrates a human capacity for communicative musicality, and work by Trevarthern and Malloch (2009) defines musical elements such as pulse, pitch, rhythm, dynamic and so on that precede verbal communication. Such elements are very close to what Stern (1995) called the "proto-conversation" existent between mother and infant before speech develops. At the core of relationship before language is established, the musicality of proto-conversation expresses the infant's and parent's desire to attune to one another.

The adoptees with whom I work have experienced early loss of their maternal figure, and subsequently have not developed that first pre-verbal attuned relationship. This traumatic loss remains unconscious because it happened at a pre-verbal stage of life. Early trauma then cannot be accessed through language because the experience predates language. It remains unconscious, yet alive. Music therapy, which evokes the early situation with its use of the same musical elements that appear in proto-conversation, has value because it is accessible to a type of client that would not access verbal psychotherapy. There is extra value in accessibility for those adoptees who, because of disability, have never developed verbal language. The particularity of my music therapy approach is in working with certain clients who struggle with symbolisations. For an adopted (especially profoundly disabled) child, verbal therapy often feels dry, at best, and impossible if the child has no verbal language. The reality of the music therapy space is that it is creative, imaginative and playful. My approach then advocates more creative clinical spaces for learning-disabled clients to access unconscious early trauma.

Winnicott stated when asked about his approach, "I gather this and that, here and there, settle down to clinical experience, form my own theories, and then, last of all, interest myself to see where I stole what" (Winnicott, cited in Phillips 2007, p.16). The approach I advocate has similarly evolved with my initial theorising being adapted in the light of client narratives emergent in therapeutic work and impacted by a broadening spectrum of theory. As a therapist with my own lived experience of adoption, I engaged with the lived experience of the adoption community, in "sense-making" (Weick 2001) of the adoption-specific situation. Discussions with my own clinical and academic supervisors introduced me to other bodies of theory: other creative expressive therapies, developments in contemporary psychoanalysis, attachment theory informed by neuroscience and even to philosophy.

My approach begins from the hypothesis that the loss of attunement (Stern 1995) suffered by adopted children in early life still impacts on their current capacity to risk, trust and relate within new adoptive families. This is no less the case for children who have learning disabilities. Early traumatic experience is powerful in its ongoing ability to affect current relating. Referrals have been generated (via social services, now funded by the Adoption Support Fund who value this approach) when adoptive placements have presented at risk of break-down due to relational difficulties. In the early days of my practice, making music together with adoptees and their families showed me how Trevarthern's "communicative musicality" (Trevarthern & Malloch, 2009) had potential to provide opportunities for reparative experiences of attunement and for new relational styles to emerge and be playfully experimented with. However, each needs-led improvisation took me into unknown territory, constantly evolving my hypotheses.

The music therapist, Trondalen (2016), describes relational music therapy as "understanding lived experiences emergent in jointly improvised music." Drawing upon Daniel Stern's (1998) description of intersubjective "moments of meeting," she views change as happening through non-verbal processes at a micro level (which I term "micro-moments of attunement" in my own research as a current PhD candidate at Sheffield University, UK). Early attunement experience was lost for Lily, when that fundamental first relationship was denied. The felt experience of loss of the earliest attachment figures impacts negatively on the core of rhythmic and sympathetic impulses, which develop brain connectivity, self-regulation and attachment capacity. I hoped a music therapy relationship might provide a creative, safe space for them to be re-experienced, enabling Lily to begin to trust.

I suggest then "micro-moments of attunement" are manifest in the spaces of non-directed free musical improvisation, where adopted children might reveal their early lived experience. Transference and counter-transference experienced within client-led improvisations helped me to gain a sense of Lily's internal world. This enabled me, and ultimately her adopter, to understand ways in which early experience influenced her present life and relating.

Freely improvising music-making together powerfully affects intra- and inter-personal responses, as music exists as a temporal and affect-laden form. Working in improvisation viscerally opened up to me Lily's whole attachment process. Music makes attachment patterns audible and visible and has the capacity to regulate and shape emotional communications. All music therapists will prac-tice giving significance to musical listening and imitating. Musically, we draw on expressive and receptive methods. However, when working with learning-disabled adoptees, when we listen we must hear not just the sounds which are played, but rather the entire sounding of a client's embodied presence. Children can feel grounded in their own music-making, whilst processing and assimilating the emotional impact of their experiences. Winnicottian holding then might happen within the space that both music and relationship provide. For the adopted child who has felt dropped, such holding is most important if they are to develop relational trust.

Being dropped

From our first session, Lily dramatically re-enacted her sense of being dropped because of her learning disability, and she returned to doing so many times during our work. She rejected instruments, either by letting them drop to the floor, or by throwing them. These dismissive gestures made me painfully mindful of how she had been rejected in an instant at birth and thrown away. What a strong symbolic communication her rejection of my instruments was! And it continued for many months before we could play. After reports of similar throwing at home, I received the following email from adopted mother: *Lily has suddenly stopped throwing things! She seems to have finally accepted that she can sit on my lap and have a cuddle if she wants and doesn't need to reject me!*

Winnicott (1972) actually uses the term "falling forever" to describe how it feels to lose the experiences of holding and mirroring from the mother. "The infant may then experience libidinal mutual gazing as maternal holding and sudden aggressive looking away as being suddenly dropped, bringing about the primal agony of falling forever" (p.89). This is a relational happening, that occurs in the space between mother and child, in what Winnicott defines as the "potential space." I argue that Lily's feeling of being dropped from her birth mother's holding and her subsequent sense of "falling forever" could be met in the potential spaces of a relationship in music therapy. For Winnicott, repeated reliable experiences of a loving, mutually holding mirror gaze between mother and infant are the remedy against negative patterns arising in a baby's internal world. Winnicott has described how such gaze prevents hopelessness (or, in his terms, "primal agony") arising. The mother's face is likened to an emotional mirror which the baby looks into. As the baby sees the mother's responses through her facial expression, the baby begins to experience its own feeling world. Thus, the baby's sense of self develops as it receives a mirrored response from the mother. Such experiences had been lost to Lily.

Stern's concept of attunement has similarities with Winnicott's mirroring, but can be seen as extending the idea. Wright (2009) states Stern's attunement is "essentially non-verbal and spontaneous, and relatively outside the mother's awareness." Attunement describes the processes by which "a mother tracks, then reflects back to her infant, her sense of having shared in her infants feeling." This is subtly different from Winnicott's mirroring as it is "more continuous and communicative...and appears to attend to relational...needs." The baby's feeling states are called "vitality effects" by Stern (2010), by which he means a continuous background feeling tone accompanying the baby's actions. The mother's responses offer a background of resonant feeling activity. Her attuned response is intuitive and ongoing. She does not simply copy or mirror but captures, transposes and gives back a felt sense to the baby of being met and understood.

I understand attachment communications within the music of adopted children as expressed in such embodied ways, at levels beneath conscious awareness within the dynamic intersubjective field. In Lily's case, her body communicated the truth of the trauma, rejection and losses of her earliest moments. Stern describes the embodied relational matrix in which humans remain embedded. Lily could not escape her embedded memories and needed them to be met in the body of another. Music therapy offered her, in music therapist Sutton's (2002) words, "an experience of herself as embodied in sound and in silence." I needed then to find music which could meet and hold Lily's experience. Sletvold (2014) calls this searching for "embodied empathy," where physical play, held within music, offers a way to experience felt attunement at an empathic embodied level.

Embodied relating

It is necessary for music therapists to engage deeply in embodied listening with non-verbal clients because it is insufficient to focus upon musical elements such as melody, tone, timbre, rhythm and so on alone. Rather, we must listen with all our senses to our client's movements, recognising rhythmic forms of posture, facial expressions, alternations of music and silence. Understanding ourselves in relation to another person, is achieved not just through musical language, but also through the language of movements that gives form and allows us to share the effects of a relationship. In adoption work, this enables an understanding of the pre-linguistic nature of emotional experience and expression. As Lily's emotional states were witnessed, she knew she was heard and responded to within a space of shared embodied attention. Jean Knox (2011) suggests that such "therapeutic witnessing" of embodied truth is necessary groundwork for the expression of trauma. Embodied musical relating gave Lily a vital sense of being alive in the presence of another.

Adopted children with disabilities can find safety in embodied improvised music. As we have seen, musical elements provide core aspects of what a baby needs in early attachment and what Lily had lacked. Making music, she could trust her own play, then let me join her. This prosodic interchange in music therapy has been shown to emanate from Stern's proto-conversation of mother and baby, providing moments of synchronicity which are perhaps not unlike "the rhythm of safety" which Tustin (1981) has described. When my clients engage in embodied musical relationship, their early intuitive emotional communications are made evident in dynamic form. Musical expression directly engages and activates the core of rhythmic and sympathetic impulses in relating, which Trevarthern (1979) calls "communicative musicality." The embodied aspects *and* the music contain all the elements of attachment formation. Lily's "old present" could be more safely thought about because music therapy provided in Wilkinson's (2010) terms "a modified response, and a different affective experience through relating at the deepest levels" (p.4). Or, as a famous (anonymous) quote states, "Where words fail, music speaks!"

The reciprocal shaping of the emotional embodied experience of the other might more simply be known to music therapists as matching and mirroring. However, genuine relatedness and empathy are very different to simply copying the music that clients play, because it is the feelings behind playing music that become our referent, in imitation, from the inside out, of what our clients' experience feels like.

Year two/three of therapy

In the second year of therapy, Lily incorporated a baby doll into our musical play which became another way for her of symbolically expressing her embodiment. She gave the doll the name GiGi, which both adopted mum and I felt was a representation of her own name. For weeks, the doll's head would be bashed off the guitar, resulting in sounds I responded to vocally. Baby GiGi was thrown hard across the room, and I was provided with a visual image of damage to Lily being located in her head, in the context of her learning disability. The damaged doll, like the instruments, like Lily herself, was thrown away and rejected, which was immensely painful to witness. It felt clear that Lily had an understanding that her damage was located in her head, in the context of her learning disability (as Cottis (2009) suggests is possible).

It took a year of work before Lily became able to show kindness to the doll. Although it would still be thrown at times, this was done with far less effort, and she began instead to sing to it tenderly and softly now, wrapping it in a blanket which she sometimes wrapped around her own body. This play occurred at home too, and was supported by adopted mother, who, like me, viewed it as fundamental to Lily having reparative experiences of the early nurture she was denied. Lily was now able to internalise goodness from our sessions to take elsewhere.

A wordless sung language was easier than spoken language for Lily to express difficult emotion-laden material. I would sometimes choose not to play an instrument with her but simply hum gently under my breath, just providing a presence for her. Adopted mother was able to utilise singing like this similarly at home. Many adopted learning-disabled children find it possible to sing out (vocalise without words), rather than talk out, experiences of loss and rejection and their consequent feelings of rage and anger.

After one particular session of hummed singing, I realised that in this session I had been singing the tune *Rock-A-Bye-Baby*, a traditional English lullaby which had enormous significance for Lily's own lived experience. I will share the words of this here now for those who may be unfamiliar with it.

> "Rock-a-bye-baby on the treetop
> When the wind blows the cradle will rock
> When the bough breaks the cradle will fall
> Down will come baby, cradle and all."

The lyrics of this lullaby were perhaps a way that I, in counter transference, picked up projections from Lily about her early felt sensorial experience of being dropped. There is a risk that children relinquished at birth can feel that they somehow must be very bad inside to have been immediately given up to adoption. Lily had gradually come to know she could reveal difficult emotions and would not be rejected as a bad self. At first in our work her rage was un-regulated and she loudly dropped instruments or smashed them hard into other objects, obliterating my music and a sense of my present self in the process. As she allowed me to become more present with her raging, she settled into a more coherent affect and function. This is a state that many adoptees with trauma experience will struggle to manage, but music can help settle hyper-aroused states, as it naturally invokes embodied expression and aids regulation.

In her third year of music therapy, Lily incorporated a dragon puppet in her music, to work with her rage and monstrous feelings. Her anger could now be welcomed, and she vocalised it furiously in music echoing her feeling states. As she was feeling more securely attached, both in music therapy and most significantly in her adoptive placement, she revealed a much more whole sense of herself, rather than one which was constantly mediated for others. Our musical frame provided, as it were, a soundtrack of tolerance for difficult emotions or memories to be worked through.

Year four of therapy

There remained much yet to face, however, as during 2017, Lily experienced multiple hospitalisations, evoking memories of her early lived experience, which, of course, itself took place in a hospital. I would sing about how difficult hospital was, and gradually she allowed my supportive vocal holding to soothe her. Our relationship was a constant thing as her life underwent huge change and uncertainty. More importantly, she held on to the security gained with adoptive mother, who stated this: *This morning, Lily regressed to being a baby. I picked her up and cuddled her, gave her a bottle and held her close. She responded, accepting at last my affection. She was calm, relaxed and made brilliant eye contact. It's the first time she's ever accepted love in hospital.*

Over the first four years of our work together, music therapy offered significant reparation for Lily. When she regressed, it was never to the precise place where she had been at before. Our music together gradually became more coherent, shared, integrated and relational. Music therapy provided a rhythm to life that her early experiences had denied her. I was continually encouraged by contact with adopted mother which showed Lily taking music therapy experiences out into the wider world, offering new opportunities for styles of attachment and relating. I received a message late in 2017, shortly before Lily's seventh birthday: *Lily seems to be moving forward! She wants me to hold her a lot, and we often role-play bottle feeding. I tell her that I love "little inside-baby Lily" but I love my big girl Lily too. She allows me now to calm her enough for bedtime and I think she would even lie all evening in my arms if I'd let her!*

Year five of therapy

Sadly, this was no fairy-tale end to Lily's journey and work with me. During 2018, her health deteriorated rapidly, and on Christmas Day she was admitted in a critical state to paediatric intensive care. The complications of her Down syndrome that affected her heart and lungs were increasingly difficult to manage. Despite the multiple interventions of consultants nationwide, Lily continued to deteriorate, and in January was moved to paediatric high dependency. Lily's mum was adamant that her music therapy must continue throughout her hospitalisation, and I agreed, whilst having to be incredibly flexible working in a High Dependency Unit, which is a tense and fragile environment where all children are critically ill. Music therapy had to incorporate unknown territory: interruptions, other people present in the room, and occasionally I even played and sang while Lily underwent medical procedures.

During this time, she became insistent that she wanted to sing what she described as her "mouse" song with me. Lily had seen a child ventriloquist on TV who had a mouse puppet, and the mouse's song was in fact *Summertime* from *Porgy and Bess*. So, I took my violin and tentatively played *Summertime* there on the ward. Some staff were completely bemused by a violinist playing to this child and could not conceive of the inner meanings of the music Lily chose. This song became both anthem and mantra for her during those sessions in hospital. It was important to think about why this song, above any other, had such resonance. The minor key immediately evokes a melancholy feeling. It seemed that this music now was Lily's choice: sad, and intense, and aching. It is written as a lullaby, and often lullabies contain dark truths for children to learn. Lily certainly had a lot of darkness to contend with. She sang with such intensity, her whole body caught up in emotion, and seemed safely held in the musical world that was created, whilst also expressing her own feeling self within the music.

> "Summertime, and the livin' is easy
> Fish are jumpin' and the cotton is high
> Your daddy's rich, and your mommas good looking
> So hush little baby, don't you cry
> One of these mornings, you're gonna rise up singing
> Spread your wings and you'll take to the sky
> Until that morning, know that nothing can harm you
> With mummy and daddy standing by."

Lyrically, this song is significant too. Lily had been adopted by a single woman and had never known an adoptive father, and yet both mother and father feature in this song. Was this a legacy of Lily's memories of her birth father, and his brief attachment to her before ultimately relinquishing her to adoption? Or was it that Lily, who already experienced being different in the world, had a fantasy of wanting to belong to a "normal" nuclear family form? My supervisor wondered if her adoptive mum and myself became a parenting couple for her as we were the things that remained fixed in her life through periods of enormous change? Whatever, it was obvious to all who heard Lily sing that there was deep meaning in her expressions and that she had immense emotional intelligence.

Year six of therapy

During April 2019, Lily's health deteriorated severely until it was decided that further interventions would not be helpful and would constitute further trauma upon her now very frail body. A plan of palliative care was implemented, and she remained in the High Dependency Unit. As part of the plan, it was agreed that I would work with Lily until the end of her life, however that worked out. Lily had felt alone immediately after she entered the world, and we were determined that she would not leave it feeling similarly.

Shortly after this decision, I went to see her and when I arrived on the ward she had just hit the hospital play worker very hard. This worker had left the room in tears, partly because of her own shock and sudden pain, but also distressed because of Lily's declining state. I sat down immediately with Lily and began to reach for instruments, which she declined. Instead, we continued to play with the sand and toys the playworker had left and utilised a song we had co-developed in the early days of our work. If she had ever shown a possibility of hitting herself or myself (which never did actually happen), I would sing her safe song with her, and this felt like the song she needed now.

> "When she's cross and when she's angry
> We will keep her safe, safe, safe."

This was to be the last session that I had with Lily as two weeks later she died. I visited her that morning where she was snuggled in bed with her mum. Lily had never been able to allow her mum to cuddle her face on, but in her last hours she allowed mum to climb into bed with her, where she sat behind her and held her. Lily's sight was fading but we know that hearing is the last sense to leave the body. When she knew I was present she simply said, "mouse song" and sang as I played violin. Even in those last moments her mum said she felt Lily soothing herself, and indeed those around her, with her beautiful song. I was privileged to play the same piece of music at her funeral.

Conclusions

Lily has been a most wonderful teacher for me and a major inspiration for my own decision to formally research my approach. Her total of six years of music therapy made it eminently clear to me that as music therapists we are well placed to deal with extremely early non-verbal unconscious material. When we seek to musically hold and attune to adoptees who have profound learning disability, in improvisational music making, our music together has its own special power to allow both bodies and minds to speak truth and to be heard. Lily may not have had the opportunity to enjoy years of new relationship with her adoptive family, but she was able to die knowing that she was loved and held.

From this I argue that we should advocate for appropriate non-verbal creative modalities of therapy for clients with profound disabilities who are presenting with the earliest forms of trauma. There may be an assumption that learning-disabled adoptees do not understand (intellectually or cognitively) their early experience, because their lack of verbal skill is less than with the general population of adoptees. However, we work with an internal intelligence and truth. Work with Lily illustrates the profound, internalised, embodied knowledge she had of her early rejection and how this continued to shape her relationships. It also shows her incredible determination to engage creatively and purposefully with painful inner narratives. Such determination needs to be met and held in meaningful enduring therapeutic relationships.

Thank you, Lily, for teaching us that adopted people with learning disabilities do indeed have vast interior worlds and lives and should therefore have exactly the same access to psychotherapy.

"Spread your wings and take to the sky."

References

Cottis, T. (2009). *Intellectual disability, trauma, and psychotherapy.* London/New York: Routledge.

Niedecken, D. (2003). *Nameless: understanding learning disability.* Sussex/New York: Brunner-Routledge.

Knox, J. (2011). *Self-agency: psychotherapy: attachment, autonomy and intimacy.* New York/London: Norton.

Ogden, T. (1989). *The primitive edge of experience.* East Sussex: Routledge.

Phillips, A. (2007). *Winnicott.* London: Penguin.

Schore, A. (2012). *The science of the art of psychotherapy* New York/London: Norton.

Sinasson, V. (2000). Learning disability as a trauma and the impact of trauma on people with a learning disability. London. *British Journal of Psychiatry,* 176, 32–36.

Sletvold, J. (2014). *The embodied analyst: from Freud and Reich to relationality.* East Sussex: Routledge.

Stern, D. (1995). *The motherhood constellation: a united view of parent-infant psychotherapy.* London: Karnac Books.

Stern, D. (1998). *The interpersonal world of the infant.* London: Karnac Books.

Stern. D. (2010). *Forms of vitality.* Oxford: Oxford University Press.

Sutton, J. (2002). *Music, music therapy and trauma: international perspectives.* London: Jessica Kingsley Publishers.

Trevarthern, C. (1979). Communication and co-operation in early infancy: a description of primary intersubjectivity. In: Bullowa, M. (Ed): *Before speech: the beginning of human communication.* Cambridge: Cambridge University Press.

Trevarthern, C. and Malloch, S. (2009). *Communicative musicality: exploring the base of human companionship.* Oxford: Oxford University Press.

Trondalen, G. (2016). *Relational music therapy: an intersubjective perspective.* Dallas: Barcelona Publishers.

Tustin, F. (1981). *Autistic states in children.* East Sussex: Routledge.

Verrier, N. (1993). *The primal wound.* Baltimore: Gateway Press Inc.

Weick, K. (2001). *Sensemaking in organisations.* London: Sage.

Wilkinson, M. (2010). *Changing minds in therapy; emotion, attachment, trauma and neurobiology.* W.W. New York: Norton and Company.

Winnicott, D.W. (1960). The theory of the parent-infant relationship. *International Journal of Psychoanalysis,* 41, 585–595.

Winnicott, D. W. 1965 (1990). *The Maturational Processes And The Facilitating Environment.* London: Karnac. Hogarth Press Limited.

Winnicott, D.W. 1972/1986. *Holding And Interpretation: Fragment Of An Analysis.* London: Hogarth Press.

Wright, K. (2009). *Mirroring and attunement; self-realisation in psychoanalysis and art.* East Sussex/New York: Routledge.

12

WHAT ARE WE TALKING ABOUT?

Development of an empirical base for art therapy with children diagnosed with autism spectrum disorders

Celine Schweizer

Abstract

Art therapists are skilled in communicating with clients who are expressing them-selves when creating art. It is also an important skill to communicate effectively with different parties, such as a client's family, colleagues from other professions and policy makers. This means that art therapists have to speak with diverse stakeholders in different "languages." Talking with the client about experiences during the art therapy process is a different skill to the exchange of professional information with family, with colleagues or with other professions and policy makers. Art therapists are therefore working with varied languages. They have to deal with interdisciplinary discussions and heterogeneous perspectives to provide transference of treatment aspects, outlines and results.

Empirical research supports the development of an objective and more gen-erally understood language. Existing studies about art therapy for children diag-nosed with autism spectrum disorders (ASD) have yielded an empirical-based language for varied aspects of the treatment. This language provides an outline for art therapists on the one hand and supports communication about art therapy with third parties as well. In several studies, an empirical-based treatment pro-gramme, was developed. *Images of Self* is an art therapy programme for children and their autism-related problems. It offers a language that is meant to be under-stood by varied parties. In this chapter, these existing studies are built upon, with the development and testing of an empirical base and vocabulary for art therapy with children diagnosed with ASD. The chapter sheds light on art therapy for children diagnosed with ASD and also on several issues about conditions for development and evaluation of the programme.

Keywords: art therapy, children, autism spectrum disorder, empirical evidence, perspectives

DOI: 10.4324/9781003110200-12

Abstract in Dutch

Beeldend therapeuten zijn bedreven in het communiceren met cliënten die zich uiten bij het maken van kunst. Het is daarnaast een belangrijke vaardigheid om effectief te kunnen communiceren met verschillende partijen, zoals de familie van een cliënt, collega's met andere beroepen en beleidsmakers. Dit betekent dat beeldend therapeuten met diverse belanghebbenden in verschillende 'talen' moeten spreken. Met de cliënt praten over ervaringen tijdens het beeldend therapieproces, is een andere vaardigheid dan het uitwisselen van professionele informatie met familie, collega's met andere beroepen en beleidsmakers. Beeldend therapeuten passen eigenlijk verschillende talen toe in hun werkzaamheden. Ze hebben te maken met interdisciplinaire discussies en heterogene perspectieven om overdracht van behandelaspecten, contouren en resultaten te bieden.

Empirisch onderzoek ondersteunt de ontwikkeling van een objectieve taal die meer algemeen wordt verstaan. Bestaande studies over beeldende therapie voor kinderen met autisme spectrumstoornissen (ASS) hebben een empirische taal opgeleverd voor verschillende aspecten van de behandeling. Deze taal geeft enerzijds een schets voor beeldend therapeuten en ondersteunt ook de communicatie over beeldende therapie met derden. In verschillende onderzoeken is een empirisch onderbouwd behandelprogramma ontwikkeld. Images of Self is een beeldende therapieprogramma voor kinderen met aan autisme-gerelateerde problemen. Het programma biedt een taal die bedoeld is om door verschillende partijen te worden begrepen. In dit hoofdstuk wordt op deze bestaande studies voortgebouwd, met de ontwikkeling en toetsing van een empirische basis en vocabulaire voor beeldende therapie bij kinderen met de diagnose ASS. Dit hoofdstuk belicht beeldend therapie voor kinderen bij wie ASS is vastgesteld en ook worden een aantal kwesties beschreven die betrekking hebben op de voorwaarden voor ontwikkeling en evaluatie van het programma.

Introduction

The arts therapies have a professional tradition with psychological and art-making processes as the main instruments in the treatment. In the Netherlands, policy-makers, insurance companies and colleagues from other disciplines are asking for evidence-based treatment protocols and concrete information about treatment aims and results. These developments may be the same in other countries.

In clinical practice, art therapists mainly base their treatment on experience and intuitive knowledge, which is hard to verbalise (Bosgraaf, Spreen, Pattiselanno & Van Hooren, 2020). "Inside" the treatment the art therapist should be able to understand and conduct the art expressions and processes of clients who are telling their own stories in their own art language. The art process has to be recognised, understood and conducted as personal expression. For communication with "outside" parties, it is often a challenge to transfer this clinical and therapeutic-oriented language. How can the nonverbal character of art-making processes be translated into an objectivated language which is understood by these "outside parties"? A generally accepted view is considered valid only if supported by objective statistics and research data.

Studying art therapy as a treatment for a specific diagnostic group offers an opportunity to look at how languages and approaches might be developed in art therapy. A diagnosis is an empirical and objective description and offers a shared language that may function as background information about opportunities and the challenges of a client in art therapy. Among art therapists there are different preferences for being informed about diagnostic information of a client before or during treatment. This kind of background information offers an opportunity for art therapists to prepare observations at the start of a treatment and explore if, and in what way, a client behaves during art-making. An important result from one of the studies by the author (Schweizer, Knorth, Van Yperen & Spreen, 2019a) is that referrers and art therapists agree that during treatment the art therapist works in contact with the personality of the client. An art therapist works with the behaviour of the client during art-making.

The word autism derives from the Greek word *autos*, which means self. It refers to people who are isolated in their own world, which is one of the many characteristics of people with autism and has many appearances. Eugen Bleuler, a Swiss psychiatrist, was the first person who used the term around 1911 (Feinstein, 2010). Nowadays ASD is recognised as a neurodevelopmental condition with the main problem areas defined as social-communicative deficits and repetitive/restricted behaviours and interests (American Psychiatric Association, 2013; World Health Organization, 2012). Prevalence of autism spectrum disorders (ASD) is uncertain and is reported with numbers from 1 to 3% in several studies in the US, United Kingdom and the Netherlands (Baio et al., 2018; Houben-Van Herten, Knoops & Voorrips, 2014; Kogan et al., 2016). The ratio of boys and girls diagnosed with ASD is 3 or 4:1. Regarding children with an ASD diagnosis it is reported that 44–70% are also treated for mental health problems. Quite a high amount of people with ASD have intellectual disabilities (ID); 50–70% have IQs < 70 (Centers for Disease Control and Prevention, 2006; Fombonne, 2003). Besides ID, people with ASD often have also psychiatric disorders (70%), such as an attention deficit hyperactivity disorder, an anxiety disorder or an opposite defiant disorder (Dekker & Koot, 2003; Leyfer et al., 2006).

Although the diagnosis indicates the selection of children being studied, in our study a consensus is found among art therapists and referrers about the importance of working with or adapting to the *individual* child and his/her behaviour and not with their diagnosis (Schweizer, Knorth, Van Yperen & Spreen, 2019a).

Development and first evaluation of images of self, an art therapy programme for children diagnosed with autism spectrum disorders

Children with severe problems which are related to ASD are regularly referred to art therapy. Nevertheless, empirical evidence about the reasons why they are referred, treatment aims, results and processes is still scarce and only recently developed (Schweizer, Knorth, Van Yperen, & Spreen, 2020a; Snir & Regev, 2013; Van Lith, Woolisher Stallings & Harris, 2017).

The PhD from the author (Schweizer, 2020b) researched the treatment, its aims, results and contextual influences. In five successive studies, typical elements of art therapy for children diagnosed with ASD have been identified and tested. The children being studied have normal or high intelligence profiles and are aged between 6 and 12 years.

The main reasons for referral were identified as: severe problems with sense of self, emotion regulation, flexibility and social behaviour. The sense of self problems are understood in a theoretical continuum of self-related problems which also involves self-esteem, self-image and self-concept. The children were referred to art therapy because they felt insecure about themselves and had a strongly negative self-image. The emotion regulation problems involved strong emotional outbursts and also depressed feelings and anxiety. Flexibility problems appeared as difficulties with even small, unexpected changes. The child may be strongly dysregulated by another brand of peanut butter at home, or a book that's put upside down on the desk in school. And social behaviour was described as not understanding how to cope with interactions with other children and adults and also difficulties with giving words about their own experiences.

The Images of Self programme was developed during the five studies mentioned and is an evidenced-based art therapy intervention. The name of the programme refers to the self-image of the child, which is often an important reason for referral and an issue during treatment. The title of the programme also refers to the art work that appears as images created by the child during therapy. Every image represents the way the child has been working on it by him/herself. The Images of Self programme provides a framework composed with consensus-based criteria. This evidence-based outline supports insight in the unique individual experiences which are part of art therapy processes. It increases transparency, transferability and verifiability of this treatment for client, client system, professionals, referrers and other interested parties.

The next parts in this chapter will explain more about the research background, the process, challenges and results.

Multilinguality

During treatment, art therapists are guided by their own professional intuitive approach and at the same time apply the same ethical principles, diagnostic categories and standards of care that other mental health professionals are using (Kapitan, 2010). Inside the treatment the art therapist aims to understand and conduct the art expressions and processes of clients who are telling their own stories in their own imaginative art language.

Varied perspectives on art therapy have been described before (Gussak & Rosal, 2016; Kapitan, 2010). In practice, an art therapist has to deal with diverse points of view. With the aim of helping clients with their problems, (s)he has to relate to expressive and creative forms on the one hand. On the other, (s) he has to comprehend more rational realities, such as psychological theories, diagnostic information, the discipline-specific languages of other professionals and of course the spoken language of clients and their relatives. In this way, art therapists have to be multilingual: attuning to the needs of each individual client, speaking and understanding the languages of art and body and being versed in different professional vocabularies as well.

When I started working with children diagnosed with autism, I felt challenged in finding my own way of communicating with these children. Although I was familiar with developmental theories, I didn't feel certain how to apply it in practice.

> *My first experiences as an art therapist working with children diagnosed with autism spectrum disorders (ASD) included feelings of insecurity and failure. I might have got a bit stuck in my own imagination about expected art therapy processes… The art materials did not invite these children to create and explore in the way I was used to with other children. The children with autism strongly held on to their own interests and behaviours and it took me some time to find ways to develop understanding and look at how to treat their problems, how to invite them to develop new experiences, and create expressive art work.*
>
> *The theoretical perspectives of Daniel Stern (1985) and Evans and Rutten-Saris (1998) about early development and the detailed descriptions of it supported me to understand these children more deeply. Differences between calendar age related behaviour and social emotional behaviour, seemed confusing. This psychological theory provided another perspective to understand their behaviour and when I applied this view in art therapy it was helpful for working with the children with ASD and their art work.*

In an objectivated vocabulary, words are applied to describe treatment characteristics on an empirical level. It describes concrete and recognisable behaviours from the client during art-making, or in relation with the art therapist, or with art therapy group members. These kinds of descriptions are expected to be recognisable by everyone and are meant to provide a language to communicate with various professional fields. The objectivated language can be applied in treatment reports and supports systematic evaluation of treatments and other research aims that may generate evidence-based knowledge. These verbalised representations of art therapy elements may support an understanding by other parties of treatment conditions, aims and results.

Empirical evidence

It is a challenge to develop a language that covers different characteristics of non-verbal and verbal languages and that may be understood by other parties. Any language with words will never fully cover the experiences during art-making.

But it may function as a framework to communicate about art therapy processes and results. For instance, the word *behaviour* may function as an outline for when someone is in a flow of creating something, shapes emerge in interaction between inner movements and art materials. The experiences, feelings and expressions are hard to describe in words. Words that describe observable behaviour will never replace these kind of experiences but may provide an objective framework that supports studying art processes.

Images of Self is an art therapy programme for children diagnosed with ASD. The treatment programme entails 15 sessions and is based on a series of practice-based investigations. It provides a general outline with observable criteria for a child's behaviour as well as an art therapist's actions. The outline supports insight into (conducting) unique individual experiences which are part of art therapy processes. The starting point is that the art therapists adapt the supply of art materials and workforms to the interests and skills of each individual child, because every child with autism is different. Also, because every art therapist is different, it is hard to prescribe a very detailed programme outline. The programme is balanced between clear outlines and space for individualities.

Five studies were conducted according to the "stages of evidence" for practice-based research, representing ascending levels of evidence regarding the effectiveness of psychosocial interventions (Van Yperen, Veerman & Bijl, 2017, p138) (see Fig. 12.1).

These studies were conducted with the aim to enable systematic evaluation of art therapy (AT) for children diagnosed with ASD (Schweizer, Knorth & Spreen, 2014; Schweizer, Spreen,& Knorth, 2017; Schweizer, Knorth, Van Yperen & Spreen, 2019a).

According to the first level of this model, the level of descriptive evidence, elements of art therapy for children with ASD was described based on interviews with eight art therapists who were experienced in treating these children (Schweizer, Spreen & Knorth, 2017). The main question asked to the interviewees was: "what are characteristics of art therapy with children diagnosed with ASD?"

The descriptions of the art therapist's stories about art means, forms of expressions, actions of the art therapist, collaboration with parents and teachers,

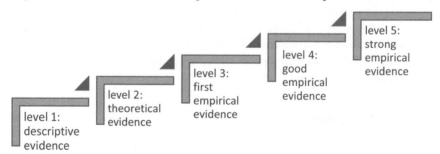

FIGURE 12.1 Ascending levels of evidence on the effectiveness of interventions. C Schweizer.

treatment aims and results, treatment duration, etc., were analysed and further developed with grounded theory principles (Charmaz, 2006; Strauss & Corbin, 1998). This means that stories from different art therapists were compared, specific items were selected and labelled. Corresponding items were grouped and labelled again. This inductive procedure is based on varied stories from art therapists and offers an objectivated perspective on core elements in art therapy for children diagnosed with ASD.

> *In this study many rich examples from art therapy practices described the art expressions of the children that were treated and also the main actions from the art therapists, the main contextual conditions and the main problem areas. This included the "tendency to sameness" of the children with autism during art making; the active structuring attitude of the art therapist; the use of varied art materials; the opportunity to connect words to experiences. Also, transference from more flexible behaviour in art therapy to the situation at home and in school was mentioned. For instance: in art therapy a child became more flexible in the choice for art materials. At home the child became more flexible about the brand of peanut butter.*

The practice-based evidence from the art therapist's stories about their practices led to more curiosity for more knowledge. After the first explorations of art therapy practices due to art therapist's tacit knowledge, a second study was undertaken. This second study, a review on the literature yielded 18 case studies. No experimental study or randomised study was found. A content analysis lead to comparable and additional descriptive information about art therapy practices with children diagnosed with ASD (Schweizer, Knorth & Spreen, 2014).

> *An important finding in this study was that these case studies mainly concerned success stories which were unsystematically reported. For example, some studies did not mention the problems for which the child was referred to art therapy. Also, the (choice for an) amount and frequency of sessions remained unclear. Some treatments took five weeks, others five years.*

It is recommended to apply a systematic way to describe case studies when aiming to provide insight in art therapy and its results to outside parties, and also for transference of knowledge about treatments and, of course, when publishing (Abbing, Ponstein, Kienle, Gruber & Baars, 2016).

In a third study (Schweizer, Knorth, Van Yperen & Spreen, 2019a), "typical elements" were established, based on the identified elements from the former two studies. With a Delphi study and a focus group in a mixed methods design, consensus was achieved by determining the level of agreement between 32 art therapists and referrers. Agreement about 46 typical elements has enhanced objectivity of these elements that are part of art therapy for children diagnosed with ASD.

The 46 consensus-based items added insight about the outlines for the treatment. For instance:

- *A diagnosis is not leading the treatment, but the behaviour of the child is.*
- *The same therapeutic aspects of making art are valuable for both verbal and non-verbal children, verbal children may profit more from the opportunity to connect words to experiences.*
- *It is important that the art therapist introduces variation in experiences and expression when the child creates art.*

The 46 consensus-based items were used for constructing evaluation instruments. One instrument for observation of the child with ASD in art therapy, the other instrument to evaluate the handling of the art therapist. Besides some general items, most items focused on the four problem areas of children with ASD who were referred to art therapy: sense of self, emotion regulation, flexibility and social behaviour.

The fourth study in this series was conducted to develop and test two measurement instruments on interrater reliability. The aim of this study was to develop the items in both measurement instruments to be understood the same way. This was achieved with test ratings and comments of users. The first scale is aimed at observation of the child in art therapy (OAT-A), and the other scale is for evaluation of the actions of the art therapist, working with a child diagnosed with ASD (EAT-A) (Schweizer, Knorth, Van Yperen & Spreen, 2019b). Determining interrater reliability was an interesting experience in the light of one of the themes in this chapter: objectivity. In several rounds, 74 art therapists and art therapy students watched videos from art therapy sessions with children diagnosed with ASD and rated the measurement instruments. Scores were compared and discussed, and items adapted to become more precise. Information about the procedure was mentioned before as an example for how an empirical language may support professionals and students.

A group of art therapists were invited to rate items from the two assessment scales with the aim to develop interrater reliability of these items. The scales were constructed with 46 consensus-based items about art therapy for children diagnosed with ASD. These items were distilled from interviews with experienced art therapists and from literature about art therapy practices.

When starting with this exercise many art therapists said they felt insecure as to whether they would understand the criteria. Many also communicated in advance that they wanted to support the research and development of the instruments but were afraid that they would not agree with the items. Students mentioned they were afraid they might be not able to understand and observe well enough. After having watched the videos, after the scoring and discussion most participants shared an enthusiasm about the instruments. The art therapists reported that the items represented their work and they felt relieved about the ability to use such kinds of instruments for treatment evaluation. Since the instruments were constructed and validated with practice-based information from the participating art therapists, they confirmed that the objectivated language in the measurement instruments are covering their art therapy practices.

For art therapy students it was informative to contribute to this research: they reported to have learned about observation in art therapy in general and also developed their understanding of specific characteristics of art therapy for children diagnosed with ASD.

It has to be mentioned that when a student develops skills to become an art therapist, it may be helpful to use an instrument for systematic observation. But this way of learning has to be additional and cannot replace discovery and development of "intuitive ways of observing" in the art therapeutic triangle as a basic skill of an art therapist.

The fifth study involved a treatment evaluation with 12 individual children. The treatment was tested with the "Images of self – programme"[1] (Schweizer, Knorth, Van Yperen & Spreen, 2020a). This art therapy programme for children diagnosed with ASD was developed and based on the previous studies and serves several aims. The evidence-based programme supports conveyance of information about treatment conditions, aims and results of art therapy for children with autism-related problems. It provides an outline for art therapists and art therapy students and also gives information for other parties such as family, colleagues from other disciplines and insurance companies.

When starting the first studies of my PhD I was desperately looking for collaboration with schools and institutions for child and youth psychiatry. I expected that implementation in the institutions would be very helpful for contributions from art therapists and clients to the research projects.

Finally, when the evidence-based Images of Self programme was written and the two first studies were published in blind peer reviewed journals, institutions were happy to collaborate.

The value of language and empirical evidence never appeared more clear to me.

The study was conducted in a mixed-methods pre-test–post-test design, with regular assessments during and after treatment. A multiple systemic single case study was applied with active involvement of children, parents, teachers and art therapists as respondents. Results were not only scored in art therapy but also at home and in school. Change in children's behaviour was expected in the following outcomes: sense of self, emotion regulation, flexibility and social behaviour.

All participating children had severe problems with sense of self, flexibility, emotion regulation and social behaviour. Results according to the quantitative data were that seven children showed reliable improvement in flexibility and social behaviour during and after treatment in AT, at home and in school. Although this concerns a small study, it is a promising result compared to general reduction of problems rates of 35–62% with psychosocial interventions for children and youth 12 months after the treatment began (Jörg et al., 2012; Nanninga, Jansen, Knorth & Reijneveld, 2018). For children diagnosed with ASD, there are a few effective treatments (Boer & Van der Gaag, 2016; Van Rooyen & Rietveld, 2017). (Young) children with ASD can make progress when receiving intensive interventions (>25 hours in a week) based on cognitive behavioural principles. These treatments have demonstrated to be effective on development of social skills (Scheeren, Koot & Begeer, 2019; Van Rooyen & Rietveld, 2017). Arts therapies are recommended for people diagnosed with ASD because of its experiential characteristics (AKWA-GGZ, 2018).

According to the qualitative data, all children were perceived by their parents, teachers and art therapists as happier and more stable, and more able to give words to their experiences. Also, improvements in emotion regulation (n = 8) and flexibility (n = 4) were reported.

Varied perspectives on art therapy for children with autism-related problems

Treatment is the core business of art therapists. Besides knowledge of client's problems, the specific actions of the art therapist, the contextual aspects of the treatment and expected outcomes are also involved. Empirical knowledge about art therapy may focus on the art processes and expressions of the client and at behavioural change. But, apart from this, we have to be aware that the processes of change are happening in a triangular relationship between client, art and art therapist. Art therapists and art therapy researchers are challenged by studies that describe the relationship between client and therapist as a more substantial contribution to the treatment result than any method (Heijnen, Roest, Willemars & Van Hooren, 2017; Van Yperen, Van der Steege, Addink & Boendermaker, 2010). Besides the therapeutic alliance, contextual influences also make an important contribution to a treatment result. In Fig. 12.2, these aspects are mapped as categories that play a role in development of empirical evidence.

In the first two studies that were mentioned before, a model was developed that visualises art therapy in the context of treatment conditions. This model was based on results from interviews and a review of the literature about art therapy for children diagnosed with ASD (Schweizer, Knorth & Spreen, 2014; Schweizer, Spreen & Knorth, 2017). The model is named the COAT model. The categories in the model are like layers wrapped around the core of art therapy, as a "coat" to wear for protecting and facilitating art therapy in its environment (Fig. 12.2).

Each layer in the model is representing a category: the **C**ontext of the treatment, the expected **O**utcomes, the **A**rt expressions of the client and the behaviour of the **T**herapist:

1. *Art means and expressions*: art materials have a potential to offer sensory motor experiences to ASD children with under- or oversensitivity. Art materials offer opportunities for development in making variations for those children

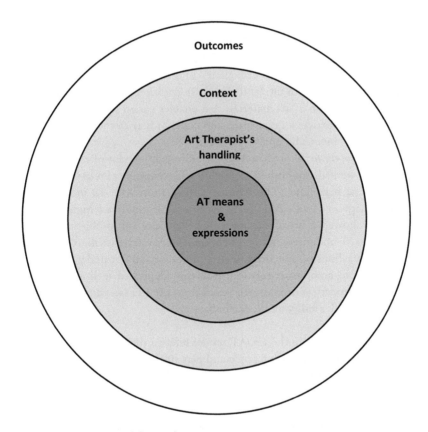

FIGURE 12.2 COAT model. C Schweizer.

with restricted behavioural patterns. One of the outcomes of the treatment evaluation was that experiences during art-making supported improvement in connecting words to experiences. When creating art, children with ASD talked about their preferences and resistances. Also, psycho education during art-making was helpful for understanding and accepting the autism-related challenges. This extension of skills transferred to the home and school situations (Schweizer et al., 2020a; 2020b).

2. *Art therapist's handling*: the art therapist has an active, attuning and structuring role and supports the child to feel at ease, to recognise and verbalise preferences, resistances, moods, tensions. Also, the art therapist supports the child to have successful experiences during art-making and supports the child in connecting words to experiences. The art therapist encourages the child to ask for help when needed and to continue creating when the child is disappointed.

3. *Contextual aspects*: in the treatment setting, several aspects are supportive for art therapy for children diagnosed with ASD. Clarity about referral criteria (see below: 4, Outcomes of the treatment) and about the number and

frequency of sessions (in the tested treatment protocol 15 sessions for children 6–12 years with normal and high intelligence profile was sufficient). For parents, psycho education will be supportive as will showing videos from art therapy sessions with their child (considering aspects of privacy) and discussing it with the art therapist. In addition an art therapy room with a broad spectrum of art materials that enables varied sensory motor experiences is supportive, a quiet space and cupboards with the potential to close for offering low audio and visual stimuli.

4. *Outcomes of the treatment*: based on the aforementioned studies, four outcome criteria were distinguished: sense of self, emotion regulation, flexibility and social behaviour. The treatment evaluation with 12 individual children diagnosed with ASD 6–12 years with normal and high intelligence profile showed a broad variation in behaviours and problems (Schweizer et al., 2020, under review). Most children were referred with (very) low self-esteem (feelings of insecurity, feeling different and not understanding why, failure) and emotion regulation problems (depressed feelings and/or outbursts of anxiety and/or anger). Seven from the 12 cases improved mainly in the areas of flexibility and social behaviour.

The four categories from the COAT model refer to different perspectives of art therapy practices which are influence and play into each other.

The first perspective is characteristic for arts therapies: the means and expressions from clients. The visual and tangible characteristics of art-making are distinctive from other arts therapies disciplines like drama, music and dance. Development of empirical knowledge about the contribution of art means and expressions in art therapy will be helpful for development of knowledge about the treatment. An evidence base of working elements in the treatment is expected to support transfer of knowledge and further systematic inquiries, for instance, about treatment results. As an example, a recent study resulted in reliability of three formal elements in art products from clients, observed by art therapists. This reliability concerns the formal elements movement, dynamic and contour. These formal elements are significantly interrelated and related to client's mental health, i.e., psychopathology, psychological flexibility, experiential avoidance and adaptability (Pénzes, Van Hooren, Dokter, & Hutschemaekers, 2020).

The second perspective from the COAT model is oriented at the actions of the art therapist. The contribution of a therapist is one of the most important factors that add to a treatment result, even more than the method (Heijnen, Roest, Willemars & Van Hooren, 2017). This implies that the therapeutic relationship is an important factor. Evidence-based guidelines may support the intuitive and critical reflective art therapist to systematic evaluation of his/her professional handling.

The third perspective, represented by the third circle of the COAT model, is oriented at organisational aspects that support the treatment: facilities in the room, choice of art materials, positioning of art therapy in the setting, collaboration with parents, frequency and duration of the treatment, etc. Art therapists work with many different practical opportunities and theoretical backgrounds. This is often expressed in the contextual and organisational aspects. Empirical knowledge about these aspects may contribute to more unity in the approach for certain problems. For instance, the choice for 15 sessions in IOS was based on several findings (Schweizer et al., 2014; 2017): some art therapists treated children with autism for 5 weeks and others for 5 years, with all kind of variations in between. The results after 15 sessions of IOS showed positive change in the measurements and in the additional comments from parents and teachers. Although most participating art therapists were used to longer treatment periods, they confirmed that they did not expect that a longer treatment should yield better results. They mentioned that they experienced the IOS programme with its systematic monitoring as supportive for the treatment. The use of the OAT-A and EAT-A and the training in small groups, with watching videos of sessions together, offered a substantive contribution to improve insight and focus in the treatment.

The outer circle concerns outcomes. Based on several studies, four behaviour areas were determined as outcomes: sense of self, emotion regulation, flexibility and social communication. Reasons for referral to art therapy in the IOS evaluation were: problems with sense of self (severe lack of self-esteem), emotion regulation problems (heavy emotion outbursts), flexibility problems and social communication problems. The main improvements were for flexibility and social behaviour. These results are confirming the practice-based evidence about Images of Self, an art therapy programme for children with autism-related problems. These kinds of results support indication policy for art therapy for these children.

Conclusion

Empirical evidence literally means originating from experiences. An evidence-based approach or treatment is not very common in art therapy yet. This chapter explains how empirical research may contribute to a transferable language for art therapy, specifically the Images of Self programme, art therapy for children with autism-related problems and the COAT model.

From the perspective of artistic processes, a vocabulary such as in the Images of Self programme, or the COAT model may be experienced as restricted room for personal expressions or interpretations. This chapter is meant as a statement for outlines with open spaces for the individual therapist and client. Do we keep reinventing the wheel? Or could we profit from existing knowledge?

The rich nonverbal professional qualities of art therapy communicate well enough for some purposes. Besides that, an evidence-based language may contribute to the improvement in the sharing of information about the treatment and its results with professionals, students, clients and other parties.

This chapter is offering insight in several ways to expand the evidence base for art therapy.

The multiple perspectives as indicated by the Images of Self programme and COAT model have the aim to support communication, professionalisation and research about art therapy for art therapists, clients and other professionals.

Note

1 An outline of the Images of Self programme is published as appendix in: Schweizer (2020). Art Therapy for Children Diagnosed with Autism Spectrum Disorders: Development and First Treatment Evaluation.

References

AKWA-GGZ (2018). *Zorgstandaard autisme [Care standards autism]*. Retrieved from: https://www.ggzstandaarden.nl/zorgstandaarden/autisme

American Psychiatric Association (2013). *Diagnostic and statistical manual of mental disorders (5th ed.)*. Arlington, VA: American Psychiatric Publishing.

Baio, J., Wiggins, L., Christensen, D. L., Maenner, M. J., Daniels, J., Warren, Z., & Dowling, N. F. (2018). Prevalence of autism spectrum disorder among children aged 8 years: autism and developmental disabilities monitoring network, 11, sites, United States, 2014. *Morbidity and Mortality Weekly Report (MMWR): Surveillance Summaries 2018, 67*(6), 1–23. doi:10.15585/mmwr.ss6706a1

Boer, F., & Van der Gaag, R. J. (2016). Ontwikkeling: een levenslang proces - de principes [Development: a lifelong process - the principles]. In: Staal, W., Vorstman, J. & van der Gaag, R. J. (Eds.), *Leerboek ontwikkelingsstoornissen in de levensloop: Een integrale medische en psychologische benadering* (pp. 15–27). Utrecht, the Netherlands: De Tijdstroom.

Bosgraaf, L., Spreen, M., Pattiselanno, & Van Hooren, S. (2020). Art therapy for psychosocial problems in children and adolescents: a systematic narrative review on art therapeutic means and, forms of expression, therapist behavior and supposed mechanisms of change. *Frontiers in Psychology.* doi: 10.3389/fpsyg.2020.584685

Centers for Disease Control and Prevention [CDC] (2019). *Autism spectrum disorders*. Retrieved from: https://www.cdc.gov/ncbddd/autism/data.html.

Charmaz, K. (2006). *Constructing grounded theory. a practical guide through qualitative analysis.* Los Angeles/London/New Delhi/Singapore/Washington, DC: Sage Publishers.

Dekker, M. C., & Koot, H. M. (2003). DSM-IV disorders in children with borderline to moderate intellectual disability. I: Prevalence and impact. *Journal of the American Academy of Child and Adolescent Psychiatry, 42*(8), 915–922. doi:10.1097/01.CHI.0000046892.27264.1A

Evans, K., & Rutten-Saris, M. (1998). Shaping vitality affects, enriching communication: art therapy for children with autism. In: Sandle, D. (ed.), *Development and diversity. New applications in art therapy* (pp. 57–77). London/Washington/New York: Free Association Books Limited.

Feinstein, A. (2010). *A history of autism. Conversations with the pioneers.* London: Wiley-Blackwell.

Fombonne, E. (2003). Epidemiological surveys of autism and other pervasive developmental disorders: An update. *Journal of Autism and Developmental Disorders, 33*(4), 365–382. doi:10.1023/a:1025054610557

Gussak, D. E., & Rosal. M. L. (2016). Part VII Research models in art therapy. In: Gussank, D. & Rosal, M. (eds.) *The Wiley handbook of art therapy* (pp. 607–608). Malden, MA: Wiley and Sons.

Heijnen, E., Roest, J., Willemars, G., & Van Hooren, S. (2017). Therapeutic alliance is a factor of change in arts therapies and psychomotor therapy with adults who have mental health problems. *The Arts in Psychotherapy, 55*, 111–115. doi:10.1016/j.aip.2017.05.006

Houben-Van Herten, M., Knoops, K., & Voorrips, L. (2014). *Prevalentie cijfers kinderen met diagnose Autisme Spectrum Stoornissen* [Prevalence of children diagnosed with Autism Spectrum Disorders]. The Hague: Centraal Bureau voor de Statistiek. Retrieved from: https://www.cbs.nl/nl-nl/nieuws/2014/35/bijna-3-procent-van-de-kinderen-heeft-autisme-of-aanverwante-stoornis

Jörg, F., Ormel, J., Reijneveld, S. A., Jansen, D. E. M. C., Verhulst, F. C., & Oldehinkel, A. J. (2012). Puzzling findings in studying the outcome of 'real world' adolescent mental health services: The TRAILS Study. *PLoS ONE, 7*(9), e44704. doi:10.1371/journal.pone.0044704

Kapitan, L. (2010). *Introduction to art therapy research*. New York/London: Routledge.

Kogan, M. D., Vladutiu, C. J., Schieve, L. A., Ghandour, R. M., Blumberg, S. J., Zablotsky, B., Perrin, J. M., & Shattuck, P. (2016). *The prevalence of parent reported Autism Spectrum Disorder among US children. Pedriatics, 142*(6), e20174161. doi:10.1542/peds.2017-4161

Leyfer, O. T., Folstein, S. E., Bacalman, S., Davis, N. O., Dinh, E., Morgan, J., Tager-Flusberg, H., & Lainhart, J. E. (2006). Comorbid psychiatric disorders in children with autism: Interview development and rates of disorders. *Journal of Autism and Developmental Disorders, 36*(7), 849–861. doi:10.1007/s10803-006-0123-0

Nanninga, M., Jansen, D. E. M. C., Knorth, E. J., & Reijneveld, S. A. (2018). Enrolment of children in psychosocial care: problems upon entry, care received, and outcomes achieved. *European Child and Adolescent Psychiatry, 27*, 625–635. doi:10.1007/s00787-017-1048-1

Pénzes, I., Van Hooren, S., Dokter, D., & Hutschemaekers, G., (2020). Formal elements of art products indicate aspects of mental health. *Frontiers in Psychology, 11*. doi:10.3389/fpsyg.2020.572700

Scheeren, A. M., Koot, H. M., & Begeer, S. (2019). Stability and change in social interaction style of children with autism spectrum disorder: A 4-year follow-up study. *Autism Research, 13*, 74–81. doi:10.1002/aur.2201

Schweizer, C., Knorth, E. J., & Spreen, M. (2014). Art therapy with children with autism spectrum disorders: A review of clinical case descriptions on 'what works'. *The Arts in Psychotherapy, 41*(5), 577–593. doi:10.1016/j.aip2014.10.009

Schweizer, C., Spreen, M., & Knorth, E.J. (2017). Exploring what works in art therapy with children with autism: Tacit knowledge of art therapists. *Art Therapy, 34*(4), 183–191. doi: 10.1080/07421656.2017.1392760

Schweizer, C., Knorth, E. J., Van Yperen, T. A., & Spreen, M. (2019a). Consensus-based typical elements of art therapy with children with Autism Spectrum Disorders. *International Journal of Art Therapy*, 24(4), 181–191. doi:10.1080/17454832.2019.1632364

Schweizer, C., Knorth, E. J., Van Yperen, T.A., & Spreen, M. (2019b). Evaluating art therapeutic processes with children diagnosed with Autism Spectrum Disorders: Development and testing of two observation instruments for evaluating children's and therapists' behavior. *The Arts in Psychotherapy, 66*, 1–9. doi:10.1016/j.aip.2019.101578

Schweizer, C., Knorth, E. J., Van Yperen, T. A., & Spreen, M. (2020a). Evaluation of 'Images of Self', an art therapy program for children diagnosed with ASD. *Children and Youth Services Review*. doi:10.1016/j.childyouth.2020.105207

Schweizer, C. (2020b). *Art Therapy for Children Diagnosed with Autism Spectrum Disorders: Development and First Evaluation of a Treatment Programme*. Dissertation, Groningen: Groningen University. doi.org/10.33612/diss.131700276

Snir, S., & Regev, D. (2013). Art therapy for treating children with autism spectrum disorders (ASD): The unique contribution of art materials. *Academic Journal of Creative Art Therapies, 2*(3), 251–260.

Stern, D. (1985). *The interpersonal world of the infant. A view from psychoanalysis and developmental psychology.* New York: Basic Books.

Strauss, A., & Corbin, J. (1998). Basics of qualitative research techniques and procedures for developing grounded theory, 2nd ed. London: Sage Publications.

Van Lith, T., Woolisher Stallings, J., & Harris, C. E. (2017). Discovering good practice for children who have autism spectrum disorder: The results of a small scale survey. *The Arts in Psychotherapy, 54,* 78–84. doi:10.1016/j.aip.2017.01.002

Van Rooyen, K., & Rietveld, L. (2017). *Jeugd en autisme. Wat werkt?* [Youth and autism. What works?] Utrecht: Nederlands Jeugdinstituut (NJi).

Van Yperen, T. A., Van der Steege, M., Addink, A., & Boendermaker, L. (2010). *Algemeen en specifiek werkzame factoren in de jeugdzorg: Stand van de discussie* [General and specific working factors in child and youth care: State of affairs]. Utrecht, the Netherlands: Netherlands Youth Institute (NJi).

Van Yperen, T. A., Veerman, J. W., & Bijl, B. (eds.) (2017). *Zicht op effectiviteit. Handboek voor resultaatgerichte ontwikkeling van interventies in de jeugdsector* [A view on effectiveness. Handbook on outcome-oriented development of interventions in the child and youth sector]. Rotterdam: Lemniscaat.

13

WHEN THE BOAT DOESN'T DARE TO SET SAIL

Working with trust issues in children

Sibylle Cseri

Abstract

The last ECArTE conference theme in 2019 of trust, truth and the unknown, celebrated in Alcalá de Henares, birthplace of Miguel de Cervantes and author of *Don Quixote*, was the inspiration for my conference presentation and this chapter, which explores and reflects on working in art therapy with children who have a fragile sense of trust. This chapter looks at the challenges of moving from inner states of alertness and mistrust to a place in therapy where the exploration of unknown territories becomes possible. Learning to trust in the creative process, gaining trust in the therapeutic relationship and acquiring trust in one's self can be an important challenge throughout the therapeutic journey, especially when working with children who have suffered early loss. But what happens when the creative path towards this discovery becomes blocked and when fear of losing control, anxiety over the unexpected and a fragile sense of trust in the therapeutic relationship challenge the unfolding of the creative process in fruitful ways?

Having developed my art therapy practice in Spain and having specialised in post-adoption services, I aim in this chapter to shed some light on the particularities of this context. It looks at the challenges of the unfolding of the creative process through case examples and draws parallels with development of trust and attachment building, individuation and transformative processes in art making when working with children in therapy who have a very particular life story.

Keywords: art therapy, adopted children, attachment disorder, trust, individuation

Abstract in Spanish

La última conferencia de ECArTE celebrada en 2019 en Alcalá de Henares, lugar de nacimiento de Miguel de Cervantes -autor de Don Quijote-, estaba enfocada

DOI: 10.4324/9781003110200-13

en la temática sobre la confianza, la verdad y lo desconocido en el trabajo de arteterapia. Estos conceptos han servido de inspiración para la presentación de mi conferencia y para este capítulo; una exploración y reflexión acerca de mi trabajo como arteterapeuta con niños de frágil confianza.

Este capítulo explora el desafío de trascender de un estado interior de alerta y desconfianza hacia un proceso creativo confiado que permite la exploración de lo desconocido. Aprender a confiar mediante un proceso creativo y adquirir confianza en la relación terapéutica y en uno mismo pueden ser retos importantes cuando trabajamos con niños que han vivido pérdidas importantes. Pero ¿Qué pasa cuando los caminos creativos hacia los descubrimientos se bloquean?, ¿qué ocurre cuando aparece el miedo a perder el control?, ¿qué sucede cuando emerge ansiedad por lo inesperado o existe una falta de confianza en la relación terapéutica? ¿En qué medida estas cuestiones dificultan el desarrollo de un proceso creativo fructífero?

Este capítulo explora las particularidades del trabajo en arteterapia especializada en el ámbito de la post-adopción, práctica que he desarrollado durante los últimos cinco años en España. De igual modo observa los retos del desarrollo de procesos creativos (a través de ejemplos), examina la construcción de los vínculos afectivos y reflexiona sobre los caminos hacía la transformación e individuación al trabajar con niños con una historia particular de vida.

Setting out on a creative process within therapy implies confidence and trust in that one may not always know the exact route nor the destination one might be aiming for, nor the exact conditions one will have to navigate through, nor the exact timing at which certain goals will be reached. Yet one trusts that after having dived through many unknown territories within the accompaniment of a significant therapeutic relationship, this process will lead to a safe shore, with meaning and insight having been gathered along the way of this experience.

But at times the fear of losing control may give way to anxiety in response to the unfolding of an unpredictable creative process. Skov's (2018) reflections on her work on shame and creativity offer valuable insight into the understanding of aspects of the self that hinder the emergence of creativity and hence the process of individuation during therapy.

> This courage of letting go of the known is an important part of original creativity and also what most individuals find most difficult, because we tend to define ourselves from what we know we are. Losing our sense of identity during the creative moment is the challenge we confront when we are working with therapeutic change.
>
> *(Skov, 2018, p.2)*

Losing the sense of identity momentarily, while being fully immersed in the creative process, gives access to the emerging of as yet undernourished or unacknowledged parts of the self and is a valuable experience in the therapeutic journey. Getting in touch with these parts of the self requires a sense of trust in the therapeutic relationship, giving way to a feeling of safety during unpredictable processes.

Children who have experienced loss in early childhood, including the loss of the biological mother in the case of adopted children, struggle to regain trust in relationships. This process is often overshadowed and marked by the fear of further loss. The experience of early infant abandonment affects physical and psychological development from that moment on, even when speech is not yet developed. In this case, there is no conscious understanding of the loss, but it marks a deep primary wound within the child that is difficult to access. In my art therapy practice with internationally adopted children, vulnerable attachment patterns lie at the heart of the treatment and mark the development of the creative process. When working with adoption, we work with unresolved history and a complex present time family constellation. In therapy, we work with multiple layers of identity issues and diverse psychological symptoms that include anxiety, insecurity, depression, low self-esteem, relational difficulties, anger issues, regressions and psychosomatic symptoms, among others. In all cases, however, attachment issues lie at the forefront and form the core aspect within the therapeutic triangle between therapist, client and art-making process. It is therefore crucial to establish a solid therapeutic bond between client and therapist that provides the necessary trusting environment so that the child may be able to enter a transformative process. Henley (2005) discusses the particular relevance of the development of affectional bonds when working with institutionalised children and adoption. He refers to Bowlby's concept of the *secure base* and Winnicott's *holding environment* as important fundaments in attachment-oriented therapy. Henley highlights how these concepts give the child security and trust, allowing them to cope with "stress, anxiety and vulnerability" (Bowlby, cited in Henley, 2005, p.31).

It is this holding environment that offers the base onto which the therapeutic process will be supported. However, establishing this solid therapeutic bond and alliance is often a challenge and an important milestone in and of itself in therapy, particularly when the fear of further loss is just as predominant, as in children who have been abandoned.

At different moments in their lives, adopted children will raise questions and seek answers about their origins and life story that their adoptive parents try to address as concisely as possible. Yet there seems to be always a piece missing in this process of acquiring the complete truth about their life story, since there tend to be gaps in knowledge around their origin. These gaps may manifest themselves by feeling lost in their identity or that something is missing inside and with others. Brodzinsky, Schechter and Henig (1992, as cited in Miller, 2003) developed identity categories in adoption. Amongst these categories, they refer to the idea of a "moratorium" and "identity diffusion" (Miller, 2003, pp.102-103). Moratorium is the lack of commitment to a set path and identity diffusion addresses a sense of being at loss in identity formation.

Coming to terms with their own unique life story, including the gaps is an important element in therapy as a means of constructing a strengthened sense of identity.

"My mom had loved me so much that she looked for someone to care for me, so that I would receive all she was never going to be able to give". This statement is often heard by the children who come to therapy. It is an explanation that is often given to them by their adoptive parents as a means of helping them to understand why they had been given up for adoption and aims to relieve that unconscious feelings of guilt and responsibility the abandonment may provoke in them.

"My mom now loves me so much, that she would never abandon me", is a sentence that is also often voiced in session by the children, however seemingly contradictory to the previous statement. Even though the child may have an official explanation of why and how they have been adopted, fantasies of their origin and further insecurities are often unavoidable. The adoptive parents most often have the need to emphasise over and over again that their child now has a safe home, stability and unconditional love with the new family as a response to the child's need for constant reassurance. This reassurance, however, could bring up contradictory feelings within the child about the idea of the love their biological mother may have had towards them, raising questions as to whether or not their biological mother had loved them enough. This process of moving back and forth between feeling safe and unconditionally loved and questioning and feeling insecure about their past and present is a constant quest in the inner world of these children.

"What if I'm not good enough? Not perfect enough? What if I frustrate you? If you get angry with me? Will you still love me? Will you still keep me?" Almost all children in treatment carry or voice some of these worries and questions, formulating them out loud or feeling them within, causing great anxiety, insecurity, fear and guilt. These insecurities, however, are not necessarily a response to their current family situation, but are rather deeply rooted, originating in their very early ruptured attachment from their biological mother and often further marked by emotionally negligent experiences at an orphanage. In response to these questions, parents often express feelings of frustration that all the love, reassurance and attention never seem to anchor within the child, as if the child were a bottomless well. This aspect is reflected in McTavish's thesis (2018) on trauma and attachment informed art therapy. Garro et al. (2011, as cited in Mc Tavish 2018, p.15) describes the effects early infant trauma has on relational development marked by mistrust, suggesting that, however nurturing the environment, the child will continuously respond in a defensive way through this lack of trust.

The following examples refer to patients I have attended at a specialised centre for psychotherapeutic services for adoptive families in Barcelona, Spain. The centre is run by a team of psychodynamic-oriented psychologists and specialists in this field who have incorporated art therapy as one of the main therapeutic services for the children. Most art therapy treatments are held weekly and individually with some small group work also facilitated. Most treatments range between two to three years, with some exceptions that may require more time. The psychologists are in charge of the diagnosis, parent counselling and supervision. The team also works closely with schools and other specialists who assist the families. I have received informed consent to use the case examples and their images.

The following patient, whom I will call Anja, was adopted at just under two years of age from Asia. She came to therapy at the age of eleven and I worked with her in individual sessions for two years. She has a close and loving relationship with her adoptive parents as well as with her two much older siblings, the biological children of her parents. At the beginning of therapy, the mother described her daughter as insecurely attached, with separation anxieties, very low self-esteem, and a highly demanding attitude towards herself that was self-imposed. She was an excellent student and yet always worried about not being good enough. She always tried hard to fit in, go unnoticed and over-adapted to all life situations. The mother explained that her daughter always tried to appear happy and pleasing to everyone, but that she observed her to be extremely fragile, often sad and to suffer greatly from her insecurities. In social circles, Anja struggled in making friendships and seemed quite solitary and lonely. In family conversation about her origins, she would become sad, cry and develop a fantasy that she must have had something monstrous within her to make her mother abandon her. On other occasions, she expressed the desire to have been brought into the world by her adoptive mother's womb. These strong and painful feelings when talking about her origins led her to close all doors for dialogue and made it difficult for her family to address. Feeling different from the rest of her family was unbearably painful for her.

When I met Anja, I perceived this fragility and her need to have herself under persistent control. I observed her as hyper-timid, showing talking anxiety, inaccessible and locked up within herself. While in session with her, I had the feeling that our relationship would have to be built up very slowly, gently and patiently in order to make her feel secure enough within this new space and within this new therapeutic relationship. At the time, I was not sure how long the process would take to build a relationship in which she would allow herself to eventually become less guarded and release some of the highly constructed mechanisms of control. Intuitively, however, I felt that although it would take a long time for her to gain trust, once achieved, we would also achieve an important milestone in the path towards our therapeutic goals. Anja's interest in the art materials and in art-making were instrumental in this initial phase of therapy, when everything was still new and unfamiliar and somewhat frightening to her. In art therapy, the different characteristics of the art materials allow the client to connect with inner needs and necessities, offering a channel of expression that resonates with the moment. The availability of the controllable materials seemed to be vital for Anja at this point and she sought them out with a sense of relief; the familiarity of the pencils or the markers, the hard and controlling quality of them, helped her to feel in charge of a situation that might otherwise feel too uncertain. I could sense that despite her interest in art-making and the sense of relief at the presence of the art materials, the results might have been unpredictable, hard to foresee

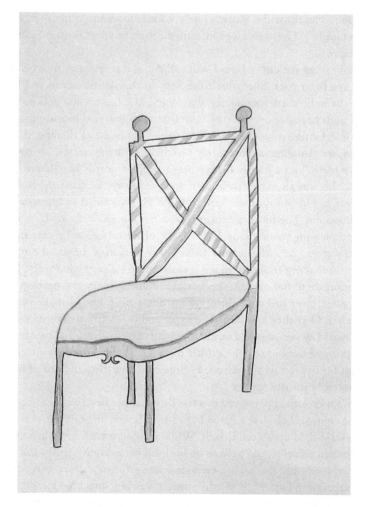

FIGURE 13.1 Anja's chair. S. Cseri.

and feel potentially frightening to her. Since Anja had such a strong sense of self-doubt and insecurity towards her own capacities as well as her relationships, the making of art became a threatening territory and a place of refuge.

During one of the initial sessions, Anja drew a chair (Fig. 13.1) with carefully drawn outlines, using coloured pencils and a fine tip marker. After we observed its unique characteristics, I asked her where she would imagine this chair to be. "It would be in a restaurant with other chairs equal to this one," she said.

This imaginary scene brought to the foreground that the chair did not want to stand out and longed to be with others and fit in with others without being different.

When looking at this chair, we observed a potential space to rest, possibly from the everyday struggles of always trying so hard to be pleasing, to be perfect and to fit in. Yet it also offers a potential place to meet, to find company and expresses the need to be together with others in a nourishing environment. As I looked at this image in session, I wondered whether she eventually would become comfortable and secure enough within this space in order to be herself.

Throughout her therapeutic process, Anja continued to reach for controllable materials and a concrete way of expression as a means of reassurance and containment. She avoided materials with less predictable characteristics and a more spontaneous means of expression, just as one would avoid wandering through swamp-like territories without the certainty of a stable ground. Moving on to more spontaneous or less predictable artistic expression could emerge further along in the therapeutic process, yet the more urgent and greater challenge was the creation of a bond that would allow her to feel accepted as she is, together with her needs and defences, without further pressure to prove herself to the other.

On one hand, the artwork and materials offered her a refuge from her insecurities within the therapeutic relationship, and on the other, they created a bridge between us, allowing us to share the experience of looking together while slowly building a bond between us. Jonathan Isserow (2008) describes the therapeutic impact on the psychological development of the client when the process of the shared gaze is fostered within the triangular setting in art therapy. Isserow emphasises the importance that joint attention has on bond making, just as the mutual gaze is central to the establishment of an infant's attachment skills. He furthermore lays out how joint attention is fundamental to building skills such as the act of giving, showing and pointing things out to one another, as well as moving back and forth between the object, the other's eye and one's own impressions. These skills develop the capacity for mentalization, just like a mother–child dyad.

> Looking back and forth between the art object and the therapist's eye requires however knowledge and toleration of the triadic relating, where two things can be held simultaneously in mind, requiring the capacity for two track thinking.
>
> *(Alvarez & Furgiuele, 1997 cited in Isserow, 2008, p. 6)*

This, however, is not a natural process; I have observed this in my practice with children who have experienced fragile or the lack of early attachment building. Looking together at the artwork of the patient implies the tolerance of the gaze of the other and the tolerance of being looked at, whether indirectly or symbolically. The experience of looking together may provoke anxiety or, as was the case for Anja, connected her with her own self-doubt, insecurities and fears of not being good enough in the eyes of the other. Furthermore, the question *what if you see parts of me I am not ready to accept* might condition not only the experience of looking together, but also the process of creation. Seeing, understanding and accepting these transferential processes provided Anja with a frame in which she was able to build up step by step a sense of trust and tolerance for looking at her images together and recognising them as parts of herself, acknowledging them and expanding on them eventually through imaginative thought and symbolisation.

Symbolic thinking is a challenge for many of the adopted children I have worked with. The capacity for constructing symbolic thought is acquired together from early on within the significant and secure attachment environment. The capacity to symbolise is favoured in an environment in which one may feel secure and contained and in which imagination can take on any form, just as playing would. Playing, imagining and expressing oneself freely may be thought of as intrinsic qualities within art therapeutic processes, especially when working with children. I have observed, however, that children who have a background of loss and trauma often acquire an inherent need for control in which ensuring the predictability and certainty of events becomes vital. Play, imagination and spontaneous art expression, something normally so inherent in children, is in this case often experienced as a threat to their highly established mechanisms of control, giving rise to anxiety when particular outcomes may not be foreseen clearly. Bowlby's secure base and Winnicott's holding environment became essential for Anja in order to be able to work through the mistrust issues that were hindering her development towards a freer and a more creative means of expression.

Playful imagination and experimentation implies the capacity for letting go and trusting in one's self and in the environment while stimulating the process of individuation of a unique self as it connects with the world. The philosopher, Merleau-Ponty (cited in Skaif, 2001), formulates this eloquently while reflecting on the phenomena of the art-making process.

> It is in the making of something that is in-between the visible and the invisible that a person becomes. And, in making something an individual contributes to what is in the world and therefore becomes connected.
>
> *(Merleau-Ponty, cited in Skaif, 2001, p.45)*

The self emerges as it engages with the act of creation that is not in isolation but in an intersubjective frame in dialogue with the world. Playful imagination fosters spontaneity and the experience of the world as something not static but flexible and at times unpredictable, where the unexpected meets one's own capacity for transformation and problem-solving. This process becomes difficult if the world, the relationships and the sense of self are experienced as fragile and as a result, refuge is sought in isolation, generated by the fear of making, as Merleau-Ponty (cited in Skaif, 2001) points out. As a sense of trust grew in Anja over time, her creative expression became more confident in size and shape, as imaginative thinking surfaced. This was not a linear process however. At times she felt the need to work with concrete elements from everyday life situations in quite controlled and rigid ways and at other times she discovered ways to experiment freely with a heightened sense of imagination. In this sense, the therapeutic process is much like the hermeneutic circle or rather spiral, where known and familiar aspects intertwine with the new and yet unknown, "connecting the parts to the whole and from the whole to the parts in ever increasing understanding" (Carpendale, 2009, p.29).

Towards the end of therapy, Anja seemed more re-affirmed in her identity within session and outside, as well as more confident in social situations. This led to her desire to take a break after two years of therapy. Despite some of these changes that manifested themselves throughout her therapeutic process, her constant reaching out and necessity for the use of controllable materials stayed in the foreground. This was a need that she recognised within herself and had to be respected. Relying on the concrete and the predictability of outcome has a vital function, especially for children who have experienced the ground as unstable and unreliable. At times for Anja this need seemed to function as a refuge and a secure base from which, at other times, she would feel enough trust to let go in her creative process.

An adolescent boy, who I will name Mario, had a history of traumatic neglect and abuse in his early childhood that resulted in a reactive attachment disorder. At age five, he was placed in foster care and was adopted at age seven together with his younger biological sister by a loving and highly dedicated couple. Shortly after the adoption, he had a psychotic breakout and was put under medication. Mario came to art therapy for five years. Throughout therapy, he reproduced objects, landscapes or events that were familiar to him repeatedly and often obsessively in a highly realistic manner. He seemed to fear experimentation, the exploration of materials and entering into a more spontaneous and less predictable art-making process. He preferred to give form to his ideas through controllable materials, such as pencils or markers, using a recognisable graphic visual language. He aimed to reproduce highly realistic images that gave him a sense of calm, control and manageability in response to underlying moments of anxiety. He continued to experience life often as unpredictable and potentially threatening despite his stable and loving family situation.

As Mario carefully drew out the image (Fig. 13.2) of this cruise ship over a number of sessions with different pencils, he felt the need to make a highly realistic representation of treasured memories of his last summer vacation, which he had experienced together with his entire extended family.

The slow and detailed process of drawing and giving concrete form to this memory throughout various sessions seemed to reinforce in Mario a heightened sense of belonging and permanence that remained firm, even outside the familiar home environment. The revisiting of a journey from known to unknown territories and the reproduction of this experience appeared to strengthen feelings of safety and containment, even in unpredictable waters. While drawing out his memories and searching for each line that corresponded to this important life

FIGURE 13.2 Mario's cruise ship. S. Cseri.

event, he sought reassurance and confirmation through our shared gaze as his inner experiences came into being in visual form.

However, this image-making process was also an aesthetic experience for him. This experience seemed to reinforce feelings of being loved unconditionally as well as a sense of permanence and harmony in contrast to the anxieties, doubts and fears he continued to struggle with in many everyday situations. Dannecker (2006) describes the phenomenon of the aesthetic experience in the art-making process as experiencing bliss. In her reflection, she refers to the ideas of Bell, who talks about the world of aesthetic elevation and its force of immersion as the contemplation of art is experienced. In this contemplation, a sense of letting go and flow is experienced; this creates a sensation of floating above what she calls the stream of life. This parallels with the ideas of Dornes (cited in Dannecker, 2006), who reflects on the moment in a child's life when they experience a momentary sense of fusion and harmony with the mother. This feeling of being perfectly held in a symbiotic experience forms a continuum in development in terms of psychological, as well as artistic, growth. Dannecker parallels this thought with Stokes, who holds the idea that the experience of art leads to the emerging of oceanic-like feelings as it renews awareness in the object (object-otherness). According to Stokes, the base of the aesthetic process, similar to the ideas of Bolas, is a faithful intra-psychic repetition of the experience of fusion with the mother during breastfeeding (Dannecker, 2006, p.57).

Throughout the entire therapeutic process, Mario needed to reach out to themes that would repeat themselves over and over again or he would work with repetitive mark making and concrete forms. This way of expressing himself appeared to give him a sense of security as well as a means for integrating the aesthetic experience of his art-making. At the same time, he would avoid expressing himself with abstract or less recognisable shapes, just as he struggled with symbolic and imaginary thinking. At times, his creative process would give a sense of being "stuck" in some ways without showing signs of new possibilities. However, at other times this repetition and search for security in his art-making process seemed to generate the creation of a solid ground or a safety-net in preparation for further growth.

A ten-year-old girl, whom I will call Adama, was adopted from an African country by a single mother at the age of one. She was described by her mother as overtly dependent with constant separation anxieties. Adama over-identified with her adoptive mother and struggled in accepting their differences physically and in character. This led to a fragile self-esteem and an unresolved sense of identity. She expressed on various occasions, her inability to imagine herself moving into adulthood and leading an autonomous life away from her mother. These insecurities brought out in her regressive behaviour and fear of growing up. She started therapy at the age of eight.

Adama also always reached for markers or pencils in a concrete and controlled way of visual expression in order to create images that confirmed over and over again the close relationship with her mother, yet were marked by her constant fear of further loss, a feeling that caused her a significant sense of anxiety. She also avoided the use of less controllable materials or a play-like approach to her creative process, along with any free flow of associations or use of metaphors for most of her therapeutic process. She preferred to depict concrete elements and often turned to repetition and the need to reaffirm her relationship with her mother in visual form. This gave her the possibility to explore her deeply rooted insecurities and fears within a context that sustained her through a secure and constant attachment frame in therapy.

Adama chose to create images (Fig. 13.3) in which she was able to visually explore her relationship with her mother and their connection while at the same time bringing to the surface aspects of over-identification and insecurities of being different from her both physically and personality-wise.

As she repeatedly reaffirmed herself through the exploration of her relationship with her mother in her artwork, she slowly began to dare to try new and different materials and different ways of expression within her creative process. Imagining, symbolising, playing and exploring more freely was at times still interfered with her anxiety and felt like a challenge, but she progressively dared to take on new initiatives as she felt reaffirmed in her relationship with her mother as well as within our therapeutic relationship.

We entered a next stage (Fig. 13.4) eventually in which playing and symbolic expression started to emerge. The previous process of constant reassurance

FIGURE 13.3 Adama and her mother. S. Cseri.

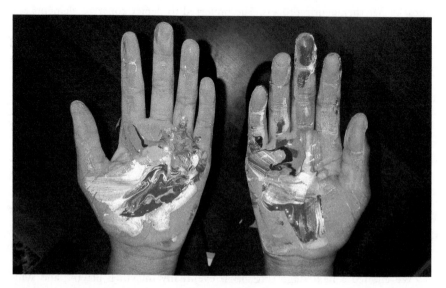

FIGURE 13.4 Adama's playful expression. S. Cseri.

seemed to be helpful to Adama in allowing her to enter a stage where creative play, learning to trust in her inner voice and the connection with her own resources became feasible.

By gaining a position in which she felt more secure and less anxious, she allowed herself to be less controlling in her means of expression. To feel in control of her circumstances, her surroundings and her actions had a vital function, just as in the previous examples. In her therapeutic process, Adama had come to a stage in which she was able to move from a persistent state of alertness or hyperawareness, manifesting itself through the constant need for control, to a state of increasing trust, which allowed her to let go and give way to imagination more frequently. She became interested in the use of paint and watercolours, daring to draw with her eyes closed, creating abstract and symbolic imagery that was improvised during the process while trying new ways of creating, essentially discovering different ways of being within her creative process.

At the end stage of therapy, after a near three-year process, Adama became interested in creating a body map on a large piece of mural paper (Fig. 13.5), which she developed over the course of eight sessions.

It was the largest format she had worked on so far and it required her whole body to be involved in the process. Within this format, she clearly moved out of her comfort zone, amplifying to a great extent her usually much smaller working format. She began exploring the body map first on the lower part, which related to her origins, her roots and early infant childhood memories and stories she had been told. On the lower left side of the mural (from the viewer's perspective) she placed in and around the body references to her early infancy with regard to her birthplace and origins. These elements refer to memories or fantasies around that first year of her life before adoption and her life at the orphanage. On the other side she placed current references to her upbringing together with her adoptive mother. As she drew, we explored each stage throughout her life with memories and references that marked important milestones in her development. The central part of the body map included the most important people in her life, those who gave her a sense of belonging, support and solid, unconditional love. This invited us to discover and discuss her relational aspects within the immediate and less immediate environments of her everyday life. Higher up on her torso, she chose to depict the qualities she felt she carried within herself as her very own resilient capacities. Each quality was covered up but could be opened at any time. She chose this format, she said, because these were qualities that are not always visible to the outside, and the acknowledgement of these qualities was in fact an inner process of self-awareness. In the depiction of her facial features, she searched for self-resemblance. It was important for her to recognise herself in her own features as a means to self-reaffirmation and differentiation from her mother. At the end of the process, she chose to place a crown of coloured feathers on the top of her head, giving her body image a sense of uniqueness and empowerment that instilled in her feelings of enthusiasm and pride. While working on the upper part of the image, it was also of great importance to her to try to find

FIGURE 13.5 Adama's body map. S. Cseri.

the right tonality for the skin colour in her portrait. She aimed with precision to find the colour that she could now accept as her own. Through this work, she seemed to gain a sense of ownership and pride over her body, reinforcing her feelings of independence and differentiation from her mother. This process seemed to facilitate in her a strengthened sense of identity moving out of a state of identity diffusion (Miller, 2003). Finally, at the very end of this work, Adama placed the words "keep calm and imagine" above the head as a reminder of her discovery throughout this process and encouragement for the future. Before and during an important part of the therapy, any notion around future provoked in Adama a sense of anxiety, as it indicated to her a process of growing and separation. She felt afraid and insecure about imagining a future life as an independent person from her mother. This fear of separation provoked in her a tendency towards regression. However, throughout the exploration of her creative process, she was able to experience a growing process of self-awareness and individuation, coming to terms with her own life story, with her identity and a way of being in the world in her own and very unique way while daring to imagine new possibilities for her future self.

Conclusion

Throughout my work as an art therapist with children in post-adoption, I have observed that art therapy treatment offers a powerful tool for coming to terms with aspects of loss, attachment difficulties, identity issues, complex family constellations and other psychological symptoms, such as depression, anxiety, low self-esteem, and somatisations, among others. This work entails a complex spectrum of aspects that often requires a long-term therapeutic process for the gradual unfolding of the multiple layers the child carries within.

This chapter is inspired by the conference theme of trust, truth and the unknown. These are aspects that stay in the forefront when working with children who have a fragile sense of trust, struggle to cope with the unknown and are in search of connecting with the true self, as identity is experienced as diffused. With these aspects in mind, I have described an area that stood out to me while working with this particular client group, often presenting itself in timid and quiet forms: the struggle for and fear of entering a creative process where anxiety, insecurity, a state of alertness and the need to be in control challenge trust in the unfolding of the creative process.

In all three cases, Anja, Mario and Adama experienced fear of further loss and separation anxieties. Their state of alertness, inner insecurities, fragile sense of identity and lack of trust manifested itself through the constant need to be in control during their creative process. Their need to control had a vital function for them because feeling in charge and giving concrete form to their expression provided them with a sense of safety and reassurance. Yet by fostering attachment building through the shared gaze, by enabling a secure base and a holding environment, by experiencing an aesthetic and symbiotic connection with the art work and by working through identity diffusion and mistrust, each child eventually would find ways of experiencing trust in the creative process, the therapeutic relationship and the self. It is through this development of trust that the capacity for play, imagination and symbolic thinking would emerge; finding ways to eventually unfold into a process of individuation with an increasing sense of true and authentic self. These transformative processes were, however, not linear. At times the creative process would become stagnant or stuck and would challenge further exploration. There would be a back and forth movement of opening up or retracting, of trying out the unknown or seeking safety in the familiar, of feeling uncertain, controlling and then daring to let go. These dynamics don't always manifest themselves in tangible forms, yet they pave the way to a process much like the hermeneutic spiral, where the known connects with the unknown in a non-linear means of self-emergence or, as Merleau-Ponty would formulate, "It is in the making of something that is in-between the visible and the invisible that a person becomes" (Merleau-Ponty cited in Skaif, 2001, p.45).

References

Carpendale, M. (2009). *Essence & praxis in the art therapy studio*. Canada: Trafford Publishing.

Dannecker, K. (2006). *Psyche und Ästhetik, Die transformationen der Kunsttherapie*. Berlin: MWV Medizinische Wissenschaftliche Vertragsgesellschaft OHG.

Henley, D. (2005). Attachment disorders in post-institutionalized adopted children: art therapy approaches to reactivity and detachment. *The Arts in Psychotherapy*, 32, pp. 29–46.

Isserow, J. (2008). Looking together: joint attention in art therapy. *International Journal of Art Therapy*, 13 (1), pp. 34–42.

McTavish, J.Q. (2018). *Using trauma and attachment-informed art therapy to promote healing in children in the welfare system: a literature review*. (Thesis for Expressive Therapies Capstone) USA: Lesley University,. https://digitalcommons.lesley.edu/expressive_theses/24

Miller, W. (2003). 'Metaphors of identity and motifs of expression: clinical observations on international adoption and the use of the sand tray process in art therapy with internationally adopted children'. In: Betts, D.J. (ed.) *Creative arts therapies approaches in adoption and foster care*. Springfield, Illinois: Charles Thomas Publisher, pp. 219–220.

Skaif, S. (2001). Making visible: art therapy and intersubjectivity. *International Journal of Art Therapy: Inscape*, 6 (2), pp. 40–50.

Skov, V. (2018). *Shame and creativity; from affect towards individuation*. London and New York: Routledge.

T - #0044 - 070222 - C0 - 234/156/14 - PB - 9780367626693 - Matt Lamination